Blossoming the Child

Blossoming the Child

A Guide to Child-Friendly Parenting

Tamarack Song

SNOW WOLF PUBLISHING

7124 Military Road, Three Lakes, Wisconsin 54562

www.snowwolfpublishing.org

Song, Tamarack, 1948—
Blossoming the Child: A Guide to Child-Friendly Parenting
ISBN: 978-0-9966561-3-9

Cover, text design, and layout by JamesBookDesigns.Weebly.com
Cover artwork by an anonymous contributor.

To send correspondence to the author of this book, mail a first-class letter
to the author c/o Snow Wolf Publishing, 7124 Military Road,
Three Lakes, Wisconsin 54562; or email the author
at office@snowwolfpublishing.org.

Visit the author's websites at www.healingnaturecenter.org,
www.teachingdrum.org, www.snowwolfpublishing.org, and www.
brotherwolffoundation.org.

References to Internet websites (URLs) were accurate at the time of
writing. Neither the authors nor Snow Wolf Publishing are responsible
for URLs that may have expired or changed since this book was
published.

All proceeds from the sale of this book go to non-
profits supporting child-friendly parenting practices.

DEDICATION

Takeshi and Diindiis (Ojibwe for Blue Jay), the youngest children of my extended family when I started this book twenty-plus years ago, were its inspiration. While watching them be themselves, guided by their intrinsic beings and the voices of Nature, I would wish that all of our young could do the same. As this book is merely my transcription of what they gave to me, I present it to you in their honor.

Also by Tamarack Song

Becoming You
3 Steps to Emotional Freedom and What Keeps You from It

Like a Shadow
The Life and Training of a Guardian Warrior

Becoming Nature
Learning the Language of Wild Animals and Plants

Entering the Mind of the Tracker
Native Practices for Developing Intuitive Consciousness and
Discovering Hidden Nature

Extreme Survival Meat
A Guide for Safe Scavenging, Pemmican Making, and Roadkill

A Forest Bathing Companion
The Rejuvenating Power of a Healing Nature Trail Walk

The Healing Nature Trail
Forest Bathing for Recovery and Awakening

Journey to the Ancestral Self
Remembering What It Is to Be Human

Truthspeaking
Ancestral Ways to Hear and Speak the Voice of the Heart

Whispers of the Ancients
Native Tales for Teaching and Healing in Our Time

Zen Rising
366 Sage Stories to Enkindle Your Days

Song of Trusting the Heart
A Classic Zen Poem for Daily Meditation

Fat Moons and Hunger Moons
The Turn of the Seasons for Northwoods Natives

See www.snowwolfpublishing.org for an
updated list of Tamarack's books.

CONTENTS

Part V

How Children Learn • 165

Part VI

The Serious Business of Play • 211

Part VII

Be a Blossoming-Supportive Parent • 237

Part VIII

Are You a Childhood-Deprived Parent? • 291

LIST OF CHARTS

Need Immediate Help?

Even though you might want to read this book from start to finish, there may be times when you need help sooner rather than later. For quick reference, here are the fourteen topics that come up most often in my counseling sessions with parents, and where they are addressed in the book.

Topic	Location
Parenting role	Part VIII
Starting a family	Chapters 2 and 3
Have a new baby	Part II
Crib use	Chapter 7
Bullying	Chapter 18
Homeschooling	Part V
Control issues	Chapter 38
Toys	Chapter 26
Food	Chapter 31
Craving attention	Chapters 32 and 33
Approaching adolescence	Chapter 14
Communication problems	Chapter 39
Feeling overwhelmed	Part III
Living for your children	Chapter 36

As a child, I discovered more of myself by Becoming other animals. Yet as a young adult, I struggled with how that translated to Becoming as a Native.

 *Prologue*

Welcome to a Different Kind
of Parenting Book

You and I think, feel, and act like hunter-gatherers. When we shop the aisles of a supermarket, we are doing the same thing as we would if we were foraging along a seashore or woodland path. Genetically, there is virtually no difference between us and our indigenous ancestors who got all of their sustenance directly from the Earth.

The same is true of our *children.** They are born wild, and their *natural* inclination is to be their fully engaged, spontaneous selves. Yet they run head-on into contemporary parenting practices, which are geared toward domesticating them. Many parent-child conflicts boil down to nothing more than the child fighting to retain her precious innate nature in the face of pressure to think, feel, and act like someone who is not her.

Our children come into this world as complete beings. Only our cultural perception of them is that they are incomplete (How often have you heard a baby referred to as *it*?), and they need our help to mature into full-fledged adults. And the quicker, the better. We are encouraged by our cultural value system to look admiringly upon children who are the first to walk, talk, read, or play a musical instrument. We are expected to reward children for acting maturely, and to view childlike behaviors as inappropriate.

Those who are drawn into conventional parenting practices risk doing two things:

---

* Glossary terms are italicized upon first use at the bottom of the page where this term appears.

- **Triggering their child's survival response,** which puts children in defensive-aggressive mode. When children struggle to survive, they cannot dream.

- **Judging their child's actions from an adult perspective.** The parents see a clingy child as immature, when her truth is that she is seeking an emotional recharge.

Children need safe, supportive environments, so they can dream. And they need to have their thoughts and feelings respected, so that they can be recognized for who they are. That's often easier said than done. Most parents bear sole responsibility for their children, which means dividing time between working, childcare, and personal needs. The only viable option for many parents is to turn to outside institutions for help.

Even though a parent might be committed to the parenting style that is variously referred to as *child-friendly, child-centered, emotionally connected, primal, free-range, unparenting,* or *rewilding,* the institutions parents rely upon are often not. Early childhood educators in my state (Wisconsin) make about $10 an hour, only 17 percent are eligible for employer-provided health insurance, and only 30 percent are included in retirement benefits.[1] A third of them are on federal assistance. That's a formula for survival mode, which isn't very conducive to being present and caring. And there is virtually no incentive—much less the wherewithal—for training in progressive childcare practices.

The early childhood educators' fallback, then, becomes what they already know: the status quo. Unfortunately, the same ends up being the go-to for many isolated and struggling parents as well. As much as we might like to think otherwise, we instinctively resort to the old and familiar in times of stress and need.

Compounding issues are the limitations intrinsic to isolated nuclear families, the lack of a full-time *Children's Culture,* and the separation anxiety suffered by children who do not receive adequate nurturing in their first year of life (all of which are covered in the text).

Yet There Is Hope

The dingy picture I just painted may be the reality for many children and parents, but it does not need to be their fate. The book in your hands is a metaphor for how you hold your children's lives in your hands. Yet you are not alone. In the next pages, you are going to immerse yourself in the parenting wisdom of the ages. Implementing it is entirely within your grasp. It doesn't take money, and it doesn't take a radical change in lifestyle. What it does take is *embracing children for who they are,* and *listening,* as they know best what they need.

Blossoming the Child is a different kind of parenting book because it is more child-centered than parent-, educator-, or therapist-centered. Those approaches have their place, yet here we are going to get to know children from the inside, out. What we learn is going to help make us parents worth descending from. By sidestepping much of the clutter and confusion around contemporary childrearing practices, we free ourselves to find out who our children are, rather than who others think they should be.

The parenting approach you'll find here is based upon the *Circle Way,* which is variously known as the *Old Way,* the *Ancestral Way,* the *Original Instructions,* and the *Beauty Way.* It is the way of life once common to all of Earth's People, and it is still being practiced to varying degrees by indigenous people wherever they persist. The Circle Way exhibits these characteristics:

- The Human People, the other Animal Peoples, the Plant Peoples, and the Mineral Peoples all live together in community.

- All of the various Peoples, including our children, are regarded as complete beings and equals.

- Relationships amongst the Peoples are based on listening and mutual respect.
- All resources, including emotional and nurturing resources, are shared openly and without preference.

My Role

At this point, you may be wondering who I am to be speaking with any authority about parenting practices and the Circle Way. In truth, you know just as much about the Circle Way as I do, as we both have the same access to its wisdom and guidance. You may know the source by one of these names: *primal memories, ancestral wisdom, the genetic library, intuition, superconsciousness, the Dreamtime,* or *the Voice of Spirit.* I have been fortunate in gaining Circle Way experience and putting it into practice.

It all began with me growing up as a wild child. My parents encouraged me to follow my instincts regarding Nature. I headed for the woods every afternoon after school, sometimes not coming home until dark. Homework took a back seat to watching baby birds hatch and grow, nursing wounded and orphaned wild animals, and gathering wild nuts and berries. I had few friends, I got bullied, and family life was dysfunctional; yet I found the nurturance I needed in Mother Nature.

As a young adult, I lived with a pack of Wolves. They accepted me as one of them, and in doing so, they taught me how to accept myself. When I was struggling and painted on a happy face, they ignored the façade and related to the true me. Such emotional honesty would sometimes bring me to tears. They were my family—I felt closer to them than to any human.

Based on what I learned as a child of Nature and a brother to Wolves, I founded Coldfoot Creek Community—a group of twenty-two children, women, and men who wanted to live in *Balance* with each other and the *Circle of Life*. With indigenous Elders and the voices of Nature as our guides, we gradually reawakened to the *clan* ways that were second nature to all of our pre-Civilized ancestors. What a joy it was for me to again experience the trust, camaraderie, and sense of self I had with the Wolves!

I went on to help establish three other Circle Way-based communities. While living in child-supportive communities for my entire adult life, I have helped parent more than a hundred children (see Acknowledgments). During that time, I have been involved with indigenous communities in various ways, and I have had the continual guidance of their Elders.

Professionally, I serve as a consultant for intentional communities. In that role, I assist in setting up community and Nature-based childcare and homeschooling programs. I have served as a consultant for the Mille Lacs Band of Ojibwe, to help them develop their Youth Therapeutic Center, and I have served as Intern Supervisor for the University of Victoria School of Child and Youth Care. I counsel parents from the United States and Europe on childcare issues, and I offer relationship and parenting workshops.

In 2012-2013, my staff and I at the Teaching Drum Outdoor School conducted the Family Wilderness Guide Program—a year-long isolated wilderness-immersion course in primitive living. Of the forty-two people who enrolled, ages ranged from two to seventy-five, and there was a total of seventeen children.

Educationally, my undergraduate studies were in Wildlife Conservation and Intentional Community Design, and my doctorate work is in childhood trauma recovery.

The Circle Way in Voice

Throughout *Blossoming the Child*, you are going to hear the voices of Native Elders. More than once they said to me, "Remember not my words, but rather what they bring alive in you." My grandmother from the Black Forest of Germany told me essentially the same thing. I ask you to do so as well when you are touched by the Eldervoices herein.

To hear what the Elders' words are telling you personally takes what one of the Elders referred to as *Deep Listening*. I relate to her description of Deep Listening, as it's the same way my Wolf kin listened to me, and it's the same way I learned from Nature as a child. Here is how to Deep Listen:

- Make no assumptions
- Take nothing out of context
- Give recognition to source
- Embrace the spirit of the words
- Consider the cultural/environmental context
- Personalize by finding how it fits for you

The Elders I apprenticed to seldom corrected me when I was not Deep Listening. They were respectful of the time I needed to learn in my own way, and at my own pace. However, my Native friends who were peers were often more direct. When I referred to Wolves as animals, they would ask, "Are you not an animal, just like them? And are they not people, just like you?"

They would respond similarly when they were referred to as *Native Americans:* "That is cultural theft. We belong to our own nations, and we are Indians." Wanting to respect their wishes and encourage Deep Listening, I use the terms *indigenous*, *Native*, or *Indian* in this text rather than *Native American*.

An Ojibwe Elder from Michigan (whose name I no longer remember) helped me see that by not taking the time to learn the ways of her people, I was not only failing to Listen Deeply, but I was appropriating their culture. The Elder gave me this example to help me understand: "The language I speak is not mine; it belongs to the Earth. To learn the language honors not only me and my people, but Earth Mother. It supports our way of life.

Otherwise, we need to speak your language to communicate with you, which robs us of our culture and creates distance between us and our Ancestors."

Another Elder, John Neconish from the Menominee Nation (in Wisconsin) impressed the ultimate significance of Deep Listening upon me by saying, "We are all in this boat together, and we are either going to sink or float together. What do you think the Earth Mother would like: for you to live in Balance with Her, like our ancestors did, or for you to continue exploiting Her, like your ancestors did? Your people are just as much children of the Mother as my people are. She does not separate and label the way we do. She loves all her children equally." Prior to his words, I couldn't see separation as exploitation, because I didn't allow myself to hear the deeper truth.

Coming 'Round

When the Elders first asked me to go beyond hearing and Listen Deeply, I was conflicted. With my childhood, I could grasp Becoming Nature, and as a young adult I viscerally experienced Becoming Wolf, yet I struggled with how that translated to Becoming as a Native. Only when voices from Natives (such as John Neconish) both encouraged and sanctioned my Deep Listening, could I begin to see how cultural sharing by indigenous people might cultivate understanding and empathy with the non-Native population. And I realized how the sharing would support the survival of Native cultures—and our survival.

At the same time, I could see the law of attrition at play: we were either going to become more like them, or they were going to become more like us. I was then able to grasp the wisdom the Elders were alluding to: For the sake of life on this planet, there was no question about which direction the attrition needed to take.

For the sake of our families—particularly our children—there is no question. The journey of *Blossoming the Child* is working through the travail that has been created by our disconnect from what it is to be authentically human. When there is no more them and us—when we can all come together in the Circle Way—we can all revel together in the *Blossoming* of our children.

Now, with the voices of Elders and children as our guides, let's get to the work of becoming parents worth descending from.

◇◇◇◇◇◇◇◇◇◇◇◇◇◇◇◇◇◇◇◇

Prologue Endnotes

1 Laura Dresser, Javier Rodriguez S. and Mel Meder, "Executive Summary," in *Wisconsin's Child Care Workforce* (WECA, 2016), 5, https://wisconsinearlychildhood.org/wp-content/uploads/2018/11/2016-Workforce-study.pdf.

Part I

A Child's Nature

Children are Nature.

 *Chapter 1*

Our Children, Our Selves

When parents cease to parent,
There will be no more childish children

When right and wrong become *care* and *listen*,
There will be no more need for rebellion

When children are once more let to raise themselves,
There will come adults who can take care of themselves

When there are no more needy children,
There will be no more greedy adults

When children are again nursed on love,
There will be no more lonely adults

When children are once again raised on touch,
There will be no more desperate, lusting adults

When all bodies are once again deemed sacred and beautiful,
There will be no more shame in children

When children can once more see all life being cherished,
There will be no more pollution, no more disease, no more killing

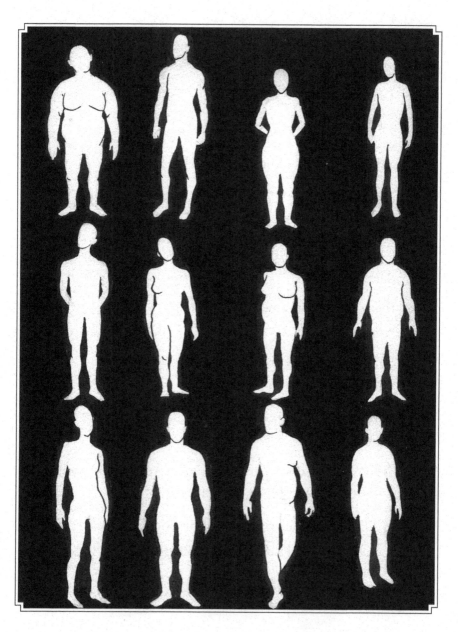

Our culture conditions us to value an ideal physical form.
A child places primary value on relationship.

 *Chapter 2*

What Is a Child?

For nearly all of the time we have existed as a species, our off-spring were manifestations of Nature. They could be nothing else, because there was nothing other than the nature of the child and Nature surrounding the child. Everything the child thought, felt, consumed, and became was an aspect of the natural environment.

When we humans began to manipulate Nature with agriculture and urbanization, we initiated a process of separation from Nature. We started to perceive our children differently: No longer were they children of Nature, but rather *our* children, who existed separate from Nature. We could no longer trust in our children's ability to follow their natural urges, as there were ever-increasing aspects of human life that were not Nature-related.

In our modern-day culture, it is common practice to condition children from the moment of birth to suppress their inner natures by denying them their spontaneity. We have them adopt the delayed-gratification and people-pleasing survival strategies of our urban-virtual reality.

Such a makeover would be virtually impossible under Mother Nature's influence. However, the outdoor-immersion time that currently exists in children's lives is typically watered down by being stylized, scheduled, regimented, and made safe and sanitary. Our playgrounds, parks, and yards may be found outside, but precious few of them are examples of unfettered Nature. For many children, the *kids are Nature* effect survives only in the stories of their parents' and grandparents' childhoods, or in movies. Some unfortunate adult souls do not become aware of the concept of kids being Nature until they run across it in a college anthropology course.

Becoming Nature

Would you like to experience for yourself what it is like to be a child of Nature? My book *Becoming Nature: Learning the Language of Wild Animals and Plants* can take you there.

Knowing a Child's Soul

To support our children's Blossoming, we need to understand that at one time there was no choice regarding whether to be indoors or outdoors. Communing or not communing with Nature was simply not an option. To be alive was to be immersed in all of Life. Everybody and everything coexisted: humans, wind, trees, animals. Like clouds being in the sky and fish being in the water, it was just the way things were. There was little reason to explore any other way to be, any more than one would question whether it might be better for fish to live in trees or clouds to burrow underground.

The same was true of the soul of a child, as illustrated by the following story about the child of a hunter-gatherer father and an agricultural mother, told by an elder woman of the Northern California Yurok named Che-na-wah Weitch-ah-wah, who lived in the 1800s.

A little son came to their home in the wilds, and they were both very proud of him. They watched their baby grow into a robust, handsome little fellow, who by nature inherited the ways of his father. As soon as he was big enough to walk and talk, he would run away from his mother and skip among the trees, romp among the bushes, and seemingly never grow tired of his wild revelry. He would talk and whistle to himself; and this grieved his mother very much, as she had tried every plan to subdue him from his wild romping, but to no avail.

When the boy was about six turns of the seasons in age, his mother became very lonesome for her people. She wished very much to see them again, so one day she summoned up the courage to ask her husband to allow her to return to her home on a visit. She said her folks were mourning for her, as they had given up hope of ever again seeing her alive.

He consented to let her go home on a visit, and to take their little boy with her. Immediately they began to make ready for the journey, as it was a long distance and the country was very rough.

The husband, who was a gifted hunter and fine craftsman, dressed his wife in the most beautiful of dresses, and the little boy was also finely clad. And so they started on their journey.

The wild man guided them until they neared the village. As they came into a small opening overlooking the village, he parted from his wife and little son, and they crossed the river and entered her home community.

She was most beautiful to behold, dressed in a gorgeous dress, with her little son by her side. Startled friends and relatives were greeted with much surprise, as

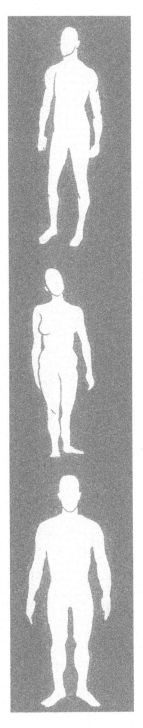

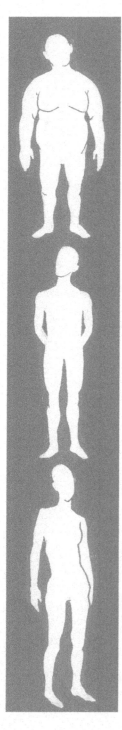

they had mourned her loss for nearly nine turns of the season.

During the first days of her visit, she encouraged her boy to associate with the children of the village. But all of his mother's pleadings proved to no avail in changing his character. He could not resist the calling of that wild nature he had inherited from his father. He would watch for opportunities to run away from the other children and play by himself among the dense bushes, jumping and whistling as he went. His mother soon gave up in despair her efforts to change his ways.

She remembered the day and place where she had promised to meet her husband and return with him to their home, but she refused to go. The boy pleaded earnestly for her to return to their home in the canyon. Holding her longing gaze on the boy's eager face, she eventually replied that he could choose between her and his father: he could either remain with her in the village or go with his father back into the lonesome wilds. Stating immediately that he preferred to be with his father, the boy sadly bade his mother farewell.[1]

The Primal Voice

Many people who first hear the story above see the child faced with this difficult decision. Yet for him, there is no choice but to follow his natural urge. I suggest that those who hear this story not judge the correctness of the boy's decision, but rather ponder the metaphor: that returning to Nature's way of child upbringing is not always straightforward or without pain.

We humans are all born wild: intrinsically Native and attuned to Nature. For most Western-culture parents, childrearing is largely a process of domesticating their children. Do you remember struggling with your child to get him to first wear clothes and keep them on, or to sit still, or to not relieve himself outside? That is the *wild* in the child—so instinctive and intrinsic to his being that it takes concerted effort to break him of it and train him otherwise.

This book advocates another approach to childrearing: allowing and encouraging our children to be their natural selves. It's the way they are happiest; and it's the way that they, in turn, are able to make the greatest contribution to their society. However they choose to live, they then know who they are and their reason for being. They have little reason to impulsively rebel against their society's cultural paradigms by engaging in either socially destructive or self-destructive behaviors.

Those children mature into the types of adults we need to lead us back to Balance in the face of the troubled times that are sure to come. The world has enough traumatized and chronically depressed automatons. Let us

gift the coming generations with individuals who know what it is to be human and what it is to be a caring and responsible citizen. Let us gift ourselves with the knowledge and the skills to start our self-healing—and allowing ourselves, along with our children, to be who we really are.

Chapter in a Page

For nearly all of the time we have existed as a species, our off-spring were manifestations of Nature. They could be nothing else, because there was nothing other than the nature of the child and Nature surrounding the child. Everything the child thought, felt, consumed, and became was an aspect of the natural environment.

When humans began to manipulate Nature with agriculture and urbanization, we initiated a process of separation from Nature. We started to perceive our children differently: No longer were they children of Nature, but rather *our* children, who existed separate from Nature. We could no longer trust in our children's ability to follow their natural urges, as there were ever-increasing aspects of human life that were not Nature-related.

In our modern-day culture, it is common practice to condition children from the moment of birth to suppress their inner natures by denying them their spontaneity. Rarely do they have opportunities for outdoor immersion. Instead, their lives are stylized, scheduled, regimented, and made safe and sanitary.

To fully support our children's Blossoming, we need to understand that at one time there was no choice of whether to be inside or outside. To be alive was to be immersed in all of Life. Communing or not communing with Nature was simply not an option. Knowing the soul of a child means knowing the inner nature of a child, which means knowing Nature itself. Let us gift the coming generations with individuals who know what it is to be human and what it is to be a caring and responsible citizen. Let us gift ourselves with the knowledge and the skills to start healing ourselves and allowing ourselves to be who we really are.

◇◇◇◇◇◇◇◇◇◇◇◇◇◇◇◇◇◇◇◇◇

Chapter 2 Endnotes

1   Lucy Thompson, *To the American Indian* (Indians of North America, 1916), 223-26.

Older children frequently share their interests with younger siblings.

 *Chapter 3*

A Being Complete

"What is a complete child?" asked a participant in one of my child-drearing workshops. I turned the question back to the group, and they fumbled around for an answer. I then asked if they could define a complete adult, and they had no problem with that. Here's what they came up with: A complete adult knows herself, has healthy relationships, and dwells consciously and completely in the now. "You have just described a complete child," I told them. "Because we live in an adult-oriented society, we tend to think of our children as works in progress—as sub- adults. However, children are whole people, with autonomous thoughts, feelings, and dreams, just like you and me."

A complete person is one who is continually evolving into her own completion. *Keiki,* the Native Hawaiian word for *child,* is a verb rather than a noun.[1] As anyone who has been around children knows, they can be defined by three words: *move, grow,* and *change.* Those descriptors are action words, i.e., verbs. *Keiki* literally means *to be or to become a child,*[2] which is a Blossoming—a continually unfolding process of movement, growth, and change.

Somewhere along our march to contemporary Western civilization, a good share of us forgot that precept and decided instead that our children are to be nouns. We began referring to them with some of the same noun terms we used for animal offspring: kid, cub, sprat, whelp, youngling. Other terms had a negative subtext: monkey, rug rat, brat, urchin, whippersnapper, jackanapes, rapscallion. Still others had a dismissive undertone: bairn, tike, cherub, infant, neonate, minor.

A verb cannot be possessed. However, a noun is an entity that can be owned and molded to the owner's liking, philosophy, and personal intention. And that is just what we began doing with our children. Many of us were convinced that we were either entitled or directed to mold them, as they were blank, directionless beings, given to us expressly to *make* something of them.

Otherwise, they were merely incomplete adults, not yet capable of self-achievement, cooperative engagement, or collective usefulness. They were weak and directionless, and it was up to the powerful and purposeful to fill in the picture. Thus began parenting as the majority of modern humankind knows and believes—parenting that is failing us, our children, and our world.

The Self-Guided Child

Contrary to popular belief, the conquering of Native peoples worldwide is far from over. It happens again and again with each new generation of children who learn from birth that one of the main purposes of life is for the Powerful to rise and control the Weak. We see it played out in nearly all of our political, economic, cultural, and social institutions.

For eons, children were not raised in a parochial or rigid manner, and still they matured into self-fulfilled and socially contributing adults. Not only were they capable of perpetuating the species, but of living in Balance with other species.

To this day, many Native and natural-living people raise their children according to what some of my Elders call "our Original Instructions." It is primarily those of us who have adopted or inherited the modern way who treat our children in the same controlling way that we have come to treat the rest of Nature.

If we could step outside our *Civilized* conditioning for a moment and observe how the children of other social animals are reared, we would get a glimpse of how our ancestors raised their children.

We'd see many of the same features if we visited a group of contemporary Native-living people:

- All adults share in the parenting of all the children.
- The children discover themselves and their world under the watchful eyes of the adults, rather than by adult instruction and regulation.
- The adults intervene in the children's learning-play only when necessary, for reasons of safety. Conflict resolution is handled by the children themselves.
- Each child, influenced by adult example, willingly assumes adult-like responsibilities as part of the learning-play process.
- Children create their own culture, based upon behavior observed from the adults and examples from the Nature around them.
- Older children frequently share what they have gained with the younger children, and the younger naturally emulate the older.
- Games—a primary way of learning[3]—spring spontaneously forth from Ancestral Memories[4] and are passed down from older to younger children through clan knowledge (a group's collective intelligence).[5]

In summation, Native children are largely self-guided, rather than being parented by ongoing intervention and instruction. Nearly all of our pre-agricultural ancestors, as well as modern gathering-hunting peoples—no matter where they live or lived on our Mother Planet—unparented their children.

What does that look like? If we walked into a hunter-gatherer people's camp, we would see contented children caring for themselves and one another, within the accepting and caring context of their clan. Boredom would be virtually nonexistent, as would dependency upon parents for approval, permission, and refereeing. Each child would be integrally engaged and honored for the unique individual he or she is.

This way of knowing and cherishing children is implied in the terms for *child* used by peoples still living indigenously. The Ainu of the northern Japanese archipelago call their children *poho*,[6] and the Gamilaraay Aborigines of Australia use the term *gaay*,[7] both of which signify that each child is a special and invaluable member of the clan.

Whose Children Are They?

"When you parent, it's crucial you realize you aren't raising a 'mini-me,' but a spirit throbbing with its own signature," says Dr. Shefali Tsabary in her book, *The Conscious Parent*. She goes on to say, "For this reason, it's important to separate who you are from whom each of your children is. Children aren't ours to possess or own in any way. When we know this in the depths of our soul, we tailor our raising of them to their needs, rather than molding them to fit our needs."[8]

Alternatively, it is useful to ask ourselves, "What happens when we lay claim to children?" As with any action of ours that runs contrary to the natural order, we suffer and we cause suffering. A child who is not free is effectively imprisoned, whether it is within an excessive social construct, an urban environment where the only trees are sickly, stunted ones set into sidewalks, or a classroom where they must sit in silence and not ask inappropriate questions.

The Russians have a maxim: *Small children give you a headache; big children give you a heartache.*[9] The innate nature of our children—in effect, their wildness—can cause disruption to the Civilized adult world. However, when the nature of children is not respected, they often end up incomplete, unprepared, and destructive adults. In effect, they are maladapted children with adult strength.

One reason for this outcome is that we Humans are the primate species that gives birth to the least developed offspring, yet we modern humans tend to impose near instant post-partum independence on our offspring. At the same time, we suppress expressions of independence that run contrary to socially prescribed norms.[10]

As Turtle clan Mohawk Elder Sara Smith advises, "These children are not your children, they are a gift to you to be cherished for only so long."[11] We need to relearn that our children are not our property, to do with as we choose; but rather, they are the sons and daughters of our greater family, and ultimately of The Great Mother. They are given to us so that we can be their caretakers and guides, on behalf of their Mother. When we have completed our service, we are then to return Her children. This is what some Native people call the *Circle Way*.

One blessing of the Circle Way is that we are not alone as parents. We are supported in these ways:

1. The Great Mother's nurturing
2. The guidance of Elders
3. Cultural traditions

When we integrate these supports into our relations with our children, along with encouraging them to be outside with other children of varying ages—every day and for as much of the day as possible—they have the best opportunity to be happy, healthy, and well-nourished.[12] Matthew Henry, a seventeenth century English freethinking minister, stated to his congregation that children "do not desire authority, do not regard outward distinctions, are free from malice, are teachable, and willingly dependent on [others]."[13] By recognizing these characteristics and supporting their development under our watchful eye, we give our children the best opportunity to become secure, self-fulfilled, caring members of their communities.

Chapter in a Page

"What is a complete child?" asked a participant in one of my child-rearing workshops. I turned the question back to the group, and they fumbled around for an answer. I then asked if they could define a complete adult, and they had no problem with that. Here's what they came up with: someone who knows herself, has healthy relationships, and dwells consciously and completely in the now. This also describes a complete child. Because we live in an adult-oriented society, we tend to think of our children as works in progress—as sub-adults. However, children are whole people, with autonomous thoughts, feelings, and dreams, just like you and me.

As anyone who has been around children knows, they can be defined by three words: *move, grow,* and *change.* In fact, *Keiki,* the Native Hawaiian word for *child,* is more like a verb than a noun. A verb cannot be possessed. However, a noun is an entity that can be owned and molded to the owner's liking, philosophy, and personal intention. And that is just what we began doing with our children. Native children are largely self-guided, rather than being parented by ongoing intervention and instruction.

That doesn't mean children go unattended. It's quite the opposite, as all adults share parenting responsibilities among most hunter-gatherers. This allows children to discover themselves and their world under the watchful eyes of the adults, rather than by adult instruction and regulation.

This way of knowing and cherishing children is implied in the terms for *child* used by peoples still living indigenously. The Ainu of the northern Japanese archipelago call their children *poho,* and the Gamilaraay Aborigines of Australia use the term *gaay,* both of which signify that each child is a special and invaluable member of the clan.

◇◇◇◇◇◇◇◇◇◇◇◇◇◇◇◇◇◇◇◇◇

Chapter 3 Endnotes

1   Henry P. Judd, Mary Kawena Pukui, and John F. G. Stokes, *Handy Hawaiian Dictionary* (Mutual Publishing, 2001), 256.

2   Mary Kawena Pukui and Samuel H. Elbert, *Hawaiian Dictionary* (University of Hawaii Press, 1986), 142.

3   J. Huizinga, *Homo Ludens* (London: Routledge & Kegan Paul, 1949), 5.

4   M. Chudek and J. Henrich, "Culture-Gene Coevolution, Norm-Psychology and the Emergence of Human Prosociality," *Trends in Cognitive Science* 15, no. 5 (2011): 218-26.

5   Joseph Henrich, *The Secret of Our Success: How Culture is Driving Human Evolution, Domesticating Our Species, and Making Us Smarter* (Princeton University Press, 2015), 4.

6   Alexander Vovin, *A Reconstruction of Proto-Ainu* (BRILL, 1993), 127.

7   John Giacon, A Grammar of Yuwaalaraay and Gamilaraay, last modified October 2014, accessed 3 August 2020, 98, https://openresearch-repository.anu.edu.au/bitstream/1885/12377/1/Giacon%20J%20Thesis%20 2014.pdf.

8   Shefali Tsabary, *The Conscious Parent* (Namaste Publishing, 2010), 2-3.

9   Mineke Schipper and Wilhelmina Janneke Josepha, *Never Marry a Woman with Big Feet: Women in Proverbs from Around the World* (Yale University Press, 2003), 133.

10 Desmond Morris, *The Naked Ape: A Zoologist's Study of the Human Animal* (Delta, 1999), 142.

11 Shirley Jones, *Simply Living: The Spirit of the Indigenous People* (New World Library, 2011), 70.

12 National Academies of Sciences, Engineering, and Medicine, *Parenting Matters: Supporting Parents of Children Ages 0-8* (Washington DC: National Academies Press, 2016), 45-47.

13 Matthew Henry, "Chapter 18" in *Matthew Henry's Concise Commentary on the Bible* (B&R Samizdat Express, 2018).

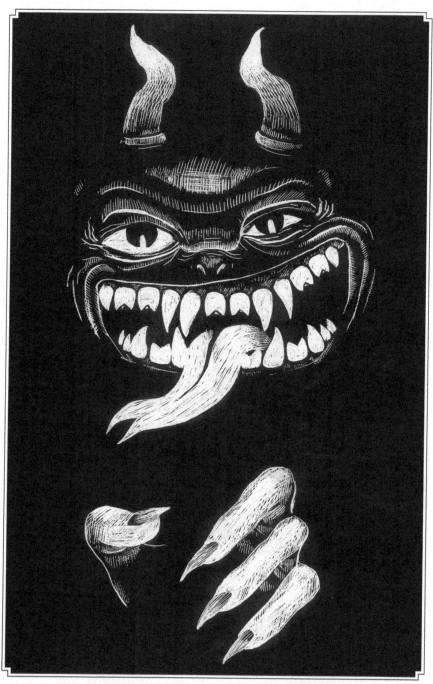

The inevitable outcome of our childhood domestication
is a lifelong relationship with Demon Fear.

 *Chapter 4*

A Child's Life Is a Verb

Our ancestors lived as nomads, moving from place to place in response to the cycles of the seasons, the ripening of nuts and berries, and the movements of animals. With the constant change and movement, life was seen to be comprised of flow and energy.

Our ancestor's languages reflected this—they were verb-based. Verbs, in conveying action or relationship, give life to nouns. A noun without a verb is worse than a fish out of water: It is merely a static object, suspended in a vacuum and frozen in time. If I say "stick," you can envision a stick; however, it has no relationship to anything and no reason for being. When I add the verb, "burns," the stick now has purpose and direction. I have given it life.

Even the names of our ancestors tended to be verbs. Referring to people named Tree and Hawk might identify them, yet adding a verb gives a better feel for who they are. Dancing-Tree and Sees-Like-Hawk speak of their character and their relationship to their people.

From Verb to Noun

Because a Native's life is a verb, he tends to think in verb-based language. This encourages him to view life as a related progression. The thought processes of a person from a modern agricultural-industrial culture are usually noun-based, which has her looking upon life as a quantified and categorized series of events.

Compartmentalizing is nearly impossible to avoid when we think in nouns. It's because we end up viewing life in person/

object/location-centered vignettes, which we rate based upon their seeming importance to us. Being noun-based, these vignettes are dense—so much so that those we have stacked at the top tend to dominate and diminish those underneath. Now our attention is not only focused on objects and things, but on those few objects and things we have placed on top of the stack.

This is typical of sedentary peoples who need to focus on and control their surroundings in order to provide for their physical needs. Unlike their ancestors, they no longer flow with the natural cycles and rhythms, as their movement patterns are no longer directly related to their sources of sustenance.

Where respect once had to do with relationship, it now becomes a matter of holding *things* in esteem. The rights to hold possessions and establish property boundaries necessitate the formation of political, economic, social, and religious systems. Without the values these systems instill and the sanctions they impose, there would not be the will or stability to maintain such an unnatural relationship with life.

The Germans have a saying, *Ende gut, alles gut*, which means *All's well that ends well*.[1] Here we see the focus on the result, the product—the noun. What about the journey?

Our Children Remember

Children know only the journey; its "end" is merely a vista in the never-ending journey of life. Imagine climbing a hill: When you reach the top, has your journey ended? If you are not fascinated by the valley below and the view of the next hill, perhaps it has.

However, we evolved as wanderers, so we have an unending curiosity for what comes next. *It is only through a dedicated process of instilling materialistic values and goal orientation into our children that we are able to derail them from continuing to lead lives of wonder and curiosity.*

With babies, first impressions so easily become lifelong patterns. When we teach nouns as their first words, we focus them on objects rather than on movement and process. We program them to live material-based lives. The Mescalero Apache have a saying, *Nutl el shihintsle angutle*: Strength comes from change. The continual change that derives from living life as a verb gives our children a strength that needs no institutions to provide or protect.

On the other hand, our children lose their strength when they learn to value things and seek to possess them. This point of view is supported in the words of Ohiyesa, a Santee Dakota who lived in the 1800s: "It is our belief that the love of possessions is a weakness to be overcome. Its appeal is to the material part, and if allowed its way, it in time disturbs the spiritual balance of the man. Therefore the child must early learn the beauty of generosity. He is taught to give what he prizes most, and that he may taste the happiness of giving, he is made at an early age the family almoner."[2]

The Circle of Life

Let's take a look at how a noun- and verb-based life looks from a place of perspective, namely the *Circle of Life* in which the individual is immersed. The first chart gives the image of a Circle whose soul is a verb, while the second chart shows a noun-dominated world.

Here is a depiction of what it's like to live as a verb. The point at which all the hoop-cycles meet is the individual. Think of it as the point of self-creation, where all the cycles of the Circle of Life merge and coalesce to form and guide the person. From that point, the individual can rotate simultaneously in any and all of the hoops, and they can rotate simultaneously within him. This dance of the hoops is what the Native recognizes as his life.

The first hoop, *The Now*, is an individual's current thoughts, feelings and impulses. The second hoop is *The Day Cycle*, which continually rotates upon itself from day to night, then again to day. *The Moon Cycle* is the third hoop, which revolves like the day cycle, only relatively slower.

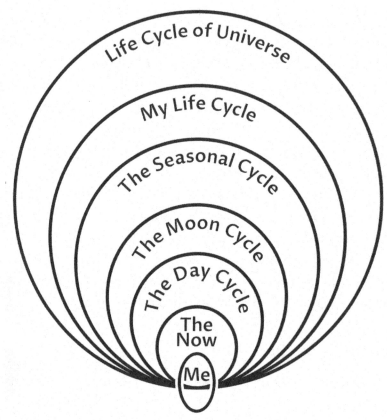

Chart 1: The Hoop Dance

Like the other hoops, *The Moon Cycle* spirals through the individual, and in synchronicity with all the cycles. The point of connection, which is the individual, is also each and all of the cycles. They are one, and the one is them—there is no distinction. Everything is of the same flow and the same force. Life is dance— a verb—with constant movement and a never-ending spiral of diverse yet interrelated energies.

Taken as a whole, the Hoop Dance chart shows that all the cycles have similar relationships to each other, and to the individual. No one cycle is more or less important than another—there is no comparison or preference. The difference in hoop sizes only reflects the relative speed of each cycle's movement.

Chart 2: The Layered Existence

In this chart, life is depicted as a noun. A person is isolated: a being unto herself. Involvements usually focus on quantifiable entities—things—so she perceives them as being separate and distinct from her; and that is the way she relates to them. On the chart, they are depicted as she sees them: Her primary vignette is directly in front of her, capturing her attention, and behind it are her other vignettes in order of decreasing importance and involvement. She has little conscious connection with (or energy for) her *Life Journey* or the cycles of the day, the seasons, and the universe.

Life in the Circle

While the first two charts gave pictures of the outer realm in which a person exists, the next two charts portray the realm within the person. Imagine that we are now viewing the "me" back in Chart 1 under a microscope. It'll show us how the inner realm can vary from verb-based to noun-based individuals.

Here the stages of life are portrayed as a verb-living person would experience them. To her, all the stages exist simultaneously: one within the other, like blossoms opening within blossoms.

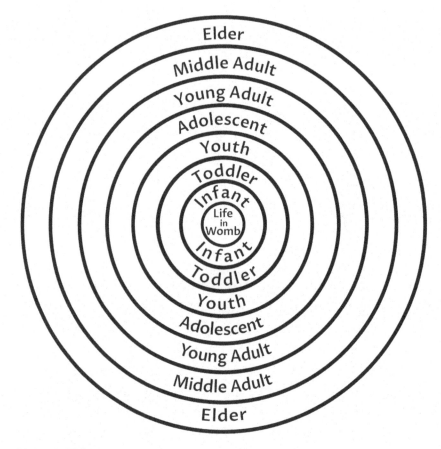

Chart 3: The Hoops of Life

From this perspective, life is a continual unfolding that gets richer and fuller over time.

This picture gives full recognition to the process of growing; because in order to reach our intended potential, we need to retain and draw from what we gained in our prior life stages. The same is true of the stages to come, as they are based on the inherited experiences of those who have walked before us.

Place your finger anywhere on the chart and imagine you are at that stage in your life. Let's say you landed on *Young Adult*. You can see that you are anything but isolated and alone at that place on your Life Journey. You are surrounded by your Adolescent, your

Toddler, your Elder, and so on. All of them make up the whole you and all walk with you together on your Life Journey.

Chart 3 could just as well be set up in reverse order, with Elder in the smallest hoop and Life in the Womb being the outer hoop. The placement is only a matter of perspective.

Each of these hoops represents a source of wisdom and awareness that walks with the individual on her Life Journey. The Youth brings inquisitiveness, the Adolescent lends fire, the Middle Adult contributes skill, and the Elder gives perspective. Ancestral memories, sensory perception, and intuition serve each of these entities within the individual.

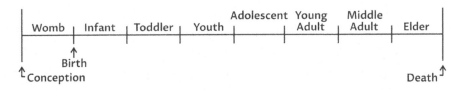

Chart 4: The Life Line

Here the stages of life are shown as nouns. As a modern person ages, he is accustomed to leaving the past stages of his life behind: A toddler leaves babyhood, an adult abandons adolescence, and so on. As the Irish say, *Youth sheds many a skin.*[3]

This linear progression is shown by the chart's layout, which is the view of personal development most of us are accustomed to. Life is a series of nouns, where a person enters and leaves distinct life stages. If you were to place your finger anywhere on the lifeline and look forward, you would only see where you were going, and if you looked back you could only see where you have been (compare with Chart 3, where at all points the individual is surrounded by all aspects of self). This narrow, noun–based view of life is what makes it possible for a person to define himself by what he sees in a mirror.

Noun and Verb Sleep Cycles

In the way The Day Cycle includes night, the human day cycle includes sleep. However, we are not intended to sleep solidly through the night, as does Sun. In foraging-hunting societies, neither adults nor children are expected to sleep all night without waking. Both adults and children sleep light, with some adults getting up in the night to eat and sit around the fire. This is verb energy. Whereas in many modern cultures, it is considered a milestone when a child sleeps through the night, solid and noun-like, and a problem if an adult can't fall right back to sleep.

How to Re-Verbalize Our Lives

In one sense, living life as a verb is easy to achieve, as it is our natural inclination. Yet most of us live our lives as nouns, as the tide of our sedentary, object-based culture is strong. That does not mean it has to be our children's default culture. Here are a number of easy-to-implement suggestions to support your child's be-as-a-verb inclinations:

1. **Teach verbs** as first words.

2. **Give experiences,** rather than things, as gifts. Experiences build on relationships and support the culture of *doing and growing* rather than *owning and controlling.*

3. **Focus on the quality of an experience** rather than its cost or location, to create a broader value system than one based solely on monetary value.

4. **Minimize personal possessions**, to give your children the space to find value elsewhere.

5. **Promote sharing.**

6. **Keep as many rooms as possible open to multiple usage**, which gives space for verb-based activities like exploring and creating.

7. **Refrain from using phrases like, "That's childish,"** "Don't be a baby," or "That's something an old fogy would do," so that all stages of life are equally valued and validated.

8. **Encourage your child to keep asking questions,** rather than being satisfied with answers. And keep asking questions of your children!

9. **Share stories of your ancestors** and their concern for the coming generations, so that children see their forebears as relevant to the present and future as well as the past.

10. **Value the transition to sleeptime** by going to bed early and making sure there is plenty of time for reflection and storytelling.

Chapter in a Page

Our hunter-gatherer ancestors lived as nomads, moving from place to place in response to the cycles of the seasons, the ripening of nuts and berries, and the movements of animals. With the constant change and movement, life was seen to be comprised of flow and energy. Our ancestor's languages reflected this, as they were primarily verb-based. Verbs, in conveying action or relationship, give life to nouns. Even the names of our ancestors tended to be verbs. Referring to people named Tree and Hawk might identify them, yet adding a verb gives a better feel for who they are. Dancing-Tree and Sees-Like-Hawk speak of their character and their relationship to their people.

Child-Friendly Parenting involves teaching our children to live as verbs, not nouns. In one sense, living life as a verb is easy to achieve, as it is our natural inclination. Yet most of us live our lives as nouns—inactive, stationary, and flat. That does not mean it has to be our children's default culture. Here are a number of easy-to-implement suggestions to support your child's be-as-a-verb inclinations:

- **Teach verbs** as first words.

- **Give experiences,** rather than things, as gifts to support the culture of *doing and growing* rather than *owning and controlling.*

- **Minimize personal possessions**, to give your children the space to find value elsewhere.

- **Encourage your child to keep asking questions,** rather than being satisfied with answers. And keep asking questions of your children!

- **Share stories of your ancestors** and their concern for the coming generations, so that children see their forebears as relevant to the present and future as well as the past.

◇◇◇◇◇◇◇◇◇◇◇◇◇◇◇◇◇◇◇◇

Chapter 4 Endnotes

1   William Shakespeare, "Act IV, Scene iv" in *All's Well That Ends Well* (Simon & Schuster, 2006), 174.

2   Charles Alexander Eastman, *The Soul of the Indian* (Boston and New York: Houghton Mifflin Company, 1911), 99-100.

3   Jon R. Stone, *The Routledge Book of World Proverbs* (Routledge, 2006), 493.

Part II

Return of the Cradled Babe

*The rebozo is the Latin-American version of the wrap-around
baby carrier found in many variations around the world.*

 *Chapter 5*

A Carrier for All Cultures

Along with wholesome food, our children hunger for a solid diet of emotional and sensory nourishment. Like nursing, it needs to be continually available, and right from birth. In order for this to happen, babies especially need to be constantly with their parents and involved in extended family activities. In order for this to happen, babies have to be as mobile as the older children and adults.

However, humans are born helpless. We are unique in the animal world in that we take the longest amount of time to progress from birth to walking. It takes us a few months after birth before we can even raise our heads, and another couple of months before we are able to crawl, and around a year before we take our first wobbly steps. In order to keep up with our family, we clearly need some form of conveyance for the time between womb and walking.

A Universal Solution

The baby carrier, found in many variations around the world,[1] handily meets the need. One version is the *sling*, which is a wraparound shawl that holds the baby or toddler close to the carrier's body. The practice, often called *babywearing,* is commonly used in traditional cultures,[2] and it is becoming increasingly popular with progressive Westerners.

Have Sling, No Colic

In countries where babies are carried by their mothers, colic is virtually nonexistent. A baby is not designed to lie in one place for long periods of time. When riding with his mother, he is in a continual state of motion, which aids his digestion.[3]

The Baby-Carrier Way of raising babies was at one time practiced by people of nearly all cultures around the globe, for perhaps 100,000 years or more.[4] Most of us are so removed from our Native roots that it might seem strange to imagine our forebears using baby carriers. Yet, there is historical evidence indicating that nearly all of our ancestors likely did so.[5]

Some of the most engrossing evidence of our past can sometimes be found in our traditional fairy tales and nursery rhymes, which are often relics of legends once told around the fire, or stories used to lull children to sleep. Following is a nursery rhyme that many of you will remember from your childhoods:

Rock-a-bye, baby, in the treetop
When the wind blows, the cradle will rock
When the bough breaks, the cradle will fall
And down will come baby, cradle and all

The reference is to the practice of hanging the baby carrier from a nearby tree branch when mom is engaged in some activity. Theories conflict regarding the origin of Rock-A-Bye Baby. Some researchers hold that it comes from early or medieval England, while others claim it to have originated in the 1600s when a young Pilgrim boy on the Mayflower observed *Wampanoag* Indian women with their babies in birch bark baby carriers hung from swaying branches.[6]

Variations on a Theme

Such varied origin theories for the same nursery rhyme show how widespread the Baby-Carrier Way once was. The baby carrier in its many forms can still be found in areas where Native and traditional cultures persist.

Rigid baby carriers, such as the one my family used and those purportedly seen by the Pilgrim boy, are commonly used in areas with temperate climates. In warm environments such as India, Southeast Asia, and Mexico, the baby is carried in a sling.

An example of a warm-climate baby carrier is the *rebozo*, a garment commonly used by Latin American women. It is made from a rectangular piece of cotton, wool, silk, or articela (a cotton-rayon blend). For such a simple garment, the rebozo is tremendously versatile: it can be used as a front or back sling, blanket, and nursing cover, along with being employed as a scarf or shawl, and to transport market products.[7]

The rebozo probably originated with the indigenous people of Mexico and Central America, and similar carriers are found in China and the Mediterranean.[8]

With tropical regions' heat and humidity, a well-ventilated baby carrier is needed. A miniature version of the commonly used open-weave hammock suits the purpose well. In the Arctic, a mother carries her baby inside her parka, in a built-in baby pouch just below the hood. That allows the mother to move the baby within her parka for breastfeeding or bodily excretions without needing to expose the baby to harsh weather conditions.[9]

Whatever the type of carrier, the concept is the same—to keep mother and baby physically close to each other, for three core reasons:

- Regular and easy access to breastmilk
- Continual psycho-emotional nourishment provided by mother's presence
- Enrichment provided by mother's activities

Regarding the first point above, some baby carrier models hold babies right next to their mothers' breast. Babies can nurse as often as every fifteen minutes. Milk is the richest when consumed regularly, as fat content drops when it sits in the breast, as the fat gets reabsorbed.[10, 11]

Bonding and the Adopted Child

It is becoming more and more common for adoptive parents to use a baby sling as a way to allow the adopted child to develop the bonding connection with the new parents that would otherwise begin in the womb.

A Foundational Childrearing Tool

Along with extended family (see Part III), rites of passage (see Chapter 14), and the Children's Culture (see Part IV), the Baby-Carrier Way is foundational to Native-based childrearing. This cornerstone supports self-knowing and the development of social skills with people of varying ages from birth on. A child's Blossoming is best provided in an extended-family environment where she can grow up in the security of people who have supported and cared for her since birth. With rites of passage, the extended family gives meaningful recognition to her phases of growth. The Children's Culture facilitates maturation and social consciousness by providing older children to emulate and younger children to mentor.

Thoughtfully incorporating these foundational elements is probably the most profound and loving thing we can do to support the Blossoming of our children. And it goes beyond that: My Elders have continually reminded me to keep in mind that what we do for our children is not just for them, but for their children as well, on to the seventh generation.

Chapter in a Page

Along with wholesome food, our children hunger for a solid diet of emotional and sensory nourishment. Like nursing, it needs to be continually available, and right from birth. In order for this to happen, babies especially need to be constantly with their parents and involved in extended family activities, meaning they need to be as mobile as the older children and adults.

The baby carrier, found in many variations around the world, handily meets this need. One version is the *sling*, which is a wraparound shawl that holds the baby or toddler close to the carrier's body. The practice, often called *babywearing,* is commonly used in traditional cultures, and it is becoming increasingly popular with progressive Westerners.

Whatever the type of carrier, the concept is the same—to keep mother and baby physically close to each other, for three core reasons: regular and easy access to breastmilk, continuous psycho-emotional nourishment provided by mother's presence, and enrichment provided by the mother's activities.

◇◇◇◇◇◇◇◇◇◇◇◇◇◇◇◇◇◇◇◇◇

Chapter 5 Endnotes

1 Timothy Taylor, *The Artificial Ape: How Technology Changed the Course of Human Evolution* (St. Martin's Press, 2010), 110-19.

2 Maria Blois, *Babywearing: The Benefits and Beauty of This Ancient Tradition* (Praeclarus Press, 2016), 30-32.

3 R.G. Barr, et al., "Carrying As Colic 'Therapy': A Randomized Controlled Trial," *Pediatrics* 85, no. 5 (1991): 623-30.

4 Sara Toth Stub, "How Babywearing Went Mainstream," *Sapiens*, last modified 3 May 2017, accessed 22 January 2020, https://www.sapiens.org/culture/babywearing-culture-mainstream/.

5 Timothy Taylor, *The Artificial Ape: How Technology Changed the Course of Human Evolution*, 110-19.

6 H. Carpenter and M. Prichard, *The Oxford Companion to Children's Literature* (Oxford University Press, 1984), 326.

7 Raúl Herrera, "El Rebozo: Tradición que se Está Perdiendo," *El Sol de Parral*, last modified 15 March 2011, accessed January 15, 2013.

8 "El Rebozo," *Artes e Historia Magazine*, accessed January 22, 2020, https://web.archive.org/web/20120512200428/http://www.arts-history.mx/sitios/index.php?id_sitio=7041&id_seccion=2722&id_subseccion=574356.

9 Betty Kobayashi Issenman, "The Art and Technique of Inuit Clothing," *McCord Museum*, last modified 2007, accessed 22 January 2020, http://collections.musee-

10 A. Hörnell, et al., "Breastfeeding Patterns in Exclusively Breastfed

Infants: A Longitudinal Prospective Study in Uppsala, Sweden," *Acta. Paediatr.* 88, no. 2 (1999): 203-11.

11 Azadeh Saki, et al., "Patterns of Daily Duration and Frequency of Breast-feeding Among Exclusively Breastfed Infants in Shiraz, Iran, A 6-Month Follow-Up Study Using Bayesian Generalized Linear Mixed Models," *Glob J Health Sci* 5, no. 2 (2013): 123-33.

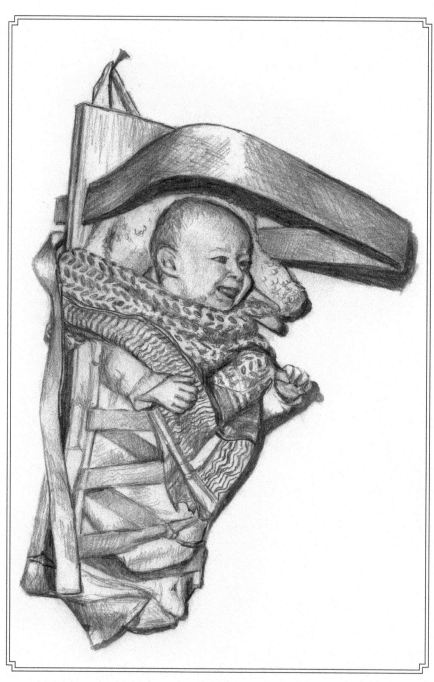

The unique benefit of the cradleboard is that it gives the parent full physical mobility while keeping the child center of activity.

 *Chapter 6*

The Cradleboard Way

In addition to lauding baby carriers in general, I would like to specifically present the benefits of the rigid-backed baby carrier. Commonly called a *cradleboard*, it is used by many temperate and far-northern climate Native peoples, particularly when their babies are between the infant and walking stages. The unique benefit of the cradleboard is that it gives the parent full physical mobility while keeping the child in the center of activity.

I raised my child the *Cradleboard Way*. The illustration opening this chapter is of my son *Wabineshi* (Ojibwe for *Little Morning Bird*) in the cradleboard I made for him. In addition, I share the guidance I received from Elders, along with personal research on the topic.

A Description

The cradleboard is a simple yet ingenious device that has served untold generations of parents and caregivers. Yet to be bested for nomadic living and active lifestyles, the cradleboard offers benefits beyond the fabric sling in support for the baby. In addition, it is easy to integrate into a wide variety of social, work, and movement contexts. Here are the main features that give the cradleboard such flexibility and adaptability:

- Provides the comfort and security of the womb
- Offers warmth, bedding, and diaper all in one unit
- Allows the baby to be continually with the caregiver

- Protects the baby's head
- Keeps the baby transport-ready
- Leaves the caregiver's hands free for other activities
- Detaches completely from caregiver, while still providing comfort and security for baby

Variations abound in cradleboard styles and construction methods. Many are made out of flat pieces of wood or bark, with holes along both sides for lacing. Basket-style cradleboards are also found. A footrest is typically secured to the bottom, along with a rollbar-type hoop at the top to protect the baby's head.

The cradleboard is usually furnished with a mattress of shredded bark or other plant material, which is covered with thick, fluffy animal furs.[1] Baby might be diapered in absorbent moss or down, and the mother may also periodically remove the baby from the cradleboard to relieve himself.

Here is a basket cradleboard description from Che-na-wah Weitch-ah-wah, a California Yurok elder woman who lived in the 1800s: "The baby is provided with a basket made for the purpose, and the child is placed in this in a sitting position. It has a strap fastened in the back so that the mother can swing it across her back, set it up against the wall, or lay it down flat just as she may choose. The baby if in health will doddle its feet and laugh when anyone takes notice of it."[2]

As Che-na-wah Weitch-ah-wah states, the cradleboard-style baby carrier is typically equipped with straps so that it can be carried over the shoulders backpack-style, or with a tumpline over the forehead. This allows the baby carrier to be easily moved from place to place and propped up against a tree, rock, or wall, or hung up in the safety of a tree.[3]

For my son, my family used the style of tumpline-carried cradleboard indigenous to the upper Great Lakes area where we live.

The Ojibwe people call it *dikinaagan*, which means *Made by the hand of a person from the body of a tree*.[4]

My family enjoyed—and benefited greatly from—using the cradleboard, even though we raised our son Wabineshi while living a largely sedentary life. Yet from our son's perspective, his lifestyle may have felt quite nomadic, with periodic hikes out to our primitive camp and wild food-gathering excursions.

In Use

Che-na-wah Weitch-ah-wah says that their basket-style cradleboards are changed out for larger ones as the baby grows; and that the outgrown baskets are burned.[5] The Ojibwe of my area follow a similar practice, by making a new cradleboard for each child, which is used by that child only.

My family kept to the tradition when our son was born, making him a personal dikinaagan and not passing it on to another child. This practice is in honor of the special attention afforded each child raised the Cradleboard Way, and of how sacred the privilege of caretaking a child of The Mother is considered to be.

When Pretty-shield, a Crow medicine woman from two centuries ago, was asked when babies were put into baby carriers, she answered that it was when they were about "six moons old ... Until that time, we carried babies in our arms, even on horseback. After they were put into back-cradles they were much less trouble."[6]

The age at which a baby is given a cradleboard varies according to tradition and the individual child. My son was about three months old when we started to use the dikinaagan, and he outgrew it around the time he started walking. His timeline fits with that of what is common to the Ojibwe people in my area, as they have told me that their children are carried in the dikinaagan for a full turn of the seasons.

In an effort to honor life as a verb (see Chapter 4), I would like to stress that it is not the cradleboard itself, what it is made of, or what tradition we might follow, but rather the Cradleboard Way that is important to embrace. Whether or not our child is literally *in* a cradleboard, rebozo, or other type of baby carrier, we can incorporate the methods of nurturance and engagement that are intrinsic to the Cradleboard Way.

Chapter in a Page

There are many benefits of the rigid-backed baby carrier in particular. Commonly called a *cradleboard*, it is used by many temperate and far-northern climate Native peoples, particularly when their babies are between the infant and walking stages. The unique benefit of the cradleboard is that it gives the parent full physical mobility while keeping the child in the center of activity. I raised my own child the Cradleboard Way.

Here are the main features that give the cradleboard such enduring flexibility and adaptability across cultures:

- Provides the comfort and security of the womb
- Offers warmth, bedding, and diaper all in one unit
- Allows the baby to be continually with the caregiver
- Protects the baby's head
- Keeps the baby transport-ready

- Leaves the caregiver's hands free for other activities
- Detaches completely from caregiver, while still providing comfort and security for baby

Many are made out of flat pieces of wood or bark, with holes along both sides for lacing. Basket-style cradleboards are also common. A footrest is typically secured to the bottom, along with a rollbar-type hoop at the top to protect the baby's head. The cradleboard is usually furnished with a mattress of shredded bark or other plant material, which is covered with thick, fluffy animal furs. The baby might be diapered in absorbent moss or down, and the mother may also periodically remove the baby from the cradleboard to relieve himself.

The Ojibwe of my area have a practice of making a new cradleboard for each child, which is used by that child only. This practice is in honor of the special attention afforded each child raised the Cradleboard Way, and of how sacred the privilege of caretaking a child of The Mother is considered to be.

◇◇◇◇◇◇◇◇◇◇◇◇◇◇◇◇◇◇◇◇◇

Chapter 6 Endnotes

1   Kavasch, E. Barrie and Karen Baar, *American Indian Healing Arts* (Bantam Books, 1999), 14-15.
2   Lucy Thompson, *To the American Indian* (Indians of North America, 1916), 42.
3   Ibid.
4   Translated by Lety Seibel, an Ojibwe language student and the author's mate.
5   Lucy Thompson, *To the American Indian*, 42.
6   Frank Bird Linderman, *Pretty-shield: Medicine Woman of the Crows* (University of Nebraska Press, 2003), 84.

Imagine a fragile Antelope fawn left alone out on the open prairie. That's the experience of a baby relegated to a crib.

 *Chapter 7*

Carrier and Crib Compared

A baby carried by her mother has an ever-changing view of—and relationship with—her environment and the people in it. Meanwhile, a baby laid in a crib is typically abandoned to the company of some dangling colored plastic, with a static bland ceiling for a backdrop. He sees the same one or two people over and over, day after day.

Imagine for a moment that you are the first baby. Then take the place of the second baby. You now have a feel for the soul of this chapter. In the coming pages, we look deeply into what life is like for each baby. In doing so, it is my most cherished dream that none of us ever again consider putting our babies through the same soul-robbing and brain-warping experience that so many contemporary babes must now endure.

How Cribs Constrict

Let's go back to envisioning the second baby we just discussed. Shortly after birth, you are placed in a stationary cradle, in your own room. Mom comes and goes, but you stay put. You are literally a prisoner of place, totally dependent upon mom to come to you—on her time—to meet your needs and desires.

However, mom is not around enough or connected enough with you to regularly read your needs and wants. You soon learn that it is entirely up to you to grab her attention and get her to focus on you. And you soon learn that your normal language: facial expressions, whimpers, and chortles, do not work over distance. You have to cry to get Mom's attention.

The upshot:

- Your constant efforts to be recognized, tended to, and touched, bring only delayed gratification.
- Your yearning becomes chronic.
- You soon come to realize that, because Mom's leaving is inevitable, contentment is only temporary.
- You become chronically starved.
- Eventually, you grow insatiable.

As you grow, you develop a hard, pragmatic outlook on life. What you can grasp, you can rely on; what is beyond your reach, you mistrust. Anything beyond your immediate control is fleeting and unreliable, so you cannot risk putting faith in it. For the sake of your sanity, you sometimes go so far as to deny its existence.

Your new outlook is reinforced by encouragement to crawl and walk as soon as you are possibly able. This suits you well, as it offers you the equivalent of an escape from prison. Finally, you have your *own* way of getting your needs met! You can satisfy your chronic yearnings by trusting in the one constant in your life—yourself.

Yet your newfound freedom is a double-edged sword, as you are relegated to a playpen (or similar) when there is no one willing or able to watch you.

It Starts at the Beginning

I see a relationship between the early relational patterns established in the stationary isolated crib and the neuroses of our culture, from overconsumption and co-dependent relationships to theft and rape. If that be the case, returning to the Baby-Carrier Way may be one approach for our culture to begin transforming itself.

In getting your needs met in the only way you know, you are perceived by others as clingy, whiny, and always getting into things.

Yet in reality, you are doing only what you have been trained for. You are literally starving for constancy and connection in your life, and no amount of admonition or discipline can sway you from your course.

How Carriers Free

Now go back to imagining you are the first child, and you are spending your first days in a portable cradle. You go wherever Mom goes; which is easily accomplished because, like a backpack, you can be slipped on and off at will. On her back (or front, when nursing) you feel secure in her presence: You smell her, hear her voice, and feel the rhythm of her movements. Whatever she is doing, and with whomever she is doing it, you are right there to be a part of it.

Your merest gurgle or moan can be sensed by Mom, and she is able to respond immediately. With such attentiveness:

- You grow to feel secure and trusting in the expression of your needs and desires, and in the ability of others to meet them.
- You have both freedom of movement and the security of being with Mom.
- You are ever a part of her circle, and she of yours, as her feet are your feet and her world is your world.
- With this foundation, you never question your oneness with the Hoop of Life as you grow in age and awareness.

When Mom is resting or occupied, she sets you beside her in the baby carrier, or she hangs you from something handy that is nearby. Either way, she has placed you in the center of activity, so you can observe and absorb all that is going on. You feel a part of it.

Whatever the situation, she makes sure you are involved and thus receive attention, both directly and indirectly. So nourished, you grow content within yourself. You have little need to grab or cling to something for fear it might otherwise disappear. And so thankfully, you never come to know the unending sickness of yearning without end, as you are blessed to continually dwell in the Circle of Relationship.

Carrier and Crib Children in Action

The French have long said that *What is learned in the cradle lasts till the grave*,[1] and another old adage states that *What we first learn, we best know.*[2] Much of who we are—outlook, personality character-istics, interactive patterns—is established at a very early age. Even before we can walk or talk, we are actively engaged in dynamic relationships with the world and the people around us. Those initial exchanges are a new being's first impressions of life, which is why they make such an imprint that they become the molders of personality and the models of future relationships.

The effect of those first months upon a person's outlook on life can readily be seen in the behavior of a toddler entering an unfamiliar room. One Native elder explained to me that if a child were raised the Cradleboard Way, her tendency would be to first assess the room, to gain perspective on the space, what it contains, and what activities might be occurring. Once she feels grounded, she then approaches what interests her.

This way of observing, which she learned from being placed in the center of activity in her cradleboard, is consistent with the Australian Aboriginal concept of *seeing*, which includes observation and perspective along with focused viewing.[3] With virtually all Native children being raised the Baby-Carrier Way, they are likely to see as Australian Aborigines do. Nineteenth century Hawaiian elder Kaili'ohe Kame'ekua, Moloka'i reflected the same seeing-with perspective when she stated, "I had tried to be ... always observing."[4]

Children who are not raised the Baby-Carrier Way are apt to go directly for what attracts them in a new environment. Without first taking in the whole picture, they might not realize what they are walking into, both literally and figuratively.

Along with other aspects of early training, the effect of being raised the Baby-Carrier Way persists into adulthood and has a life-long influence on behavior and quality of life. How vitally important our relationship with our children is from the very onset!

The Apaches of Arizona may have been such notoriously successful fighters in part because of their baby-carrier training. Captain James A. Shannon, who served in the 11th Cavalry over a century ago with the Apache scouts, described their strategy: "You tell a troop of white soldiers there is an enemy a thousand yards in your front, and they will go straight at him without questions. The Indian under the same circumstance wants to look it all over first. He wants to go to one side and take a look. Then to the other side and take a look. He is like a wild animal stalking her prey. Before he advances he wants to know just what is out in front of him. This extreme caution, which we don't like to see in the white man, is one of the qualities that make him a perfect scout. It would be almost impossible to surprise an outfit that had a detachment of Apache scouts in its front."[5]

I suspect that the stark difference Shannon's story shows between the approaches of the scouts and the soldiers has something to do with the likelihood that the Indians were raised the Baby-Carrier Way, and the soldiers were raised the Crib Way. Like the soldiers, many of our culture's children mature into adults who "go straight at [it] without questions."

Such an approach fits with our highly structured and task-oriented modern existence. Our military, educational, and manufacturing institutions would not run well if they became top-heavy with curious, independent thinkers.

Being the gatekeepers of our children's formative experiences, we make decisions that affect them for life. We can support the development of their natural ability to gain perspective and attune to their ever-expanding world. When we don't support them in this way, their yearning for relationship can drive them to become singular in purpose, willing to put their noses to the ever-turning grindstone and follow never-ending orders. Such a life approach compromises their ability to be themselves, to be adaptable, and to grasp the bigger picture before focusing. Clearly, *how—or even whether—we carry our children in their first year of life is one of the most important and far-reaching decisions we can make for them.*

A Fresh Take

Let's go back to the entering-a-room scenario. If you were a baby carrier-raised child, you as an adult are now accustomed to first gaining perspective in new situations and settings. You are generally content and centered within yourself—calmness is your natural state. Rather than being driven by frenetic gorging to get your needs met in a limited time, you can give yourself the space to absorb what an experience has to offer. You embrace life with your senses and feelings, rather than being driven by a blind yearning to grasp and possess. Venturing forth from a foundation of caring presence that you know you can rely on and return to, you are comfortably autonomous. Your needs have been respected and served, which makes you naturally respectful and willing to serve.

You are such a person because you have been honored—starting already in the womb—by being included as a full and present member of your Circle of Relations. Let us give every child we can the same gift, for it is nothing less than the gift of life.

Chapter in a Page

Even before we can walk or talk, we are actively engaged in dynamic relationships with the world and the people around us. Those initial exchanges are a new being's first impressions of life, which is why they so strongly mold our personality and become the subconscious models for our future relationships.

Being the gatekeepers of our children's formative experiences, we make decisions that affect them for life. We can support the development of their natural ability to gain perspective and attune to their ever-expanding world. When we don't support them in this way, their yearning for relationship can drive them to embrace unhealthy relationships with people, work, and substances. Such a life approach compromises their ability to be themselves, to be adaptable, and to grasp the bigger picture before focusing.

Clearly, *how—or even whether—we carry our children in their first year of life is one of the most important and far-reaching decisions we can make for them.* A baby carried by her mother has an ever-changing view of—and relationship with—her environment and the people in it. She is connected, secure, and trusting, because you are immersed in her life.

Meanwhile, a baby laid in a crib, or otherwise parented inattentively, is typically abandoned to the company of some dangling colored plastic, with a static bland ceiling for a backdrop. She sees the same one or two people over and over, day after day. She is literally imprisoned within the crib, excluded from life beyond it. She learns to strain for attention and becomes starved for connection. Even if she has meaningful time and connection outside of the crib, the experiences within it affect her and her development.

◇◇◇◇◇◇◇◇◇◇◇◇◇◇◇◇◇◇◇◇◇◇◇

Chapter 7 Endnotes

1   "21 Proverbs About Cradle," *The List of World Proverbs*, accessed 23 January 2020, http://www.listofproverbs.com/keywords/cradle/.

2   Henry Scheib, *The Thought and Its Expression* (Zetzener, 1849), 86.

3   Beulah Loue, *Yolngu-English Dictionary* (ARDS Inc., 2004), 137.

4   Pali Lee and Koko Willis, *Tales From the Night Rainbow* (Black Print, 1987), 17.

5   *Armor, Volume 27* (U.S. Armor Association, 1916), 548.

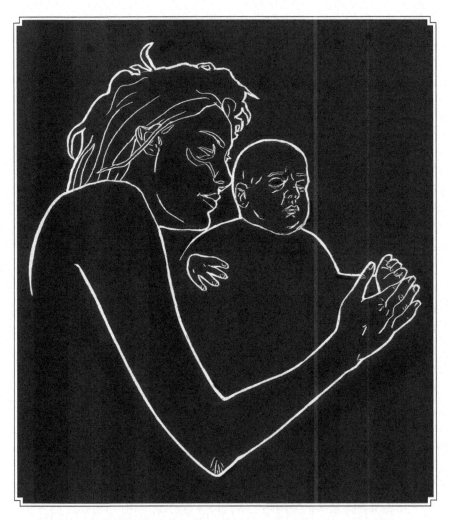

*One has to look far and wide to find the mother of any species
who would not want her baby next to her at night.*

 *Chapter 8*

But Can It Be Done in This Day?

"That all sounds good," some of my clients and readers say, "but we are no longer living Natively. I don't see how we can do the Baby-Carrier Way with our child."

Lisa and I, along with our ten-year-old daughter, Katrina, raised our son Wabineshi the Baby-Carrier Way, with Lisa working part-time and me full-time. Many others have figured out how to do it in a wide variety of family configurations and living situations. It's possible because it's the manner, not the trappings, that make it the Baby-Carrier Way.

It starts in the womb. *Kamgaabwikwe* is my Ojibwe Elder from nearby Ontario, Canada, who recently passed over. She told me about her mother instructing her on how the baby carrier is merely an extension of the womb, which is considered to be the first cradleboard upon which a child is carried. The concept and the teachings of beginning the Baby-Carrier Way in the womb are so important to her people, Kamgaabwikwe said, that they have a special word for it (which she did not divulge, as it is reserved for talk amongst women).

To illustrate how much the emotional climate can affect a child's time in the womb, Kamgaabwikwe told me the story of a woman who was hit across the back of her hand with a piece of firewood by her angry husband. The resulting black bruise remained for a long time, and her baby, whom she was carrying at the time, was born with an identical bruise on the same hand. Kamgaabwikwe finished the story by telling how her mother had cautioned her against activities when she was pregnant that would cause an extreme adrenal rush, or intense and chronic sadness, loneliness, or pain.

The point I want to make with Kamgaabwikwe's story is that emotional crises cannot always be avoided, yet we can choose ways to deal with them that encourage healthy emotional expression and quick resolution. The effect on the unborn child is then positive rather than negative.

The Essentials

Raising a child the Baby-Carrier Way does not mean that she always has to be in the baby carrier. When one is not traveling or outdoors, the baby carrier may not be necessary. Yet we sometimes put Wabineshi in the cradleboard indoors and hung it up on the wall. It was especially handy when we were cleaning the room or involved in some other engrossing activity.

At other times, we would cradleboard him just because it gave him comfort. I remember one time when he was agitated and we couldn't figure out why. His fidgeting went on for most of the morning and it was starting to wear on our nerves. It finally occurred to us to try the cradleboard, so we laced him in and perched him in the middle of our activity. He calmed immediately, and a rosy smile spread over his face.

The essential elements of raising a child the Baby-Carrier Way are for him to:

1. Always be with his mother or another close family member.
2. Have body-to-body contact with mother or other close person.
3. Be allowed to nurse on demand.
4. Have movement be a major part of his day.
5. Be in the center of activity as much as possible.

Wabineshi was nearly always with one or more of us in his immediate family, so he was an intrinsic part of our daily activities. He was nursed and slept with Lisa and me until he was in his fourth year. Up until that time, he did not know a babysitter or experience the pain of separation.

The first time Wabineshi faced being away from us for part of a day, he reacted with a torrent of tears. Yet it wasn't long before he replaced them with the curiosity and courage to venture forth without us. That first parting went well because we waited until he was secure enough to risk the unknown and old enough to know in his heart that he was not being abandoned.

With Katrina being homeschooled and Lisa and me working mostly at home, we were able to accomplish raising Wabineshi the Baby-Carrier Way as a nuclear family. An extended family could surely do it easier than we did (see Part III), yet the rewards are so high that I would encourage families of any configuration—even single parents—to come up with creative ways to make the Baby-Carrier Way happen for your children.

Is It Too Late for Older Children—or for Us?

Not at all. I prefer looking at it as being none too early to start incorporating the nourishing and supportive ways of baby carrier upbringing, whether or not it is feasible anymore to incorporate an actual child-carrying device. That deprived babe is still very much alive and unwell within each of us and our children, no matter what our current age.

Once we are aware of what is missing in our lives, going on with life as usual tends to strike our children as disingenuous. Being intuitively perceptive, they intrinsically know that something is askew. I've seen terrible internal conflicts arise within children, as they know to look to their parents for clarity, example, and inspiration. If we would like our children to be their natural selves, we can do no better for them than to be our natural selves. When we do so, the Baby-Carrier Way comes naturally to us, and to them.

We are as we envision ourselves, so if we want to re-empower our suppressed natural ways of gaining awareness and perspective, we can do it. The following four-step process puts a positive spin on the old adage that says *Give someone an inch and he'll take a mile.*[1] Starting the process can be overwhelming, but you'll find that it's easier than you think once you get going, as momentum takes over.

The initial move is usually the hardest, and you have already taken it—you have the awareness. The next move is awakening to the awareness, which incorporating the following steps does for you. It won't take long for you to see results, as every time you practice one of the following exercises, you are simultaneously breaking an old pattern of suppression and creating a new practice of expression.

Four Steps to Actualizing the Baby-Carrier Way

1. Be Present.

The Baby-Carrier Way is no more than dwelling in the presence of relationship rather than in self-absorbed ego. To encourage presence:

- Let others speak first.
- Greet people you know with touch.
- Ask them for something more than, "Hi, how are you?"
- Show genuine interest in their stories.

2. Gain Perspective.

When entering new surroundings, whether it be a room, a neighborhood, or a wild area,

First, orient yourself.

Second, survey your surroundings.

Third, take in the sounds, sights, smells, and feelings unique to the locale, such as:

- Features and landmarks
- The way the earth feels underfoot
- The sense of belonging or alienation that visits you
- Who and what are your present company
- How they are sensing you, and you, them

To break the old self-centered pattern, it is important to take an extended amount of time for perspective-gaining *every time* you enter a new area. Remember to do it right away, before involving yourself in anything else. As you become more reacquainted with this approach, you find it taking less time and coming more automatically.

3. Grow by Sharing.

We receive as we give. When we raise our children and guide others in the Baby-Carrier Way, we as well gain from the collective experience. Here are some suggestions to encourage sharing consciousness:

- Tend to someone else's needs before your own.
- Allow people to get in line before you.
- Do something special for a friend.
- Offer to share your food and snacks when in the company of others.

4. Become an Active Listener.

In order to maintain a submissive and supportive populace, our culture conditions us to be passive listeners, which means: *Hear the voice of authority, but don't respond.* Add to that the fact that we are so inundated with sensory input that we don't have to seek out or attune to our surroundings. Even if we tried, we wouldn't be able to take it all in, so only the catchiest or most dominating voices penetrate the din. To change that:

- Read the whole menu when you go out to eat, and try something new.

- Adopt the active-listener approach to a variety of events and activities in your life.

- Take an unknown trail and try a new campsite the next time you're out in the woods.

- Set aside time on a regular basis to turn off the canned sounds and choreographed sights, and take in the spontaneous dance of the wind, song of the birds, touch of the sun, and chill of the rain.

For more on listening, please see my book *Truthspeaking: Ancestral Ways to Hear and Speak the Voice of the Heart.*

Ultimately, the question isn't whether or not the Baby-Carrier Way can be practiced in this day, but rather how to bring back what has lain dormant within us for generations and cries to again see the sparkle in a baby's eyes. My final suggestion is to find other like-minded people near you, so that you can together walk the journey and share the joy.

Chapter in a Page

Kamgaabwikwe, my Ojibwe Elder from nearby Ontario, Canada, told me the baby carrier is merely an extension of the womb, which is considered to be the first cradleboard upon which a child is carried. To illustrate how much the emotional climate can affect a child's time in the womb, Kamgaabwikwe told me the story of a woman who was hit across the back of her hand with a piece of firewood by her angry husband.

The resulting black bruise remained for a long time, and her baby, whom she was carrying at the time, was born with an identical bruise on the same hand. Kamgaabwikwe finished the story by telling how her mother had cautioned her against activities when she was pregnant that would cause an extreme adrenal rush, or intense and chronic sadness, loneliness, or pain.

Raising a child the Baby-Carrier Way does not mean that he always has to be in the baby carrier. The essential elements of raising a child the Baby-Carrier Way are for him to:

1. Always be with his mother or another close family member.
2. Have body-to-body contact with mother or other close person.
3. Be allowed to nurse on demand.
4. Have movement be a major part of his day.
5. Be in the center of activity as much as possible.

The core elements of this process can be practiced even with older children and adults. They simply involve: being present and attentive to others, broadening our perspectives, being willing to share, and being active listeners.

◇◇◇◇◇◇◇◇◇◇◇◇◇◇◇◇◇◇◇◇◇◇

Chapter 8 Endnotes

1 *Cambridge Dictionary*, accessed 8 July 2020, https://dictionary.cambridge.org/us/dictionary/english/give-someone-an-inch-and-they-ll-take-a-mile.

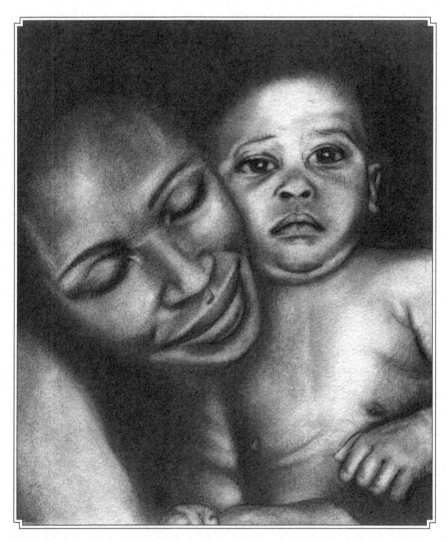

!Kung San children spend their first years in almost constant close contact with their mothers.

 *Chapter 9*

Attachment Parenting in Context

From an aboriginal perspective, parenting involves the constant connection a baby has with primarily the women and children of a clan. The biological mother, other mothers, elder women, and older children are involved in the nurturing of the baby right from birth. The baby is continually in either physical or audio-visual contact with nurturing clan members. When not being held, the baby is placed where he is in close proximity to people and has a clear view of their activities.

The aboriginal model of baby raising survived largely intact through our species' transition from a hunter-gatherer to an agriculture-based economy.

The Upheaval

Then came the Industrial Revolution, with its separation of production and processing from daily family life. Adults needed to leave home on a regular basis to run the manufacturing facilities, which led to the breakdown of the extended family. The resulting childcare vacuum was filled by institutions, which included schools, nurseries, orphanages, and child-labor shops.

Increased mechanization and analytical academics—hallmarks of the Industrial Revolution era—gained steam in the twentieth century, particularly after World War II. They inspired a form of childrearing that came to be known as *Behaviorist Parenting,* which is based on changing unacceptable behavior with practices such as timeouts, loss of privileges, and sleep training. Its signature—and most long-term hurtful—practices are bottlefeeding, the use of cribs, playpens, and strollers, and positive-negative reinforcement.[1]

At the same time, the sterility and stolidness of Behaviorist Parenting fomented a counter-movement based on emotional bonding and empathy. Dr. Benjamin Spock's hugely popular 1946 book *Baby and Child Care* both influenced and reflected the change.[2]

The momentum picked up with the publishing of psychiatrist John Bowlby's book trilogy: 1969's *Attachment,*[3] 1973's *Separation: Anxiety and Anger,*[4] and 1980's *Loss: Sadness and Depression.*[5] Thanks to Bowlby, the movement gained a handle: *Attachment Theory.*

Several influential books followed: In 1975, Jean Liedloff published *The Continuum Concept,* based on her experience with an indigenous Amazonian tribe;[6] in 1993, *The Baby Book* by Dr. William Sears and Martha Sears, RN, made a big splash;[7] and Meredith Small's *Our Babies, Ourselves* did the same in 1998.[8]

The Sears gave the movement a new name: *Attachment Parenting,*[9] which is now the most commonly used term. Other terms in use are *Immersion Mothering, Babywearing, The Continuum Concept,* and *Natural Childrearing.*

Although clinical definitions—and general understandings—of Attachment Parenting vary, in general it is perceived as a childrearing philosophy that offers methods to encourage a close relational connection between mother and child, based on the emotional attunement of one to the other. The connection is based on the mother's sensitivity, empathy, and immediate responsiveness, along with bodily closeness and touch.

A Common Misconception

There is a saying: *It takes a village to raise a child,*[10] and we need to take it literally right from conception if we want our children to reach their full potential. The village approach to parenting is clearly the way we are designed to raise our children. Even though

Attachment Parenting as a movement originated in the past fifty years, aboriginal cultures—including those of our own ancestors—practiced this concept long before the advent of the isolated nuclear family.

To see what childrearing looks like with the village as the setting and attachment parenting as the method, let's take a look at the *attachment* and *parenting* components of Attachment Parenting from a contemporary perspective. Some of us take the term *attachment* literally, believing that babies need to be in continual direct physical contact with the mother during their waking hours. The practice is commonly referred to as *Babywearing.* Today, Babywearing (and parenting in general) is practiced predominantly by couples and single parents living in their own housing units, with the female parent being the prime babywearer. She—largely alone—attempts to provide her baby with the level of nurturance once afforded by an extended family or clan.

In a traditional village, babies are always kept in close proximity to nurturing energy, which is provided *in a variety of ways, by multiple individuals, on a daily basis,* in addition to literal attachment to the biological mother. Proper terms for such practice might be *Collective, Communal, Non-Nuclear,* or *Non-Immediate Attachment Parenting.*

Attachment Parenting and the Nuclear Family

No degree of intimacy from one person can compensate for the richness and diversity of a clan environment.

In a nuclear family setting, the baby typically develops a strong attachment for the one person who is providing for the majority of her needs and wants, whether or not Attachment Parenting is being practiced. The child becomes imprinted with a single-provider relationship pattern, which she is destined to enact throughout her life. As her mother attached herself to the child, the child attaches herself to others, whether with friends, intimate partners or her own children. Put succinctly, parenting of any style in a detached social context can turn into a liability, by creating the potential for future codependent relationships.

Yet we don't appear to have many other options. So many young parents I talk with want to do the right thing. They know their baby is given only one chance to be properly nurtured in those critical first developmental years, and they are doing their very best with what they are given.

Unfortunately, no amount of overcompensation is going to make up for a child living in a detached environment. The isolated nuclear relationship format hampers parents and handicaps children right from the start, no matter what the parenting style. If we were biologically programmed for single-parent nurturance, Attachment Parenting as it is currently practiced would be a perfect fit. However, we evolved to have our children receive nurturance from a variety of people of varying ages, and I don't know of any substitute for that. It's hard to trick genetic predispositions.

This doesn't mean single-parenting or small social circles are "bad," but rather that they don't reflect the Original Instructions on how our hunter-gatherer ancestors raised children. Living in Balance with Nature, with *our* Nature, means recreating a broad, diverse clan environment for our children's Blossoming.

Here, in detail, is why an over-abundance of nurturance from one person does not adequately compensate for the diversity of nurturance that comes from a number of individuals:

- As social beings, we need the diversity of stimulus and role models that comes from a variety of people, right from the first moments of our lives.[11]

- Life-long relational patterns are established in the first two years of life.[12]

- Self-confidence, security, and the ability to trust come from interactions with a variety of trusting, caring people.[13]
- Receiving most of our developmental input from only one person can result in reverse effects.[14]

The Effects of Continual Attachment

I had a client who as a child was raised by a dedicated full-time mother. Until age three, my client was an only child; and her mother, following Attachment Parenting principles, was her near-constant companion. She developed beautifully, with strong self-confidence, fine motor skills, and the ability to listen astutely and clearly express herself.

At the same time, she wasn't ready to get potty trained until age four. Her younger sister, three years her junior, potty trained herself by two years of age, which included cleaning up after herself.

My theory on what caused the developmental difference between the siblings is that with the arrival of the second child, mom had to divide her attention between the two children. Since necessity is the mother of invention, the younger child was inadvertently given the doorway to develop a sense of autonomy and personal empowerment at an earlier age than her older sibling. Big sister had her every whim tended to, whereas little sister often had the opportunity to figure things out on her own. She was allowed to develop her innate capacity to adopt the examples she saw enacted around her by her parents and sister.

The story you just read gives ideas for changes you can make right now to give your child some of the benefits of Attachment Parenting. The next two sections of this book show how to bring your child all the advantages of clan-based Attachment Parenting. You'll learn how to renew extended family and the Children's Culture, which are essential to a child's full Blossoming.

Chapter in a Page

There is a saying: *It takes a village to raise a child,* and we need to take it literally right from conception if we want our children to reach their full potential. The stark reality is that no degree of intimacy from one person can compensate for the richness and diversity of a clan environment.

In a traditional village, babies are always kept in close proximity to nurturing energy, which is provided in a variety of ways, by multiple individuals, on a daily basis, in addition to literal attachment to the biological mother. Proper terms for such practice might be *Collective, Communal, Non-Nuclear,* or *Non-Immediate Attachment Parenting.* This village approach to parenting is the way we evolved to raise our children.

In a nuclear family setting, the baby typically develops a strong attachment for the one person who is providing for the majority of her needs and wants. The child becomes imprinted with a single-provider relationship pattern. As the mother attached herself to him, he attaches himself to others, whether with friends, intimate partners, or his own children.

Put succinctly, Attachment Parenting in a detached social context can turn into a liability, by creating the potential for future codependent relationships. The problem here is not the parent or their intentions, but the detached environment in which both the parent and child live.

As social beings, we need the diversity of stimulus and role models that comes from a variety of people, right from the first moments of our lives. This doesn't mean single-parenting or small social circles are "bad," but rather that they don't reflect the Original Instructions of how our hunter-gatherer ancestors raised children. Living in Balance with Nature, with *our* Nature, means recreating a broad, diverse clan environment for our children's Blossoming.

◇◇◇◇◇◇◇◇◇◇◇◇◇◇◇◇◇◇◇◇

Chapter 9 Endnotes

1   Clark L. Hull, "Introduction to an Objective Theory of Behavior," in *Principles of Behavior: An Introduction to Behavior Theory* (New York: Appleton-Century-Crofts, Inc., 1943), 16-32.

2   Thomas Maier, *Dr. Spock: An American Life* (New York: Basic Books, 2003), 142.

3   John Bowlby, *Attachment and Loss* (Basic Books, 1969).

4   John Bowlby, *Separation: Anxiety and Anger* (Basic Books, 1976).

5   John Bowlby, *Sadness: Loss and Depression* (Basic Books, 1982).

6   Jean Liedloff, *The Continuum Concept: In Search of Happiness Lost* (Da Capo Press, 1986).

7   William Sears, *The Baby Book* (Little, Brown and Company, 1993).

8   Meredith Small, *Our Babies, Ourselves* (Doubleday Books, 1998).

9   Bill Sears and Martha Sears, *The Attachment Parenting Book: A Commonsense Guide to Understanding and Nurturing Your Baby* (New York, Boston: Little, Brown and Company, 2001), 2f, 5, 8–10, 110.

10 Joel Goldberg, "It Takes a Village to Determine The Origins of an African Proverb," *NPR*, last modified 30 July 2016, accessed 8 July 2020, https://www.npr.org/sections/goatsandsoda/2016/07/30/487925796/it-takes-a-village-to-determine-the-origins-of-an-african-proverb.

11 Darcia Narvaez, "The Evolved Development Niche: Longitudinal Effects of Caregiving Practices on Early Childhood Psychosocial Development," *Early Childhood Research Quarterly* (2013): http://dx.doi.org/10.1016/j.ecresq.2013.07.003.

12 Robert Winston and Rebecca Chicot, "The Importance of Early Bonding on the Long-Term Mental Health and Resilience of Children," *London Journal of Primary Care* 8, no. 1 (2016): 12-14.

13 Darcia Narvaez, "The Evolved Development Niche: Longitudinal Effects of Caregiving Practices on Early Childhood Psychosocial Development,"

Early Childhood Research Quarterly (2013): http://dx.doi.org/10.1016/j. ecresq.2013.07.003.

14 N. Garmezy, "Stressors of Childhood," in *Stress, Coping, and Development in Children*, ed. N. Garmezy, and M. Rutter (New York: McGraw-Hill, 1983), 43–84.

Part III

Creating a Child–Friendly Setting

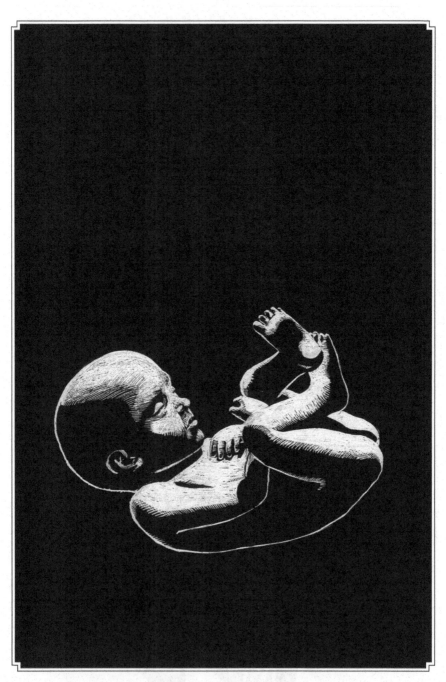

In the developed countries, there is a poverty of intimacy. The greatest suffering is to feel alone, unwanted, unloved.

 *Chapter 10*

The Extended Family and Its Devolution

Collective Parenting is a human evolutionary trait: Each and every adult is biologically programmed to help care for all the children in the clan, and each and every child is biologically programmed to relate to all clan adults as parents.[1] With all adults involved in providing for the children's sustenance, safety, and happiness, children grow up in a sea of trust and love. In such a multigenerational environment, everyone has known each other for their whole lives—and knows their ancestors. No adults, then, are strangers; and there are typically no adults to be wary of, as everyone is held accountable by the community as a whole.

In such a system, every adult has an influential role in the life of every child. With multiple role models, a child who does not resonate with one parent has several other options. In time of need, a child never has to run home from the neighbors to find a parent, because he is always home. With everything being shared, he does not have to worry about the favoritism of a particular adult, or about being deprived of what others have.

Living Examples

The children of the Ladakhi People of northern India receive unlimited and unconditional affection from everyone around them. Rather than being segregated into peer groups, they grow up surrounded by people of all ages, from babies to great-grandparents. The chain of relationships equates to a chain of giving and receiving.[2]

Hawaiians call their unstructured, extended-family parenting style *Ku i ka welo*, which literally means *children and adults fitting into the clan ways*.[3] By definition, clan ways of relationship are all-inclusive and not biologically dependent. A child's well-being, then, is determined by how well she lives the spirit of Ku i ka welo, rather than by how well she functions with her birth parents.

For nearly all of us in this day, Ku i ka welo is only a romantic notion. The closest most of us come to it is in an anthropological text, a National Geographic special, a piece of utopian fiction, or a glamorized version in a Hollywood film. Whatever the source, I see it bringing a sense of longing to some for the way of being in family that was known by their not-so-distant ancestors.

Because Ku i ka welo is such a vital part of our biology, its loss has turned the world of our children upside down. Ohiyesa, a Santee Dakota who grew up in the 1800s, was born into Ku i ka welo. It was taken from him by boarding schools, and later in life he reflected on what that meant to him: "As a child, I understood how to give. I have forgotten that grace since I became Civilized. I lived the natural life, whereas I now live the artificial."[4]

What Does Living Without Ku i ka welo Mean to Our Children?

Many of them are lucky to have two parents, and some have only one. Those one or two adults are the world to a small child, as they must provide for all her needs and wants—as unrealistic as that expectation might be. Even if the parent is lacking in some way, there is oftentimes no one else to fall back on.

For educational and employment considerations, many people have moved a considerable distance away from their biological families and close friends. When these dispersers become parents, neither they nor their children have grandparents, aunts and uncles, or cousins close by.

Even when family members live in proximity to each other, they seldom have the luxury to provide a consistent presence for the child. With our fragmented society and set schedules, children and adults are typically taken in different directions. With the adults off to work, children are placed in same-age-group environments, which makes it difficult for them to develop relationships with people of various ages.

Other complications are legalities such as custody laws, which while being set up to protect children, can also make it difficult for multiple adults to be involved in the raising of a child.

All of this places a tremendous burden upon the parent (or parents) of a nuclear family to attempt to provide the rich, multidimensional social environment a child needs in order to be healthy and whole. Never in the long history of our species has such an expectation been placed upon parents.

Anatomy of the Fall

For millions of years, stretching back to the time when our remotest ancestors were still tree-dwellers, we lived in clans. It is all we had ever known. Then, around 10,000 years ago, a few distinct populations of Humans began to abandon their clan ways. The movement gained momentum, until now only a few pockets of people in the most remote corners of the world live the clan way.

Although there is much speculation regarding the reason or reasons for the shift, the topic is likely to be explored and debated for a long time to come. What we do know is that nomadic gatherer-hunters and primitive agriculturists typically have a clan-based social organization, while industrialized peoples are largely nuclear-family structured.

Between the two extremes lies the evolutionary steps of mechanized agriculture and village living. Both require stability, which is provided by a sedentary lifestyle and dependence on set plots of land. Along with that, a relationship system capable of harnessing energy and being goal oriented was needed.

Enter the *extended family*. With a monogamous couple at the helm, many children, and aunts, uncles, and grandparents taking support roles, the fields and pastures had a reliable labor force to tend them. Yet the extended family was smaller than the clan, and crops and herds needed to be protected. Extended families responded by banding together in villages.

A village has a considerably larger social structure than clan and extended family, which tends to erode the significance of both, resulting in the breakdown of Ku i ka welo. Combine that with the fact that we Humans are biologically capable of having caring, trusting relationships with a maximum of fifteen to fifty people,[5] and you can see why village relationships become less intimate and more civil.

The Cost to Our Children

Village life has a profound effect upon children. No longer is every child their sibling and every adult their parent. Rules and social conventions now govern relationships outside their family. No more is any full breast available to a nursling; no longer can a child find food and comfort in any house.

The Birth of Cities—and the Nuclear Family

In villages, a weak form of Shared Parenting sometimes continues, when close relatives live in the same or adjacent residences. Children can then still benefit from multiple role models and compassionate, committed care from adults other than their biological parents.

However, as agriculture grows in economic importance and complexity, so do villages. With size comes specialization—the cornerstone of industrialization. We now have cities peopled by laborers who perform specialized tasks.

Here we have a radical departure from the collectivism of the farm: Rather than needing more hands to perform a task, fewer and more specialized hands are required. The upshot is the shattering of the extended family's economic base.

With the reduced need for labor to support family enterprises, we now need a new family model. Enter a stripped-down version of the extended family: the biological parents and their offspring. We know it as the *isolated nuclear family*.

Over the past 100 years, the transition from rural to urban life has greatly accelerated across the Civilized world. In 1900, 60 percent of the US population lived in the country, and 40 percent lived in the city. By 2000, the percentage of city dwellers doubled—to 79 percent.[6] During that century, fathers first entered the workforce; then during World War II, mothers joined as well. The percentage of working females dropped to around 30 percent shortly after the war, then it began to rise in the 1960s, with it resting at 71.2% in 2021.[7]

The breakdown of the extended family and the changes to the nuclear family through industrialization and urbanization have a far greater effect on our children than the breakdown of the clan. The double-income nuclear family can come nowhere near providing for a child's biologically programmed need for clan upbringing. To fill the gap, we create institutions: childcare and big brother/sister programs, recreation centers, camps, schools, clubs, and the list goes on. Surrogate siblings in the form of classmates and playmates, and surrogate parents in the form of babysitters, teachers, and counselors, attempt to further compensate.

Are Clan Replacement Systems Working?

A look at how many children are marginalized,[8] suffering from depression,[9] and socially maladjusted[10] tells me that our current familial and community structures are failing miserably.

If that's not proof enough, we can take into account the adults heading up nuclear families. Many of them are burdened with emotional and physical disease. Around 35 percent are chronically overstressed[11] and 20 percent suffer from depression,[12] both of which are major contributors to many of the health conditions that contemporary adults experience.[13] In addition, we can look at the common causes of adult debilitation and death, which bear little resemblance to those of our clan ancestors.

And how about the families these adults are heading up? A full 96 percent of US families can be considered dysfunctional,[14] with 26 percent of them engaged in some sort of physical, emotional, or sexual abuse.[15] Add to that the fact that around 25 percent of children find themselves in the care of only one parent (more on this in Chapter 13).[16] Those grim figures beg the question: Can a household that is little more than a crossroads for people coming and going in different directions, or a parent-child relationship dominated by abuse or absenteeism, or a single parent and child barely subsisting on their own, even be considered a family?

Chapter in a Page

Collective Parenting is a human evolutionary trait. Each and every adult is biologically programmed to help care for all the children in the clan, and each and every child is biologically programmed to relate to all clan adults as parents. With all adults involved in providing for the children's sustenance, safety, and happiness, children grow up in a sea of trust and love.

In such a multigenerational environment, everyone has known each other for their whole lives—and knows their ancestors. No adults, then, are strangers; and there are typically no adults to be wary of, as everyone is held accountable by the community as a whole. With multiple role models, a child who does not resonate with one parent has several other options. He always has a home.

Our fragmented society, with its set schedules, typically takes children and adults in different directions. With the adults off to work, children are placed in same-age-group environments, which makes it difficult for them to develop relationships with people of various ages. Even when family members live in proximity to each other, they seldom have the luxury to provide a consistent presence for the child.

Other complications are legalities such as custody laws, which while being set up to protect children, can also make it difficult for multiple adults to be involved in the raising of a child. All of this places a tremendous burden upon the parent (or parents) of a nuclear family to attempt to provide the rich, multidimensional social environment a child needs in order to be healthy and whole.

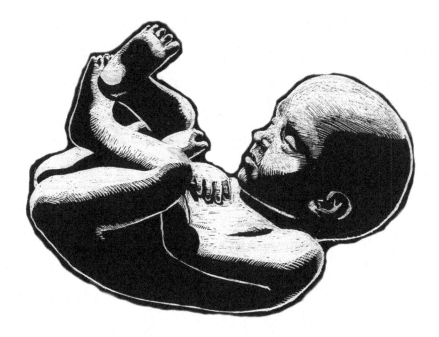

Never in the long history of our species has such an expectation been placed upon parents.

◇◇◇◇◇◇◇◇◇◇◇◇◇◇◇◇◇◇◇◇◇

Chapter 10 Endnotes

1 L. Newson, "Cultural Evolution and Human Reproductive Behavior," in *Building Babies: Primate Development in Proximate and Ultimate Perspective* (New York: Springer, 2013).

2 Helena Norberg-Hodge, *Ancient Futures* (Sierra Club Books, 1991), 66.

3 Mary Kawena Pukui, *'Olelo No'eau: Hawaiian Proverbs & Poetical Sayings* (Bishop Museum Press, 1983), 202.

4 Charles Alexander Eastman, *The Soul of the Indian* (Houghton Mifflin, 1911), 88.

5 Robin Dunbar, *Grooming, Gossip, and the Evolution of Language* (Harvard University Press, 1998), 77.

6 Hannah Ritche and Max Roser, "Urbanization," *Our World in Data*, last modified November 2019, accessed 25 January 2020, https://ourworld-indata.org/urbanization.

7 News Release, Bureau of Labor Statistics, US Department of Labor, April 10, 2022

8 Kate Offerdahl, Alice Evangelides, and Maggie Powers, *Overcoming Youth Marginalization: Conference Report and Policy Recommendations* (New York: Columbia University, 2014), 5-19.

9 "Data and Statistics on Children's Mental Health," *Centers for Disease Control and Prevention*, last modified June 2022, accessed 4 July 2022, https://www.cdc.gov/childrensmentalhealth/data.html.

10 R.L. McGhee and R.J. Short, "The Prevalence of Social Maladjustment Among School-Age Children," *Psychology in the Schools* 28, no. 4 (1991): 285-89.

11 "Stress Research," *The American Institute of Stress*, accessed 4 July 2022, https://www.stress.org/stress-research.

12 "Facts and Statistics," *ADAA*, last modified 2018, accessed 26 January 2020, https://adaa.org/about-adaa/press-room/facts-statistics.

13 "Stress Research," *The American Institute of Stress*, accessed 1 April 2022, https://www.stress.org/stress-research.

14 Lee McCormick and Mary Faulkner, *Spirit Recovery Medicine Bag* (Health Communications, 2014), 164.

15 U.S. Department of Health and Human Services, *Child Maltreatment 2018* (2020), 19, https://www.acf.hhs.gov/sites/default/files/cb/cm2018.pdf#page=21.

16 U.S. Census Bureau, *Current Population Reports OECD*, last modified Sept 2018, accessed 4 July 2022, https://www.childstats.gov/americas-children/tables/pop1.asp.

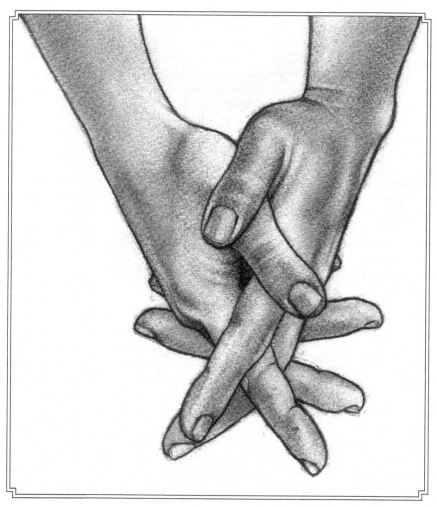

Then we look at our children, who are starved for more than food. What is missing?

 *Chapter 11*

It's All about Relationship

There is probably nothing more supportive and healing that we can do for our children—and ourselves—than to live in an extended-family environment. It doesn't matter whether we call it a clan, a commune, or a group household, just as long as there is Shared Parenting and all the children are together the majority of the day. So many personal and relational problems are created by the isolated nuclear family structure, and so many of these problems can be helped just by returning to extended-family living. For that reason, I encourage you to place extended-family living as the top priority in your family's journey to Balance.

What Really Matters

The extended family can provide for much of our essential nurturing and relational sustenance, without which we would be miserable. When we can begin relating to each child as our child, and each adult as a co-parent, our entire life starts transforming. The sole burden of responsibility lifts from our shoulders, we see new facets of our children, we realize how much our contribution means to our entire extended family.

As most of us now live, we have many concerns that consume our days, such as security, achievement, and comfort. We bear them largely alone, and they often weigh heavy on our souls. Then we look at our children, who are starved for more than food. What is missing? Why do our children not thrive on our efforts? Red Cloud, an Oglala Lakota who lived in the 1800s, addresses these very concerns in the following quote: "Look at me—I am poor and naked, but I am the chief of the nation. We do not want riches, but we do want to train our children right. Riches would do us no good. We could not take them with us to the other world. We do not want riches. We want peace and love."[1]

Extended family is a primary concern for all peoples living in the Native Way. When I am with them, much of what we talk about has to do with their relations. Whether or not an individual is currently able to live with his kin, his concerns and priorities are still with them. It's based on both long-standing tradition and practicality: When someone is separated from his people, he typically comes to realize the value of kin-relationships all the more.

As all of us have Native ancestral ways, I have sought out the voices of those who lived the Native Way to guide us on this vital topic of relationship we are exploring. The Ancestral Way has stood the test of time—even in this modern age we keep rediscovering why it is the Beauty Way. Let's begin with an eloquent definition of extended family by Kaili'ohe Kame'ekua, the Hawaiian Elderwoman who has already shared some of her wisdom with us:

"Family, to us ... was seen as a solid unit. A whole, of which we were each a part. In actuality, the family was a community or group of people living together, growing together, working out their problems the best way they could together, all connected, all learning and growing and assisting each other in their growth. We were all related in some way. Many generations—many fingers of the same hand; parts of one body...The 'aha [extended family] consisted of the flesh, or living family and the spirit family. That a person had passed from flesh did not make them less family. They were spoken of and to, remembered in *mele* [song, poetry] and chant. At meals they were remembered before the family ate the food."[2]

The Relations *Are* Family

Rather than thinking to create a community when settling in a new location, Native people see themselves joining an already existing community: that of the animal, plant, and mineral beings who are already living there in harmony. Natives ask permission to join the community, which the Ojibwe of my area call the *Hoop of Life*.

Children are especially sensitized to their relationship with the Hoop of Life. "[The children] feel that all living creatures are blood brothers and sisters," says Ohiyesa, who we met earlier in the book. "The strong wind is to them a messenger."[3]

Ohiyesa goes on to say that "The Indian mother has not only the experience of her mother and grandmother, and the accepted rules of her people for a guide, but she humbly seeks to learn a lesson from ants, bees, spiders, beavers, and badgers. She studies the family life of the birds, so exquisite in its emotional intensity and its patient devotion, until she seems to feel the universal mother-heart beating in her own breast."[4]

The same is as true for the other clan members as it is for the children and mothers. The guiding voices help them to integrate by establishing camps and leading lives that are in Balance with a particular area.

Relationship in Family

South African !Korana (an exterminated people related to the !Kung San) children called any younger boy in the clan *ti !kã-p =xam-p—my younger brother*.[5] Here is an example of a clan's unstratified social structure, which extends to all ages and relationships.

Hawaiian Elderwoman Kaili'ohe Kame'ekua echoes the same sentiment when she says, "Within the family all first cousins, sisters and brothers and half-sisters and brothers were simply called sisters and brothers. All of the generation of the parents were called *makua* (parents). All people of older generations were called grandparents. We called them *kupuna*. Individually they were called *Tutu* and their given name. We loved them all, for they first loved us. When you did not know the genealogy chants of your family it was extremely difficult to know which pair of these many were your individual line. To most of us it didn't really matter."[6]

No Child Left Behind

"Orphans and the aged are invariably cared for, not only by their next-of-kin, but by the whole clan,"[7] says Ohiyesa. Here is a vibrant case from Yurok Elderwoman Che-na-wah Weitch-ah-wah ook, who was a contemporary of Ohiyesa: "If anything happens to the mother that causes her death at childbirth or after ... they take sugarpine nuts or hazelnuts and pound them into fine flour and mix this in warm water, making a milky substance out of it. They can raise a child on this preparation as well as if it was nursed at the mother's breast. Every family ... was very careful to keep a good supply of pine and hazelnuts on hand."[8]

Chapter in a Page

Extended family is a primary involvement for all peoples living in the Native Way. When I am with them, much of what we talk about has to do with their relations. Whether or not an individual is currently able to live with his kin, his concerns and priorities are still with them. It's based on both long-standing tradition and practicality: When someone is separated from his people, he typically comes to realize the value of kin-relationships all the more. There is probably nothing more supportive and healing that we can do for our children—and ourselves—than to live in an extended-family environment.

It doesn't matter whether we call it a clan, a commune, or a group household, just as long as there is Shared Parenting and all the children are together the majority of the day. So many personal and relational problems are created by the isolated nuclear family structure, and so many of these problems can be helped just by returning to extended family living.

For that reason, I encourage you to place extended-family living as the top priority in your family's journey to Balance. When we can begin relating to each child as our child, and each adult as a co-parent, our entire life starts transforming. The sole burden of responsibility lifts from our shoulders, we see new facets of our children, we realize how much our contribution means to our entire extended family.

◇◇◇◇◇◇◇◇◇◇◇◇◇◇◇◇◇◇◇◇◇◇◇◇

Chapter 11 Endnotes

1   Edmund B. Tuttle, *Three Years on the Plains: Observations of Indians 1867-1870* (Waxkeep Publishing, 2015), 199.
2   Pali Lee and Koko Willis, *Tales From the Night Rainbow*, 10.
3   Charles Alexander Eastman, *The Soul of the Indian*, 34.
4   Ibid, 33.
5   Menán du Plessis, *Kora: A Lost Khoisan Language English* (University of South Africa Press, 2018), 327, 348.
6   Pali Lee and Koko Willis, *Tales From the Night Rainbow*, 7.
7   Charles Alexander Eastman, *The Soul of the Indian*, 101.
8   Lucy Thompson, *To the American Indian* (L. Thompson, 1916), 28.

If we want flush and plentiful fruit, we must give attention to the health and nourishment of the tree long before the fruit appears. The same is true with establishing a strong extended-family base for our children.

 *Chapter 12*

The Value of Shared Parenting

Next in importance to an extended-family environment is Collective Parenting. It gives every adult both the responsibility and privilege to be closely involved with every child, and vice versa. With the attention and security this web of relationship brings, it is seldom that a child turns out as anything other than an asset, and—from the earliest age—a contributing member of the clan. It would be hard to imagine hearing something akin to novelist Peter De Vries's quip, "There are times when parenthood seems nothing but feeding the mouth that bites you."[1]

The following quotes highlight different aspects of the Shared Parenting style of raising children. Each passage broadens the definition of relationship and how it enriches the lives of everyone involved.

> "Children belonged to all of the family, not just one set of parents."[2]
> –Kaili'ohe Kame'ekua
>
> "They all brought me up, all of them helped. My aunt brought me up; my father and mother brought me up; my grandmother brought me up."[3] –Nisa, !Kung San woman, 1900s
>
> "I said, 'Where's my mother; I don't know where my mother is.' And he [my uncle] said to me, 'OK, I am looking for her, and when I find her I am going to hand you to her, to my sister. You're my son, my sister's boy; you need not worry."[4] –Wandjuk Marika, Australian Aborigine Elder, 1900s
>
> "My mother adopted [an unrelated woman] and they became sisters. [The unrelated woman] is also my mother 'cause she always

look after me, when I get in touch with her she is always there."[5]
–Mawalan Marika, Wandjuk Marika's son

Traditional Roles and Role Models

Adults of childbearing age are usually not the primary childcare providers, for two reasons: They are best suited for providing sustenance (foraging, hunting, craftwork, exploring), and they have little parenting experience. The primary caregivers are the children themselves (who knows children better than children?) and grandparents, who have experience, perspective, and time.

With Shared Parenting, there is a variety of men and women available to serve as role models. While children are exploring and developing the masculine and feminine aspects of themselves, they can look to multiple people in any gender as role models.

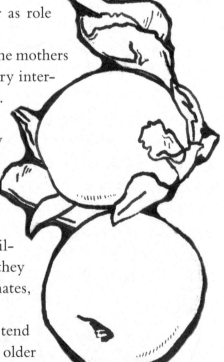

For children under age six, the mothers play a central role as the primary interpreters of the fathers' character. Children in this age group tend to imitate their mothers, so they can either elevate or degrade the fathers in the children's eyes.[6] Being very aware of how their mothers and fathers interact with each other, the children learn relational patterns they will enact with their future mates, and with their own children.

As boys grow older, they tend to shift from the mothers to older boys and men for guidance on ways to interact and explore their roles within the clan. Ohiyesa states that "[As children] we watched the men of our people and acted like them in our play, and learned to emulate them in our lives."[7]

Native mothers and fathers generally consider the following traits to be the pillars of parenting, and thus what children most need to have modeled by them:

- Firmness
- Kindness
- Consistency

In addition, these traits are beneficial for us to model in our relationship with our *child-self*.

How Elders Serve

The passing down of clan memories, skills honed from a lifetime of experience, and the wisdom distilled from deep reflection are the gifts of the elders that give extended family its lifeblood. In a myriad of ways, often unknown and unseen, the elders guide the clan on its course.

Universal among Native people is the honor and respect given elders, such as being served first at meals and being seated in the place of honor. The way this regard is shown by the youngest of children, it seems instinctual. Here are a few passages that illustrate the regard Native children have for their elders:

> "[A five-year-old Ojibwe girl of the 1800s called Oona] went to her grandparents and stood before them with eyes cast down, knowing she could not speak the many questions she wished to ask, for they who are wise must speak first. Always, the first words spoken should be from the older people."[8] —Ignatia Broker, Ojibwe elder and great-great granddaughter of Oona
>
> "I was made to respect the adults, especially the aged. [They] are old and wise. They have lived and achieved. They are dedicated

to the service of the young, as their teachers and advisors, and the young in turn regard them with love and reverence. In them, the Indian recognizes the natural and truest teachers of the child."[9] —Ohiyesa

"The elders of our family were wise. By watching the children and seeing what they did well and what interested them, they helped us to place them with an uncle or auntie who could teach them all that there was to be known about a particular area of knowledge. Many children were placed at birth or by the time they were one or two years of age, because they had already shown the path upon which their heart would lead them."[10] —Kaili'ohe Kame'ekua

Here are the words of an Ojibwe Elderwoman from the 1800s named A-wa-sa-si (Bullhead) that show the respected role of Elders in the lives of newborns:

"The children of the Ojibwe are the beloved. When they are born they are given a song and a medicine bag by a namer. The first is given in honor to its grandmother and grandfather, the parents of the mother. They cherish the child, teaching and showing the places where footsteps must tread.

"The second, third, and other children are given in honor to a namesake who must watch the growing child and speak to the parents often. Never is a child without the spoken words of the Old Ones."[11]

Extended Family and the Newborn

An expectant mother is anything but preoccupied during her pregnancy. Even though her child is yet to be born, she is fully present with him, guiding him with visualizations and her own example. She can devote time to her coming child because of the support of the clan. In a real sense, the entire clan is giving to the child.

In homage to the Circle of Life, the clan helps assure that the first influences on the unborn child are from the plant and animal members of the extended family. Here Ohiyesa speaks to the topic:

"[The mother's] attitude and secret meditations must be such as to instill into the receptive soul of the unborn child the love of the Great Mystery and a sense of connectedness with all creation. Silence and isolation are the rule of life for the expectant mother. She wanders prayerful in the stillness of the great woods.

"And when the day of days in her life dawns ... she seeks no human aid. She has been trained and prepared in body and mind for this, her holiest duty, ever since she can remember.

"Childbirth is best met alone, where no curious embarrass her, where all Nature says ... 'It's love! It's love! The fulfilling of life!' When ... a pair of eyes open upon her in the wilderness, she knows with joy that she has borne well her part in the great song of creation!

"Presently she returns to the camp ... [The baby] is still a part of herself, since both are nourished by the same mouthful, and no look of a lover could be sweeter than its deep, trusting gaze.

"She continues her spiritual teaching, at first silently—a mere pointing of the index finger to Nature—then in whispered songs, bird-like, at morning and evening. To her and to the child the birds are real people, who live very close to the Great Mystery; the murmuring trees breathe its presence; the falling waters chant its praise ... She bids [the child] be still and listen—listen to the silver voice of the aspen, or the clashing cymbals of the birch ... Silence, love, reverence—this is the trinity of first lessons."[12]

Ensuring Quality Upbringing

She lifted up the child (/koi !xo khãsi) is a metaphorical saying of the !Korana that expresses the support and caring that a child receives.[13] This is possible because many Native women space their children around four years apart, which results in less competition between children and more parental time per child. The Hawaiian idiom *Ka'ika'i i ka lima, hi'i i ke alo—Lead with one hand, carry with one arm,* refers to a mother with children born too close together.[14]

Care for Those in Need

In closing this vital chapter on coming together to raise our children the Circle Way, I'd like to feature what I consider to be one of its greatest rewards: producing children who vie for the honor of serving those unable to help themselves. The children embody the following values that are inherent to clan living:

- Giving is receiving.
- People come first.
- The strength of the individual is dependent on the strength of the Circle.

Here Ohiyesa describes how those values reflect in his people:

"We are never permitted to forget that we do not live to ourselves alone, but to our tribe and clan. Every child, from the first days of learning, is a public servant in training. It was the loving parents' pride to have their daughters visit the unfortunate and helpless, carry them food, comb their hair, and mend their garments.

"The young boy was encouraged to enlist early in the public service, and to develop a wholesome ambition for the honors of a leader and feast-maker. At such feasts [also known as *Giveaways*], the parents often gave so generously to the needy that they almost impoverished themselves, thereby setting an example to the child of self-denial for the public good."[15]

Chapter in a Page

Next in importance to an extended-family environment is Collective Parenting. As Kaili'ohe Kame'ekua said, "Children belonged to all of the family, not just one set of parents." Collective Parenting gives every adult both the responsibility and privilege to be closely involved with every child, and vice versa. With the attention and security this web of relationship brings, children grow to become valued, contributing members of the clan.

Within traditional communities, adults of childbearing age are usually not the primary childcare providers, for two reasons: they the best suited for providing sustenance (foraging, hunting, craftwork, exploring), and they have little parenting experience. The primary caregivers are the children themselves (who knows children better than children?) and grandparents, who have experience, perspective, and time. Mothers and fathers still serve as fundamental role models, and seek above

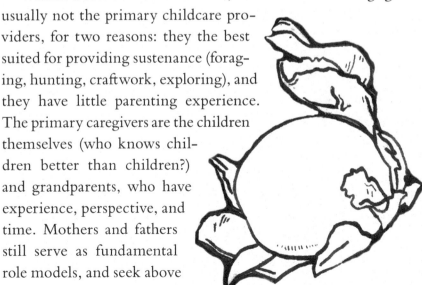

all to model the following three traits: firmness, kindness, consistency.

The passing down of clan memories, skills honed from a lifetime of experience, and the wisdom distilled from deep reflection are the gifts of the elders that give extended family its lifeblood. In a myriad of ways, often unknown and unseen, the elders guide the clan on its course. For that reason, it is universal among Native people that honor and respect is given to elders, such as being served first at meals and being seated in the place of honor. Many young children demonstrate such honor to elders almost instinctively, and indeed one of the greatest honors as parents is raising children who are attentive to demonstrating honor and respect to elders.

◇◇◇◇◇◇◇◇◇◇◇◇◇◇◇◇◇◇◇◇◇◇◇◇

Chapter 12 Endnotes

1   Peter De Vries, *The Tunnel of Love* (University of Chicago Press, 2014), 45.

2   Pali Lee and Koko Willis, *Tales From the Night Rainbow*, 28.

3   Marjorie Shostak, *Nisa: The Life and Words of a !Kung Woman* (Harvard University Press, 2000), 56.

4   Wandjuk Marika and Jennifer Isaacs, *Wandjuk Marika: Life Story* (University of Queensland Press, 1995), 48.

5   Ibid, 5.

6   Elise Frank Masur and Jennifer E. Rodemaker, "Mothers' and Infants' Spontaneous Vocal, Verbal, and Action Imitation During the Second Year," *Merrill-Palmer Quarterly* 45, no. 3 (1999): 392-412.

7   Kent Nerburn, *The Wisdom of the Native Americans* (New World Library, 2010), 17.

8   Ignatia Broker, *Night Flying Woman: An Ojibway Narrative* (Minnesota Historical Society Press, 1983), 22.

9   Charles Alexander Eastman, *The Soul of the Indian*, 34-35.

10 Pali Lee and Koko Willis, *Tales From the Night Rainbow*, 20-21.

11 Ignatia Broker, *Night Flying Woman: An Ojibway Narrative,* 57.

12 Charles Alexander Eastman, *The Soul of the Indian*, 29-32.

13 L.F. Maingard, *Korana Folktales* (Witwatersrad University Press, 1962), 59.

14 Mary Kawena Pukui, *'Olelo No'eau: Hawaiian Proverbs & Poetical Sayings*, 151.

15 Charles A. Eastman, *The Soul of an Indian* (New World Library, 2001), 26-27.

What parents do, children will do. Once we open the doorway, all we have to do is stand back and they will take to clan ways like Bees to Flowers.

 *Chapter 13*

Goodbye Guilt, Hello Clan

The Hawaiians have a saying: *I maika'i ke kalo i ka'ohā*, which means *The goodness of the taro root is judged by the young plant it produces.*[1] Many parents take this outlook to heart and blame themselves for the condition of their children.

Then there is the flip side of guilt: blame. Others are quick to heap the burden of responsibility on parents. After all, they *are* the parents; so if their child fails, it must be their fault, right?

Wrong.

One or two parents—even if they are exceptional in every way—can barely begin to provide their children with a clan upbringing. For parents to assume the burden of guilt for the breakdown of the clan is unrealistic and defeatist. And those who point fingers at parents might do well to notice who the other fingers of their hands are pointing back to. Let us remember that we are social beings, which means that much of who we are is a reflection of our culture. No individual can shoulder responsibility for a culture that has been careening off course for so long that the very reasons for its woeful condition are lost to the dim reaches of the past.

Where to Go with Blame

In her book *Ancient Futures: Learning from Ladakh*, Helena Norberg-Hodge states that "If our starting point is a respect for Nature and people, diversity is an inevitable consequence. If technology and the needs of the economy are our starting point, then we have what we are faced with today—a model of development that is dangerously distanced from the needs of particular peoples and places and rigidly imposed from the top down."[2]

When we grow frustrated with the situation seemingly beyond our control that Helena refers to, many of us deal with it by externalizing, i.e., blaming someone else. For those of us who had troubled childhoods, that "someone else" is often our parents. With them having a major—if not *the* major—influence on our young lives, we can easily trace our struggles back to them.

That makes it easy to forget that they had parents also, who also had parents, and so on, all of whom imprinted their children with epigenetically and culturally inherited patterns and behaviors. Is it fair to hold any one parent liable for such a legacy?

Many of us use externalizing and blaming to create distance between ourselves and our parents, so that we can commit ourselves to raising our children differently than we were raised. However, in doing so we deny one fundamental truth: *To a large degree, we are our parents.* Time and again I see young mothers and fathers reenacting the same patterns and behaviors they were raised with.

Sadly, these parents are not aware that they are doing it. Sometimes the old approach is disguised by different jargon or a supposedly new childrearing philosophy. At other times parents just revert to the old and familiar, which is a natural tendency in times of stress.

To distance ourselves from our parents is to lose touch with who we are and how we have learned to function. Our parents are our mirrors, plain and simple. When we accept that and recognize that they live on in us, we recognize and accept ourselves. We have then opened the doorway to change.

Blaming our parents does the opposite—it reinforces the behaviors of theirs that we carry. When we look outside ourselves for the cause of our actions, we become blind to ourselves. No matter how strong a case we create against our parents, and no matter if they take the blame, it does nothing to change us, who are the current practitioners of our family's dysfunctional childrearing methods.

Awareness is the first step in healing: Without embracing our primary role in perpetuating our parents' ways, we will most assuredly carry on our family childrearing tradition. The same holds true for our cultural tradition.

A Bridge for Skeptics of the Blossoming Way

Recently a couple asked, "Is there anything we can do to bridge the gap between us and our friends and relatives who don't agree with Natural Childrearing?" I suggested that they focus on what they have in common with their friends and relatives that goes beyond childrearing philosophies. For example, a mother or grandmother might be able to help a parent understand the language of babies. A friend with older children could give some insight into the changes a child goes through at puberty. When someone is able to make a valued contribution, she feels validated. Time and again I've seen this approach reduce tension and lead to acceptance.

Return to Clan

Many parents I know have turned to extended family out of need or desperation. They have gone back to live with siblings, parents, or grandparents, or they have entrusted children to their care. This fits with the history of extended family, which was born out of need. Clan, on the other hand, is born out of an innate yearning to manifest what it is to be human. Some people I know call this intrinsic longing *real love*.

"Easy to say," you might be thinking, "but how do you do it?" The good news is that all we have to do is get out of the way and allow it to happen. Remember that we are already clanspeople to the core—every cell in our bodies sings out Ku i ka welo. It is only our conditioning that has us living any other way. And our children? The Hawaiians say, *Ka hana a ka mākua, o ka hana no ia a keiki—What parents do, children will do.*[3] Once we open the doorway, all we have to do is stand back and watch them take to clan ways like bees to flowers. They progress much faster and easier than us, because they have not been as numbed to their intrinsic voices to the extent that we have.

We can help the process by identifying the areas in our lives that prevent clan connection, then make changes for cultivating a fertile environment in which clan-style living can grow. Here are some ideas to get you started:

- Organize playtimes and other activities where your children interact with other children of varying ages.

- Either avoid or revamp events geared toward same-age children.

- Cultivate relationships with other families having children of a range of ages, so that you can have shared meals, outings, and other activities.

- Either homeschool your children in conjunction with other families, or have your children attend schools that are not based on a one-age class structure.

- Choose living situations where you are in close proximity to clan-minded families. Possibilities include shared housing, adjacent rental units, neighborhood blocks, and intentional communities.

- Organize a study-envisioning group, to share ideas and concerns, educate yourselves, and explore/develop possibilities for realizing elements of clan living.

Why Can't I Love Every Child as Much as My Own?

The answer lies in the story of clan, where biological relationship is secondary to clan relationship. Bonding is a matter of time, not blood. Adopted children feel just as close to their mothers as do birth children, and mated relationships—the closest of all human ties—have no shared blood. In a clan living situation, deep and lasting bonds with children and adults become established through the lifelong sharing of life and *lifeway*.

This is in deep contrast to our contemporary lives, where there is seldom anyone with whom we have close daily relationship other than our children. The answer, then, to why someone in this day can't love others as well as their children is that there is usually no one other than their children to love. As the old saying goes, *Every mother's child is handsome.*[4]

Yet that is not the way it has to be. If I had to summarize this book in a few words, it would be *a return to clan ways*. With each page of this book, you reawaken more to our intrinsic clan ways, and you obtain the tools and guidance to renew them. Nearly all the quotes and references are reflective of clan lifeway, because they are the voices of people living in clan.

Clan Living Brought to Life

To gain a sense of what it is like to live in clan, as all humans once did, please see my book *Fat Moons and Hunger Moons: The Turn of the Seasons for Northwoods Natives*.

When we realize *we* are our only limitation, we can start healing our wounds and renewing our indigenous ways. We then empower ourselves to live our lives as intended and to let our children grow as they are intended. Together we can then live in bliss with all our relations on our beautiful Mother Earth.

Chapter in a Page

Let us remember that we are social beings, which means that much of who we are is a reflection of our culture. We live at a time when clan culture has largely been left behind or broken, though many are working to revive it. One or two parents—even if they are exceptional in every way—cannot recreate the clan way of living by themselves. Yet for parents to blame others or assume the burden of guilt for the breakdown of the clan way of living is unrealistic and defeatist.

The impulse to separate ourselves from where we have come from, and to blame others for it, is an impulse worth examining more closely. Many of us use externalizing and blaming to create distance between ourselves and our parents, so that we can commit ourselves to raising our children differently than we were raised.

However, in doing so we deny one fundamental truth: *To a large degree, we are our parents.* To distance ourselves from our parents is to lose touch with who we are and how we have learned to function.

Our parents are our mirrors, plain and simple. When we accept that and recognize that they live on in us, we recognize and accept ourselves. We have then opened the doorway to change. Awareness is the first step in healing: Without embracing our primary role in perpetuating our parents' ways, we are most assuredly going to carry on our family's childrearing tradition. The same holds true for our cultural tradition.

◇◇◇◇◇◇◇◇◇◇◇◇◇◇◇◇◇◇◇◇◇◇

Chapter 13 Endnotes

1 Mary Kawena Pukui, *'Olelo No'eau: Hawaiian Proverbs & Poetical Sayings*, 133.

2 Helena Norberg-Hodge, *Ancient Futures* (Sierra Club Books, 1991), 163.

3 Mary Kawena Pukui, *'Olelo No'eau: Hawaiian Proverbs & Poetical Sayings*, 141.

4 Lois Kerschen, *American Proverbs About Women: A Reference Guide* (Greenwood Publishing Group, 1998), 137.

The Hawaiians have a saying: *Each child born has at birth, a Bowl of perfect Light. If he tends his Light it will grow in strength and he can do all things.*

 *Chapter 14*

Rites of Passage: A Sense of Belonging

In the preceding chapters on extended family and the Cradle-board Way, we laid a solid, supportive foundation for our children's Blossoming. Now, as they grow, they reach milestones in self-discovery and skill development. The ceremonies and celebrations by a child's community that recognize these milestones are called *rites of passage*. Intrinsic to the rite of passage ritual is the sending off of the child on the journey to his next rite of passage.

Because we come from a culture focused on goal-oriented linear progressions—expansion, development, accumulation of wealth—we tend to view a child's growth as a steady progression from birth to adulthood. If we were to chart it out, we would begin with birth and plateau at adulthood, as shown in Chart 5 below. Any mile-stones that might be noted are viewed merely as stepping stones to the pinnacle—adulthood.

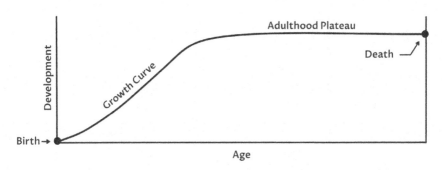

Chart 5: The Growth Curve

The only problem with the stepping-stone model is that a child—or anything else, for that matter—does not grow in a linear fashion. Like the changing seasons, growth has its times of increase and rest. A tree extends its branches in the summertime and lies dormant in the wintertime; an animal gathers food in the day and uses that nourishment to grow in the night while resting.

A Native person sees each peak in growth, each milestone, as being as complete and significant as any other. The Hawaiians have a saying: *Each child born has at birth, a Bowl of perfect Light. If he tends his Light it will grow in strength and he can do all things.*[1] This means that a child has reached a milestone with birth, and is a complete being, ready to journey to the next milestone. A person, then, matures

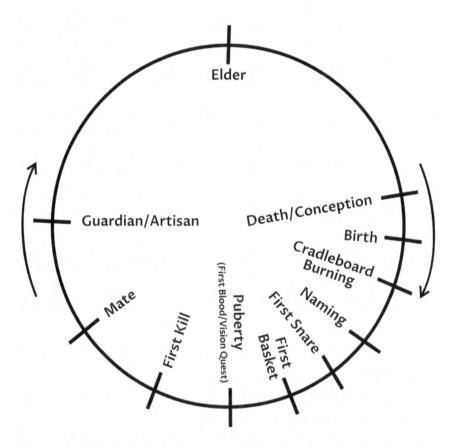

Chart 6: Rites of Passage

not once in his/her life, but a number of times, and each time into a complete being.

These milestones are marked by rites of passage (see Chart 6, which gives emphasis only to a child's rites of passage). As depicted in the chart, life is a continuum from one rite of passage to another, from birth to death to birth again. Each rite is a rebirth in itself—a fresh platform from which to rejoin life. (The rites as shown on the chart are a generalization from Native cultures worldwide and vary somewhat from locale to locale.)

The Ritual of Passage

All cultures, whether Eastern or Western, whether contemporary or Native, celebrate rites of passage. The difference among these various peoples is only in the number of milestones acknowledged and the degree to which they are honored. One culture may pay little more than lip service to a couple of milestones in a child's life, while another culture may put on a dozen celebrations in that time, involving the whole community and sometimes lasting for days.

Following is a brief description of childhood rites of passage common to many aboriginal cultures worldwide.

1. **Death/Conception** At this point where the Hoop of Life laps itself, the ancestral memories of the people—all they have gained in their journey of countless generations—are carried forth to the coming generations. This might be a time of quiet celebration by the women, or if the pregnancy has been awaited, the entire clan gives thanks and feasts.

2. **Birth** Because of close relationship and Shared Parenting, a child is born to the entire clan. In the tradition of my Ojibwe kin, a baby is anointed with Oil of Cedar immediately upon birth. Cedar, the most sacred of trees, is called

Nokomis—Grandmother, and the anointing is the ritual presenting of the child to the Grandmother of Life.

3. **Cradleboard Burning** At about a year of age, the child is ready to walk and no longer needs the cradleboard. When there is distance to cover, her back and neck are now strong enough that she can walk on her mother's legs by riding on her hip. The cradleboard is ritually burned to infuse the strength of the cradleboard into the babe's legs.

4. **Naming** Only when a child gains the autonomy of being able to move under her own power do certain aspects of her personality begin to reveal themselves. In some cultures, it is at this time that the Elder chosen to name the child starts to watch her closely for clues to her name. This name is going to both define and help shape her character until she receives her adult name.

5. **First Snare** In emulation of their parents and older siblings, young girls and boys learn to trap and snare around the camp. When they come proudly in with their first animal, no matter how small, a great feast is held to commemorate the occasion. It's as though they presented a great, fat animal to the clan, since their tiny kill is so highly valued because of the skill exhibited in the feat.

6. **First Basket** Craftwork is not as important for the goods that are produced as for the preservation of clan knowledge. The evolution of a craft involves many generations of input, and the mastering of a craft by a young person helps to assure that it survives to be passed on to the coming generations. This is similar to the First Snare rite.

7. **Puberty** As much as a puberty rite is considered by Westerners to be a coming-of-age, puberty is only one of several milestones to be reached in becoming a full-fledged adult. A girl's puberty rite is usually held on the occasion of her first moontime (menstrual bleeding), and the reason for a boy's is much

more varied. In my area it is often associated with a successful *Vision Quest*.

8. **First Kill** A !Kung San boy usually kills his first large animal when he is fifteen to eighteen years of age. He is honored in two ceremonies: one each for successfully hunting his first male and female animals. Even though he has made his first kill and may be several years into puberty, he still spends a number of years honing his hunting skills before he takes a mate.[2]

Our Dearth of Relevant Rites

Because modern culture is a hybrid of many, we have a rich and varied blend of traditions. It would seem that rites of passage should abound, and in fact they do. Our culture is so diverse that rites can vary considerably from region to region, and even from family to family in the same neighborhood. Socioeconomic status, religion, and ethnic background all play their roles in determining which rites are practiced and whether or not the greater community participates. Following are some of the most common and familiar rites:

1. **Baby shower** Akin to Native women celebrating a conception, this is a gathering of the (usually female) friends and family of an expectant mother, who literally shower baby gifts upon her, along with giving support and sharing in her joy over the upcoming birth.

2. **Birth** A generation ago, the typical middle-class birth occurred behind closed doors in a sterile hospital, with a couple of strangers in attendance and family members excluded. The only involvement of the greater community was reading the birth announcement. Times are changing, with immediate family, and sometimes close friends, now often being in attendance.

3. **Baptism** An initiation ritual into the religious community, it is performed soon after birth by most Christians and in adulthood

by some others. In recent times, baby Baptism for most people has degraded from a congregational celebration to a formality attended only by the practitioner, the immediate family and sponsor(s). In that Baptism allows the baby eternal salvation, it runs parallel with the Ojibwe Oil of Cedar Anointing.

4. **A baby's first word or step** Cards announcing the event, perhaps along with a picture, are often sent to relatives and friends. The event is noted in a *baby book*, a diary of the child's growth and progress kept by the parents.

5. **Birthday celebration** This ritual celebration of another year lived gives time to reflect over the past year as well as to plan and make resolutions for the upcoming year. Because Natives do not keep daily-monthly calendars or keep track of age, and because they have other rites satisfying the role of birthday celebrations, they have no parallel rite.

6. **First Communion** For Christians, Communion is a reen-actment of the Last Supper, the sharing of bread and wine the night before Jesus' crucifixion. In some traditional Christian denominations, a child's first participation in the Communion ritual occurs at age seven, when the child has reached the "age of reason" and is thus able to understand the symbolism of the ritual. First Communion is often an elabo-rate affair, complete with elaborate dress, photographers, and a large family gathering.

7. **Confirmation/ Bar Mitzvah** Like Baptism, these Christian and Jewish parallels to the Native puberty ceremony have lost most or all of their profundity to everyone but devout adher-ents. For a contemporary Western adolescent, the following rite has all but supplanted it.

8. **Driver license** The ability to drive a car—symbol of free-dom, power, independence and individuality—gives an ado-lescent the means to independently explore the world around

him, along with greatly facilitating sexual and other adult-sensitive explorations.

9. **Club ceremonies** Many boys and girls clubs have initiation, achievement, and graduation rites. Some of them are patterned after Native practices. Their primary drawback is that they are usually disconnected from the child's community, and sometimes also from his family.

10. **Sports and academic achievements** For many children, sports and academics are their lives. Recognition and self-esteem, as well as advancement, come from standings and awards gained from dedication and practice.

11. **Graduation** Similar to the driver license, graduation is a coming-of-age rite that is deeply significant to most children, whether or not they are academically or athletically inclined. Graduation from elementary, middle, and high school are clear signs to children that they have accomplished something recognized by their community and are sanctioned by it to move on to the next stage in their lives.

12. **First Kill** In families with hunting traditions, a youth's first kill of a deer or game bird, or the first catch of a prized fish, is often celebrated with a feast, accolades from the family's elder hunters, and requests to tell the story of the hunt in front of an attentive and admiring audience. Because hunting is seldom relied upon for sustenance, the First Kill rite is not infused with as much significance or ritual power as in cultures where hunting skills are relied upon for survival.

What Demarcates Coming of Age in This Day?

We may be able to vote, drink alcohol, serve in the military, and be considered adults in the legal system, and at the same time we are marrying and starting families at later dates than is traditional for our culture, and we could still be financially-dependent students, covered by our parent's medical insurance. The time at which we clearly pass into adulthood has become clouded.

In summary, many contemporary rites of passage are but hollow observances. Our children's hearts are often not in them, as they lack a most vital element—community involvement. There are several reasons for this state:

1. **An evolving culture** with changing values, which is rendering some rites obsolete while creating others.

2. **Regimentation** of our children's lives by schools and other institutions, which dictates values, imposes goals, and dampens personal aspirations.

3. **Depersonalization** resulting from large schools and neighborhoods of strangers, which isolates individuals from their communities.

When there is no celebration in a child's life that is relevant to whom he is, when there is no ritual to honor a threshold surmounted, he is often left feeling hollow and disconnected. In an effort to find a place for himself, he might overachieve or rebel. Or he protects himself by sinking into depression and retreating into isolation.

Can Culture Survive without Ritual?

If the boys in clan-based cultures are not initiated into manhood through being shaped by the tutelage of mentors and the caring guidance of Elders, these boys often end up destroying the culture. When they cannot add the fires that burn inside them to the hearth of their community, they must continue feeding their fires on their own. Just to feel the warmth of the culture they so yearn to be a contributing part of, they often end up burning down their culture's very fiber.

In a big sense, it does not matter what is ritualized and celebrated, because it is the *act* of ritualizing and celebrating, *within the context of his community*, which nourishes and supports the child. As noted a number of times in this book, the breakdown of community is at the core of our children's alienation. Here is yet another instance where we can note deprivation caused by the lack of extended family.

Along with restoring community, we can model our children's rites of passage after the Native Way, by adapting traditional rites common to many Native cultures to fit the child and be relevant to this day. For example, the coming-of-age ritual often culminates with the discovery of one's Life Path—the unique talent or gift that defines the individual and gives him a reason for being through serving his people. With this discovery, the youth is welcomed into his clan as a new person, just as when he was born. This infusion of a new person with a valued gift signifies fertility, which is essential for the continued life of the clan.

Neither another person nor a unique talent are so important to the maintenance of modern cultures, most of which are over-populated and discourage individuality in favor of conformity. And yet the coming-of-age ritual need not be discarded. Even in this day—especially in this day—every child yearns to know how he is special and how he can gain fulfillment by helping others. When we emphasize the self-discovery aspect of the ritual, it works just as well today as it did for the youth of our forebears. After all, we are the same people, with the same needs and desires.

The fulfilling of these needs by the clan is one reason for high self-esteem and their deep respect for each other that is found in those living the Native Way. A person feels richly satisfied when she accomplishes something and is recognized for it because of who she is, as opposed to the fleeting ego-stoke that comes when being acknowledged for how many possessions or accolades one has accumulated. Let us raise our children to be richly satisfied.

Chapter in a Page

As children grow, they reach milestones in self-discovery and skill development. The ways we recognize these milestones through ceremony and celebration are called *rites of passage*. All cultures, whether Eastern or Western, whether contemporary or Native, celebrate rites of passage.

The difference among these various peoples is only in the number of milestones acknowledged and the degree to which they are honored. Some childhood rites of passage common to many aboriginal cultures worldwide are: death/conception, birth, cradleboard burning, naming, first snare, first basket, puberty, and first kill.

Because we come from a culture focused on goal-oriented linear progressions—expansion, development, accumulation of wealth—we tend to view a child's growth as a steady progression from birth to adulthood. Any milestones that might be noted are viewed merely as stepping stones to the pinnacle—adulthood.

The only problem with this perception is that a child—or anything else, for that matter—does not grow in a linear fashion. Like the changing seasons, growth has its times of increase and rest. A Native person sees each peak in growth, each milestone, as being as complete and significant as any other.

While modern cultures have many rites of passage—including baby showers, birthdays, and graduations—they are often merely superficial as they lack a most vital element: community involvement. In a big sense, it does not matter what is ritualized and celebrated, because it is the *act* of ritualizing and celebrating, *within the context of his community*, which nourishes and supports the child. As noted a number of times in this book, the breakdown of community is at the core of our children's alienation.

◇◇◇◇◇◇◇◇◇◇◇◇◇◇◇◇◇◇◇◇◇◇

Chapter 14 Endnotes

1   Charles Francis, *Wisdom Well Said* (Levine Mesa Press, 2009), 78.
2   Funso S. Afolayan, *Culture and Customs of South Africa* (Greenwood Publishing Group, 2004), 221.

Part IV

Restoring the Children's Culture

When we were a people who gathered around the evening hearth, all the clan members were storytellers. Everyone contributed their chapter to the day's storybook.

 *Chapter 15*

Stories: Their Cultural History

The *Teaching Trail* is paved with stories. Each step is guided with a story, and each stumble and fall has a story to help it not happen again. Without stories, the Teaching Trail would degrade to an endless gauntlet every child is forced to run. Stories give children the life experience they have not yet had the opportunity to gain, and stories paint enticing visions of where the Teaching Trail is about to take them.

For the vast majority of human existence, people would gather around the evening hearth and tell our stories of the day. Men returned from the hunt and women from gathering would relive their adventures. This was not only entertaining, but essential to the clan's survival. When things did not go well, telling the story served as a psychological and emotional cleansing, and opened the avenue for empathy and guidance. When the day's activities were successful, storytellers gained recognition for their contributions. By comparing stories, the best gathering areas were found and the movements of animals were kept track of. Comparison with past stories brought long-term trends to light.

Throughout the stories, wide-eyed children would listen intently. They were being taken to places their small feet could not yet carry them, and they could experience some of the thrill of the adult world. Additionally, they learned about being an adult, and about how the Gifting Way works in the world beyond their small childhood realms. Stories of both past and present hunts taught them the lore vital to a successful hunt.[1] They learned the habits of plants and animals, the ways of the weather and the seasons, and how to honor and show respect for each other and their non-human relations. (You can find examples of such teaching stories in my book *Entering the Mind of the Tracker: Native Practices for Developing Intuitive Consciousness and Discovering Hidden Nature.*)

Storytellers were emulated, with children retelling the stories the next day in play. The stories would become role-playing games the children would act out, and in this way the stories taught through the example of the storyteller and their own experience of playing out the story.

Why Stories Work

When a fact is given as education, it lies cold on the heart. A fact is a thin slice of life frozen in time. When this fact appears alone, outside the context of its story, it is like a dry bone stripped of all skin and flesh. On the other hand, when the fact appears in the context of a story, it is part of a living experience that can touch the heart. This is why facts only give knowledge, while stories are able to impart wisdom.

Children's Stories Today

We might take the storytelling tradition to be a part of our ancestral past; but this is far from so. Every time we sit down in the evening to a movie or television show, and every time we tell our children a bedtime story, we—and our children—respond to our DNA coding to wrap up the day with story. How often have you heard "Story, story!" from your sparkly-eyed little one when bedtime neared? Even—and often especially—our media-obsessed children are enacting stories with computer-based interactive and role-playing games. One reason they are glued to the screen is because of their thirst for story.

Many stories are designed to implant values or promote ideologies, and probably all stories inadvertently do so. Because of this, children's stories have become central in the debate over gender bias, racism, and cultural appropriation. In response, a new breed of story has arisen, with each story being crafted to standards of political correctness. Are these the only stories a child ought to hear?

The Story of Stories

From the perspective of traditional cultures, all stories come from the storyline—the Great Story which contains all stories, and which guides the rhythms of the universe. Because all stories told, and all stories that will be told, already exist, our judgments hold no sway. Because everybody has access to the storyline, our attempt to control access is futile.

When a story no longer has anything of value to convey, it fades away. Stories that live on are those that capture the imagination. That is why the same story is continually dressed up over the centuries, and from culture to culture, whether it is retold around the hearth, in books, or in film.

A lasting story has these features:

- Multiple layers of meaning
- Speaks to a deeper part of the self
- A storyline that gradually unravels
- Different themes stand out at different stages of one's Life Journey

Raising my children with this premise, I have encouraged them to seek out stories from as many sources and persuasions as possible. Because stories have layered meanings, the traditional storyteller shares the same story with an audience comprised of all ages. I have done the same with my children, allowing them to listen to some stories, read some books, and see some movies that others might not consider to be age-appropriate.

Your Child's Story within the Story

By observing what has captured your child's imagination within a particular story, you can help her explore that theme as it relates to her life. Do so by asking questions that help her bridge from the narrated story to her life story.

Story is life, and every life tells a story, so there can be no bad stories. Besides, it is not the story itself that teaches as much as how the story is told. I can say with a benevolent smile, "Robin Hood stole from the rich and gave to the poor," yet it means something entirely different if I were to say it with narrowed eyes and a furrowed brow. A storyteller merely taps into the storyline and gives voice to what already exists. From a Native perspective, to claim authorship of a story is plagiarism. Realizing that she merely gives the cultural context of the story, the Native storyteller usually gives credit to the person from whom she learned the story, if not to the storyline directly.

Our Storytellers

When we were a people who gathered around the evening hearth, all the clan members were storytellers—everyone contributed their chapter to the day's storybook. Nothing has changed: We still yearn for the day's story, only we get it in the car on the way home, on the phone, or around the dinner table. Our world has grown from what our eyes could scan to what our surrogate electronic eyes can bring us, so part of our story of the day comes from newspapers, newscasters, and talk show hosts.

Children help tell their family's story of the day; and having their own Children's Culture, they also have their own day story to create. Wherever they gather, whether it be at school or coming home from school, on the playground, or at a friend's house, they fill each other in with their piece of the story.

Along with day stories, our ancestors had teaching stories. They were timeless, traditional tales from the storyline that brought guidance and perspective to the deep questions of life and daily living, such as:

- Where did we come from?
- Why do we live as we do?
- How can I best serve my people?
- How do I deal with contrary thoughts and feelings?

These teaching stories were often structured around a culture hero, who represented the clanspeople and whose antics and adventures were metaphors for the listeners' life struggles and aspirations.

Each clan had a storyteller with a special gift for accessing the storyline and personalizing the story to meet the needs of the people. "It is like looking for things in a bag," said Pretty-shield. "I just feel around till I find something."[2] Ohiyesa described his people's storytellers in this way: "There was usually some old man whose gifts as a storyteller and keeper of wisdom spread his fame far beyond the limits of his immediate family … It is reserved for them to repeat the time-hallowed tales with dignity and authority, so as to lead the child into the inheritance of the stored-up wisdom and experience of the race."[3]

Much respect was afforded the storyteller, so after the evening meal and when the day story was finished, children and adults would quiet to hear their hallowed tales come to life. This was especially true in the wintertime, as Ohiyesa relates: "In [an Elder's] home at the time of the winter camp, the children of the band were accustomed to gather. The long winter evenings are considered the proper time of those traditions that have their roots in the past and lead back to the source of all things. And since the subjects lie half in the shadow of mystery, they have to be taken up at night, the proper realm of mysticism."[4]

Pretty-shield describes the Crow having a similar tradition: "Winter was our time for storytelling. Old ones told of Old Man Coyote until the fires grew dim, and listeners fell asleep. Evenings were long, and there was not much excitement, because the men did not often go to war while the snow was deep. There was dancing, and we girls liked to watch the women when they danced the owl-dance."[5]

The Yupik of coastal Alaska and far eastern Russia are another example of winter being the time for the old stories. Traveling in family groups to gather and hunt during the warm season, the Yupik would spend the winter in often interconnected subterranean communal lodges. Each band would have two: the women's was called the *ena* and the men's was the *qasgiq*. The band would gather in the qasgiq for winter stories, along with ceremonies, dancing, and singing.[6]

Where to Begin

Because our forebears abandoned clan storytelling traditions such as those of the Yupik, Crow, and Dakota, it is now up to each of us to bring storytelling back to our families. Thanks to our innate thirst for stories, nearly anything we do whets appetites for more. Few of us have wizened elder storytellers in our family circles, and yet we can find them nearby. Here are some possibilities:

1. **Ask your family and neighborhood Elders** if they know any stories that have been passed on to them.
2. **Check in with your local cultural communities** to see if any of their storytellers share their stories with those outside their community.
3. **Watch local event calendars** for storyteller appearances.
4. **Attend storytelling festivals.** For listings go to www.loc. gov/loc/cfbook/bkevents or google Storytelling Festivals.

5. **Join the National Storytelling Network** (132 Boone Street, Suite #5 Jonesborough, TN. 37659, 1-800-525-4514; www.storynet.org). Members receive *Storytelling Magazine*.

6. **Get stories via book, CD, and DVD** from friends, libraries, and bookstores.

Valuing nearly all stories, I hesitate to make suggestions when asked for written story recommendations. At the same time, I realize that with the seemingly endless selection of books and recorded materials, the neophyte storyteller can easily become overwhelmed. Following are a few author and collection recommendations to get you started. In this grouping can be found stories for children of any age, and you'll likely find that you are already familiar with many of the stories. I chose stories that sparkle children's imaginations, give them great role-playing material, and can be easily found in libraries, bookstores, and online.

Eastern and Western Culture: Classic and Contemporary

- *One Thousand and One Nights* (also known as *Arabian Nights*)
- The Robin Hood tales
- Grimm's fairytales
- Tales found in *Women Who Run With the Wolves*, by Clarissa Pinkola Estés
- Hans Christian Andersen's fairytales
- Any of Dr. Seuss's books
- Any of Byrd Baylor's books
- The Wise Child Series, by Monica Furlong
- *When the Sea Turned to Silver*, by Grace Lin
- *Hatchet*, by Gary Paulsen
- *Julie of the Wolves* and other novels by Jean Craighead George

Indian: Classic and Contemporary

- Any of Joseph Bruchac's books
- The Birch Bark House Series, by Louise Erdrich
- Any of Paul Goble's books
- *Two Old Women*, by Velma Wallis
- *Whispers of the Ancients,* by Tamarack Song & Moses (Amik) Beaver
- *The Legend of the Indian Paintbrush* and *The Legend of the Bluebonnet*, by Tomie dePaola

Children need stories because there is no more powerful or gentle teacher. No matter what a child's inclinations or struggles, a story finds his heart and lifts him to his feet. Jesse Bowman, grandfather of renowned Indian storyteller, Joseph Bruchac, said: "My father never hit me, no matter what I done. He'd just talk to me, tell me a story. There was times I think I would of rather had him hit me. Them stories was strong."[7]

Chapter in a Page

The Teaching Trail is paved with stories. They give a child the life experience he has not yet had the opportunity to gain, and they paint enticing visions of where the Teaching Trail is about to take him. For the vast majority of human existence, people would gather around the evening hearth and tell the stories of the day. Each clan had a storyteller with a special gift for accessing the storyline and personalizing the story to meet the needs of the people. Storytelling was not only entertaining, but essential to the clan's survival, as stories provided a source of emotional cleansing, empathy, guidance, peer recognition, and knowledge transfer.

From the perspective of traditional cultures, all stories come from the storyline—the Great Story which contains all stories, and which guides the rhythms of the universe. Stories that live on are those that capture the imagination.

By observing what has captured your child's imagination within a particular story, you can help her explore that theme as it relates to her life. Children need stories because there is no more powerful or gentle teacher. No matter what a child's inclinations or struggles, a story finds his heart and lifts him to his feet.

Because our forebears abandoned many clan storytelling traditions, it is now up to each of us to bring storytelling back to our families. Few of us have wizened elder storytellers in our family circles, and yet we can find them nearby through local elders, cultural centers, festivals, and libraries.

◇◇◇◇◇◇◇◇◇◇◇◇◇◇◇◇◇◇◇◇◇◇

Chapter 15 Endnotes

1   Gregory Cajete, *Native Science: Natural Laws of Interdependence* (Clear Light Publishers, 2000), 159.

2   Frank Bird Linderman, *Pretty-shield: Medicine Woman of the Crows* (University of Nebraska Press, 2003), 39.

3   Kent Nerburn, *The Soul of an Indian: And Other Writings from Ohiyesa* (New World Library, 2010), 25.

4   Ibid.

5   Frank Bird Linderman, *Pretty-shield: Medicine Woman of the Crows*, 41.

6   Liam Frink, *A Tale of Three Villages: Indigenous-Colonial Interactions in Southwestern Alaska* (University of Arizona Press, 2016), 43-47.

7   Jospeh Bruchac, "Introduction to Our Second Catalog of Native American Literature," *Ken Lopez Bookseller*, last modified 1996, accessed 8 July 2020, https://lopezbooks.com/articles/bruchac/.

With fast-maturing animals like Dogs, their children's culture disappears when the pups mature. Humans, being slow-maturing, have overlapping childhoods, which perpetuates their children's culture.

 *Chapter 16*

Culture through Their Eyes

Contemporary society is an adult world, in which children are accommodated. From our cultural perspective, children are incomplete in their development and in the process of becoming fully actualized. This is reflected when we refer to someone as childish, which means he is acting immaturely. The upshot is that we treat children as second-class citizens, expected to defer to adults and conform to adult standards. Is this the natural state of affairs for our species? With such upbringing, can we realistically expect our children to grow up and assume roles as independent, self-reliant, freethinking adults?

Their Own Culture

Our ancestors were self-directed people, clear on who they were and intimately involved in providing for the welfare of their people. How did they achieve this? As children, they were part of an independent culture that allowed them to develop as individuals and assume roles of responsibility and guidance. Their Children's Culture was separate and distinct from the adult culture. It functioned semi-autonomously, with the adults overseeing it yet allowing it to evolve on its own and serve its own needs.

Intrinsic to a successfully functioning culture is its ability to provide for its members' needs. When children have their own culture, they grow up in an environment that allows them to learn firsthand the ways of respect, conflict resolution, cooperation, and providing safety and security for their own members. When the time comes for their rite of passage into adulthood, they are naturally ready to assume parallel roles in the adult culture. The existence of the Children's Culture is the primary reason you'll read in anthropological accounts of children sometimes as early as five and six years of age assuming roles of responsibility.

From the children's perspective, they are complete unto themselves and content with being who and how they are. In fact, there are adults who admire the ways of children. They refer to those adults who emulate the qualities of children and remain connected with the child within as childlike rather than childish. Two of the most well-known and respected adults of all time, Buddha and Jesus, both encouraged their followers to become as children.[1, 2] The childlike qualities of being totally immersed in the moment, sensitive to one's surroundings, and capable of great love and trust are associated with some of the most esteemed people of our culture—poets, geniuses, artists and inventors.

With children being complete beings, it should not be surprising that they also have a culture unto themselves. It is a well-developed culture, complete with its own rituals, social activities, initiations, judicial, legislative, and educational systems, songs, games and stories, and even its own physical and sexual training.

A Secret Culture

Even though this culture is well established and regularly functioning right under adults' noses, most of us are barely aware it exists. This is partly because most adults are not interested, and partly because children keep it secret to protect it from adult scrutiny and control. They practice their culture mainly when they are not in the presence of adults.

The Children's Culture is passed on from older friends and siblings, and occasionally from parents and grandparents. It is perpetuated through games, riddles, jump-rope rhymes, and stories—in other words, play.

How is the Children's Culture different from adult culture? Unlike adults, children do not distinguish between play and life. To a child, play *is* life, his life, and games are real (more on this in Part VI). To the chagrin of many adults, children, when left to their own devices, incorporate games into what adults insist ought to be more serious pursuits. "But games are serious, games are life," a child says by his perplexed expression. The culture gap is broad; the child has no words to bridge it when a stern-faced adult is looming over him from the other side of the gap.

What about Friends?

Only in modern society do children have to make or win friends. That forces children to function from their *egos* rather than their hearts: How they appear to someone becomes more important than who they are. A Native child is born into trust and friendship; the modern child is supposed to earn it.

Birth of the Children's Culture

Aboriginal peoples generally chronicle the turns of the seasons by the Moon, rather than by the Sun, as we do. They named each Moon by a significant event that occurs during that lunar cycle, such as the *Berry Gathering Moon, Long Night Moon,* and *Moon When the Geese Return.*

There is one Moon that is particularly relevant to the topic of Blossoming, and to children themselves—all children, whether they be human, bird, fish or plant. This Moon is referred to as the *Transition Moon* by many indigenous people. It occurs at the beginning of the Green Season, when nearly all of the plants and animals (who are primarily adult) turn their energy toward perpetuating a new generation of their kind.

The Transition Moon is a time of magic, and all of life heralds it—frogs sing from the ponds, birds from the treetops, and insects from the grasses. Males are calling mates and marking territories, and females nervously chirp when predators draw close to their nests. Even the plants cry out in ecstasy: Their narcotic essences and clouds of pollen fill the air. There is such an ecstatic explosion of life that *if one is quiet enough* she can even hear the plants grow.

All of this hullabaloo involves the transition that is about to happen: Life is bursting at the seams, and relationship is about to transform from two-dimensional (adult-adult) to three-dimensional (adult-adult-child).

Culture is the flower of relationship. The culture prior to the Transition Moon is primarily adult-based: The adults of most species are more than preoccupied with getting through the winter, and in the affairs of mating and preparing for the coming young.

The Transition Moon turns the world topsy-turvy—all of a sudden there are young everywhere and the attention of the adults shifts dramatically from each other to the children.

While the adults are busy foraging and defending, the Children's Culture is being reborn. The children are together all the time, sharing in all the experiences of life. Together they grow, explore, discover, and learn, and in this process of intense relationship they evolve a culture of their own, which is separate and distinct from the adult culture. Children have different sets of needs and priorities than adults, so they naturally act and behave differently from each other than they do with adults.

With animals who mature within a year, the Children's Culture gradually fades as the young mature into adulthood, and the culture comes back to life again with the birth of a new year's young. With humans and others who take more than a year to mature, such as our fellow primates, elephants, many fish, and some birds such as Eagles and Cranes, the Children's Culture is perpetual, being passed down from older to younger children.

Even when the Children's Culture is perpetual, it is invigorated during the Transition Moon, as all of the surrounding life energy is transitioning from two-dimensional to three-dimensional. Those who are observant can see it in their children—there is a new lust for life, a more intense yearning to be with other children, and their activities show a zest that had been gradually fading in the moons prior to the Transition Moon. With some Native peoples, births are most common during the Transition Moon, which feeds the spirit of renewal of the Children's Culture.

Chapter in a Page

Contemporary society is an adult world, one into which children are molded and accommodated. From our cultural perspective, children are incomplete in their development and are in the process of becoming fully actualized. This is reflected when we refer to someone as childish, which means he is acting immaturely. We treat children as second-class citizens, expected to defer to adults and conform to adult standards.

Is this the natural state of affairs for our species? With such upbringing, can we realistically expect our children to grow up and assume roles as independent, self-reliant, freethinking adults?

Our ancestors were self-directed people, clear on who they were and intimately involved in providing for the welfare of their people.

As children, they were part of an independent culture that allowed them to develop as individuals and assume roles of responsibility and guidance.

This Children's Culture was separate and distinct from the adult culture—because children have different sets of needs and priorities than adults, so they naturally act and behave differently from each other than they do with adults. It functioned semi-autonomously, with the adults overseeing it, yet allowing it to evolve on its own and serve its own needs.

The Children's Culture is passed on from older friends and siblings and occasionally from parents and grandparents, perpetuated through games, riddles, jump-rope rhymes, and stories—in other words, play. Unlike adults, children do not distinguish between play and life. To a child, play *is* life, his life, and games are real (more on this in Part VI). For this and other reasons, the Children's Culture is an essential ingredient in Child-Friendly Parenting, and in helping our children to Blossom personally.

◇◇◇◇◇◇◇◇◇◇◇◇◇◇◇◇◇◇◇◇◇◇◇◇

Chapter 16 Endnotes

1   "Matthew 18:2-4," *New International Version* (Biblica, 2011), https://www.biblegateway.com/passage/?search=Matthew+18%3A2-4&version=NIV.

2   Lao Tzu, "Chapter 28" in *Tao Te Ching* (Harper Perennial Modern Classics, 2006), 38.

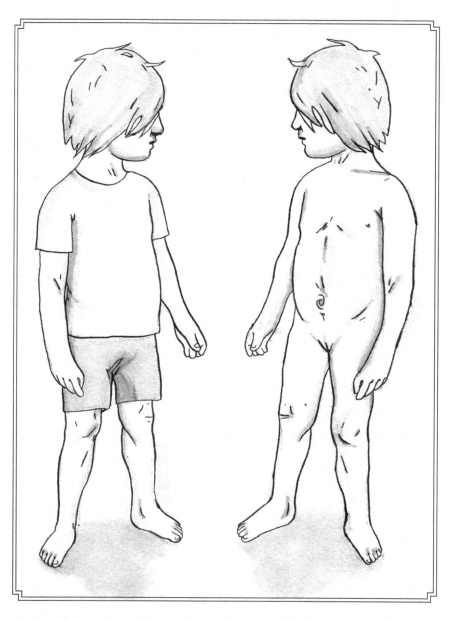

*The Hawaiian God's loved bodies the way they were
made. The foreign God wanted every man, woman, and
child covered up. He was ashamed of his children.*

 *Chapter 17*

The Hub: Children's Camp

Regardless of culture or era, children like to play grown-up. They assume the roles of adults and imitate nearly everything they observe adults doing. When I was a child, the girls would try to entice us boys to *play house* with them, whereas we preferred more active male-related activities such as digging and building. The one exception was *playing doctor*, where the girls allowed us to explore a bit of their anatomy. Otherwise, we would usually negotiate trade-offs: Us boys would play house for a while, followed by the girls helping us build a fort.

It is much the same for the !Kung San children of the African Kalahari. They play house, complete with getting married and having children. The younger play the roles of children and the older play the parents.[1] Games are often patterned after adult activities such as gathering and hunting, rituals, and chants. Sometimes they actually gather or trap some food.[2]

The stage for playing grown-up is usually a miniature of the adult world, either self-constructed or provided by adults. In modern Western cultures, dollhouses and tree houses are common. Aboriginal children construct miniature versions of their camps or villages. Here is an example from Pretty-shield, a Crow medicine woman from the 1800s: "Once several of us girls made ourselves a play village with our tiny tepees. Of course our children were dolls, and our horses dogs, and yet we managed to make our village look very real … One day several of us girls and a boy were going to have a play sun-dance … We believed that our dance was real. We felt very serious."[3]

Nisa had similar memories growing up in the Kalahari: "We would leave our parents' village and set up a small, 'grown-up' village of our own nearby. We played at gathering food from the bush, at bringing it back and eating it. Then we 'married' and played sexually together. We played like that all day. If one of our fathers had killed an animal, we would go back to the village to get some meat ... One boy would sit with one girl and another boy with another girl. We would sit there, cooking meat and giving presents of it to one another, just like adults ... Only when the sun stood late in the sky would we return to our parents' village to stay. But even there, we would just continue to play."[4]

The Foundation

The oral tradition provides the entire foundation of the Children's Culture. Aspects of the culture can be traced back centuries, even millennia. Much of the culture is the result of imitation of adult cultural forms. In fact, many extinct adult practices are preserved in children's games and rhymes. They are relics of a time when there was no real distinction between the Children's Culture and the adult culture—when one was a shadow of the other.

Adults and children would participate in ceremony together, along with undertaking the hunt, doing craftwork, and virtually all of the other activities of life. Each individual, whether child or adult, participated in the way relevant to him or her.

Ritual and sexual practices were openly shadowed by children, as it was one way they learned about such matters. They had no need to act in secrecy or feel shame, as adults did not stigmatize or censor them. Rather, they condoned the enactment of such activities, which were considered a normal part of everyday life.

The Governing System

This culture has its own system of law, which exemplifies some of the distinguishing qualities of children—direct, applicable to the moment, and peer-administered. Expressions have different psychological implications; *Time out!* brings safety and respite, *Dibs* establishes claim, *Cheater* identifies someone who is unfair, *Take-back* is for changing one's mind, *Butts* is used for slipping into line, *Save my place* makes it possible to go and return, and *Cross my heart* professes sincerity and trustworthiness.

Children's law is based on voluntary participation and consent, and it is voluntarily obeyed. This is the form of governance with which we humans evolved. It is our indigenous way, and fortunately for all of us, children still practice it. The adult world has moved away from it; however, we have our children for examples. Unfortunately, our children's form of governance does not prepare them well for today's adult world, which may be why children struggle with *fair* when talking with adults, and why many adolescents and young adults struggle with *the law*.

What about Morals?

"But aren't adults needed to teach the children right from wrong?" I'm often asked. As covered in Chapter 21 under *Can Children Teach Themselves Values?* Recent research shows that morality is intrinsic to our species.[5] Contrary to popular belief, religion does not instill morals—there is no difference in the basic morality of atheists and that of Christians, Jews, Buddhists, Hindus and other faith-holders. Neither do parents instill morals in their children: It appears to be innate, and like other innate abilities, it needs only to be exercised. The Children's Culture provides an excellent format for that.

Number of Children Needed

In order for there to be a viable Children's Culture, there needs to be a minimum of four children, and they need to be of varying ages. With three children, one invariably ends up feeling left out. When there are only two children, relational energy tends to bounce back and forth between them. If anything goes wrong in their relationship, or if one of them becomes dysfunctional, there is nothing to carry relationship momentum. Fears of abandonment can be triggered, and one or both children often feel victimized.

Lone children struggle even more, usually turning to pets, toys, fantasies, the media, adults—anything to feel part of a culture. A child, being a social being, has no choice but to seek culture where he can find it.

Sibling Rivalry

One of the earliest manifestations of sibling rivalry is competition over toys. In small families especially, it starts with competition for Mom's attention, which is endemic to isolated nuclear families. The emotional unfulfilledness of the children and the resulting competitiveness for attention spills over into other arenas, whether it be playing with friends, getting served first at a meal, or having exclusive time with the toy.

The Necessary Level of Engagement

The Children's Culture can evolve and sustain itself as a viable culture only if children are with each other full time. The only child, or the child whose siblings are too far apart from him in age, is often with other children only part-time, so for him the Children's Culture is but an adjunct to the primary culture he has adopted to sustain himself.

Without a full-time Children's Culture, the teachings and examples of adults usually influence children to become little adults. Within the supportive context of their own culture, children more naturally apply what they learn to who they are as individuals. This allows a child to discover her own talents and abilities through the context of play and pretend, where she is free to take on different roles and try out being different people. Self-discovery is more fluid and less confining than when talents or inclinations are pointed out or praised in an adult setting.

Two Cultures Interlinked

According to Nisa, a !Kung San woman from South Africa's Kalahari Desert, adults would respect the individuality of children and their autonomous culture by witnessing, but not interfering, in their play. Those in the adult culture as well as those in the Children's Culture seem to have a level of trust and security around the roles that they each take in the community. "When I sit in the village and my children are playing around me," Nisa said, "I don't worry; I just watch what they do."[6] The observation was mutual: "Whenever my father brought back meat," said Nisa, "I'd greet him 'Ho,ho, Daddy's coming home with meat!' And felt happy for everything and there was nothing that made my heart unhappy."[7]

Chapter in a Page

Regardless of culture or era, children like to play grown-up. They assume the roles of adults and imitate nearly everything they observe adults doing. The stage for playing grown-up is usually a miniature of the adult world, either self-constructed or provided by adults.

In modern Western cultures, dollhouses and tree houses are common. Aboriginal children construct miniature versions of their camps or villages. Amongst our ancestors, adults and children participated in daily life together—including the hunt, doing craftwork, and virtually all of the other activities of life. Children participated, observed, and later reenacted these things amongst themselves in the Children's Culture.

In order for there to be a viable Children's Culture, there needs to be a minimum of four children, and they need to be of varying ages. After it has been established, it can evolve and sustain itself as a viable culture only if children are with each other full time.

Within the supportive context of their own culture, children more naturally apply what they learn to who they are as individuals. This allows a child to discover her own talents and abilities through the context of play and pretend, where she is free to take on different roles and try out being different people. Self-discovery is more fluid and less confining than when talents or inclinations are pointed out or praised in an adult setting.

◇◇◇◇◇◇◇◇◇◇◇◇◇◇◇◇◇◇◇◇◇◇◇

Chapter 17 Endnotes

1 Marjorie Shostak, *Nisa: The Life and Words of a !Kung Woman* (Harvard University Press, 2000), 97.

2 Ibid, 74-75.

3 Frank Bird Linderman, *Pretty-shield: Medicine Woman of the Crows*, 10-11, 14-15.

4 Marjorie Shostak, *Nisa: The Life and Words of a !Kung Woman*, 116.

5   J. Kiley Hamlin, "The Origins of Human Morality: Complex Socio-moral Evaluations by Preverbal Infants," *Research and Perspectives in Neurosciences* 21 (2014): 165-88.

6   Marjorie Shostak, *Nisa: The Life and Words of a !Kung Woman*, 96.

7   Ibid, 79.s

In indigenous cultures, older children begin teaching younger ones the ways of adulthood when they are mere toddlers.

 *Chapter 18*

The Folly of Peer Groups

A man should not be struck when he is down, states a Russian proverb.[1] Nor should a child. However, it happens regularly, and it can be done by children themselves. The Children's Culture functions cooperatively only if the children are of varying ages. As soon as a group of the same age—a *peer group*—forms, the climate turns from cooperative to competitive. No longer are the natural distinguishing characteristics that exist among children of different ages, so in an effort to find their uniqueness, they scramble over one another. Whether in the form of bullying, competitiveness, or favoritism, it's essentially the same scenario playing itself out: The weak and meek get demeaned and exploited, and the bold and forceful get exalted and rewarded. Hindus have this to say about pecking orders: *When an elephant is in trouble, even a frog will kick him.*[2]

To Teach Is to Learn

Largely lacking in peer groups is the teaching-learning process that occurs in mixed-age children's groups. There are three steps in the learning process:

1. Awareness
2. Practice
3. Teaching

Joseph Joubert, a French moralist and essayist, wrote, "To teach is to learn twice over."[3] It speaks to the last step, which is critical in the learning process, because in order to teach, we must review and organize what we have gained and present it in a coherent-enough fashion that others can understand it.

The competition and self-consciousness inherent in peer groups inhibits this learning-teaching process. This serves the purposes of a hierarchical society because its primary goal is to educate children to serve the hierarchy.

Peer groups squelch the play of imagination, the direction of creative urges, the sound of voices within, and the sensitivity to external powers and energies. In addition, peer groups encourage children to reinforce in each other the quirks of their age, while at the same time not allowing for the diffusion of its traumas. It magnifies their age-dimensioned view of their reality.

The way most school systems are designed makes them the primary agents in this process. By having children sit, think, walk, and urinate in unison, the schools create citizens suited to the routines of Civilized existence. (Churches, scout and other youth groups, daycare agencies, and other similarly structured organizations also contribute.) The peer pressure this system generates is its own regulating and conforming agent.

Growing at One's Own Pace

Children grow at different rates physically, mentally, and emotionally. In mixed age groups, a child is much more free to grow at his own speed, without outside pressure or comparisons being made. This is largely because the child is not automatically associated with a specific, homogenized age group.

Children Teaching Children

People living in the Native Way encourage their little ones to play with others of varied ages. This gives them the opportunity to emulate older children, and to be an inspiration to those who are younger. They learn responsibility and the skills of caring for and teaching others. Their shared time is a multi-dimensional experience, a microcosm of the life their play is preparing them for.

Health Benefits from Mixed-Age Groups

A recent study revealed that older siblings appear to help strengthen the immune system of younger siblings by virtue of exposing them to more pathogens.[4] This would suggest that humans are immunologically stronger when living social, interconnected lives.

Having a healthy mixed-age Children's Culture is vitally important because children may play a greater role in raising themselves than do their parents. Older children begin teaching younger ones the ways of adulthood when they are mere toddlers. Small Kalahari !Kung San boys are given bows and arrows by children who may not be much older than themselves.[5]

Nisa, a !Kung San woman, gives us an inside picture: "I started to carry my little brother around on my shoulders. My heart was happy then; I had grown to love him and carried him everywhere. I'd play with him for a while and whenever he would start to cry, I'd take him to mother so he could nurse. Then I'd take him back with me and we'd play together again ... [My older brother would] put me up on his shoulders and carry me. That's part of the reason I followed him around all the time! When he'd see an animal, he'd put me down, track it, and shoot it. If he struck it, we'd return to the village and he would always let me be the first to tell, 'My big brother killed a gemsbok!'"[6]

The indigenous Hawaiians have a deep, long-standing tradition of honoring the roles older and younger children play for each other. They have a saying, *Nana i waele mua i ke ala, mahope aku mākou, na pōki'i,*[7] which means *The older one first cleared the path and then younger ones followed.* This is said with affection and respect for the oldest sibling, who is referred to by the special term, *hiapo*.[8] (Sibling can also mean a cousin or child of another clan member.)

Another saying, *Ku i ka māna*,[9] which means *Like the one from whom he received what he learned*, is paid as a compliment to the child who walks in the footsteps of the older children who reared him. *Māna*,[10] which is food masticated by an older person and conveyed to the mouth of a small child, symbolizes knowledge and example being passed on.

The great affection between brothers and sisters, especially for their younger siblings, is expressed in the saying, *Oke keiki he loa'a i ka moe, o ka pōki'i 'a'ole*,[11] which means *One can produce a child by sleeping with a mate, but he cannot produce a younger brother or sister.*

Chapter in a Page

The Children's Culture functions cooperatively and effectively only if the children are of varying ages. As soon as a group of the same age—a peer group—forms, the climate turns from cooperative to competitive. No longer are the natural distinguishing characteristics that exist among children of different ages, so in an effort to find their uniqueness, they scramble over one another.

Peer groups squelch the play of imagination, the direction of creative urges, the sound of voices within, and the sensitivity to external powers and energies. In addition, peer groups encourage children to reinforce in each other the quirks of their age, while at the same time not allowing for the diffusion of its traumas. It magnifies their age-dimensioned view of their reality.

People living in the Native Way encourage their little ones to play with others of varied ages. This gives them the opportunity to emulate older children, and to be an inspiration to those who are younger. They learn responsibility and the skills of caring for and teaching others. Their shared time is a multi-dimensional experience, a microcosm of the life their play is preparing them for.

A recent study revealed that older siblings appear to help strengthen the immune system of younger siblings by virtue of exposing them to more pathogens. This would suggest that humans are immunologically stronger when living social, interconnected lives. It is just one example of the reasons why intergenerational communities support healthy, thriving children.

◇◇◇◇◇◇◇◇◇◇◇◇◇◇◇◇◇◇◇◇

Chapter 18 Endnotes

1   Abel Adekola and Bruno Sergi, *Global Business Management: A Cross-Cultural Perspective* (Ashgate Publishing, 2012), 278.

2   Paul G. Blacketor, *Everyday Useful Quotes* (Xlibris, 2009), 302.

3   Joseph Joubert, "Chapter XVIII. Of Education," in *Joubert: A Selection from His Thoughts* (New York: Dodd, Mead & Co., 1899), 163.

4   H.M. Wolsk, "Siblings Promote a Type 1/Type 17-Oriented Immune Response in the Airways of Asymptomatic Neonates," *Allergy* 71, no. 6 (2016): 820-28.

5   Marjorie Shostak, *Nisa: The Life and Words of a !Kung Woman*, 75.

6   Ibid, 63, 82.

7   Mary Kawena Pukui, *'Olelo No'eau: Hawaiian Proverbs & Poetical Sayings*, 247.

8   Mary Kawena Pukui and Samuel H. Elbert, *Hawaiian Dictionary*, 413.

9   Mary Kawena Pukui, *'Olelo No'eau: Hawaiian Proverbs & Poetical Sayings*, 202.

10 Mary Kawena Pukui and Samuel H. Elbert, *Hawaiian Dictionary*, 235-36.

11 Mary Kawena Pukui, *'Olelo No'eau: Hawaiian Proverbs & Poetical Sayings*, 267.

To honor our children is to honor ourselves, because they are both reflections of, and windows to, who we are.

 *Chapter 19*

Supporting the Rebirth

To honor our children is to honor ourselves, because they are both reflections of, and windows to, who we are. To honor our children is to honor our ancestry, because it is they who carry on our lineage. If we remember that we were once children, we'll remember how important—or rather, essential—our children are. Those of us who come from a strong and sustaining Children's Culture are most able to contribute to a strong and sustaining adult culture.

In the days when we lived in Balance with our own kind and our non-human relations, the Children's Culture was strong. Children lived joyous lives, as in this scene from Nisa's childhood: "[We] went back to live again at our old water hole. All my friends were there, and when I saw them I was happy again. We played and played and danced and sang, played music and sang and danced, and my heart was happy to be with the children I liked."[1] How could anything but joyful, capable, and self-assured adults emerge from such an upbringing?

Witness a Dying Culture

Then there is our present reality—an increasingly structured society appearing to methodically orchestrate the death of the Children's Culture. The leading causes of its demise are:

1. **Compulsory education.** Schools are standardizing a large part of the childhood experience, along with structuring and supervising recreation and exercise (in the form of physical education).

2. **Structured "free" time.** Due to time constraints and the desire to provide quality experiences for their children, caregivers feel increasingly pressured to over-structure their children's time by enrolling them in a myriad of recreational, educational, sports and entertainment activities.

3. **Adult game role models.** In imitation of adults, we encourage children to play organized sports. The result is children emulating adult sports figures, along with adopting the sports mentality. Less and less, children create their own games or pass games down from the Children's Culture.

4. **Modernization.** In Japan, jumping rope is discouraged by adults who do not see it as a practice that fits into a contemporary industrial society. Along with jumping rope, the attendant rhymes—a large segment of the Children's Culture oral tradition—are dying out.

What We Can Do

As caregivers, we have a unique opportunity to lay the groundwork for the rebirth of the Children's Culture. The beauty of the processes is that no midwife is needed. All we need to do is provide the birthing room, then step back and watch. The children know what to do—they've been taking care of their own cultural needs from the dawn of our species' appearance on this Lovely Planet, and there is no reason to think they still can't do it. Here is all we need to do:

- **Acknowledge** our children's reality. Refrain from the urge to orchestrate or rescue, as neither make sense to children who already have everything they need.

- **Give credence** to what our children dream up by showing respect for it, and by listening with interest when they choose to share it with us.

- **Create space.** Structuring our children's lives is one of the worst things we can do for them. They need the time and sanction to learn in their own way how to invent, organize, and participate in spontaneously evolving group play.

- **Avoid judgment.** There may be times when children appear to us to be unfair with each other, argumentative, or out of control. These are their learning opportunities, when the organic processes of the Children's Culture come to the fore.

Our primary role is to act as hands-off, discrete overseers. Our children need to know we are there if needed; and at the same time, they want us to be engaged in our own lives, rather than theirs. Casting an occasional eye their way—discreetly, so that it goes unnoticed—is all that is wanted by them, and all that is needed from us.

Salvation for Single and Paired Parents

As covered in Part II of this book, we are not physically or psycho-emotionally designed to be solo parents, or even to parent as couples. In such contexts, children often grow up wanting, and parents sometimes end up stressed beyond their limits. As children largely raise themselves in a vibrant Children's Culture, even single parents seldom feel overburdened when living in a community that supports a Children's Culture.

When Two Become One

Coming from a culture with dichotomous perspective and detached observation as two of its foundations, we tend to view aboriginal communities as having separate child and adult cultures. And that has been our approach in this book up to this point. I did so in large part because the Elders have impressed upon me the importance of meeting people (myself included) where they are at.

In actuality, there is no clear demarcation between the two cultures. They are so enmeshed, and the transition from one to the other is so gradual, they are more like different sides of the same circle than separate circles. In such an all-embracing hoop, how could any child feel forsaken or unloved?

This way of circle living with our children that we are exploring is our intended way of being, as given to us in the Original Instructions. As you now know, those Instructions are literally us—they are our biology; they are encoded in our DNA. It should be no surprise, then, that both children and adults are the happiest and healthiest when the Children's Culture flourishes.

At the same time, I think it goes beyond that. As the Elders have told me, *Giving is receiving*; and as Mahatma Gandhi said, *Be the change you wish to see in the world.*[2] Perhaps returning to the Circle Way—of which the Children's Culture is an integral part—could help return us to the personal, cultural, and planetary Balance we so sorely miss and dearly need.

Chapter in a Page

To honor our children is to honor ourselves, because they are both reflections of, and windows to, who we are. Honoring our children is also honoring our ancestry, because it is them who carry on our lineage.

One of the best ways to honor our children is to support the emergence of a Children's Culture, which becomes the template for learning to become healthy, thriving adults. Those of us who come from a strong and sustaining Children's Culture are most able to contribute to a strong and sustaining adult culture. In the days when we lived in Balance with our own kind and our non-human relations, the Children's Culture was strong.

Today, in our increasingly structured, mechanized society, this culture is weak and often non-existent. As caregivers, we have a unique opportunity to lay the groundwork for the rebirth of the Children's Culture. The beauty of the processes is that no midwife is needed. All we need to do is provide the birthing room, then step back and watch. The children know what to do—they've been taking care of their own cultural needs from the dawn of our species' appearance on this Lovely Planet, and there is no reason to think they still can't do it. Our primary role is to act as hands-off, discrete overseers. Our children need to know we are there if needed; and at the same time, they want us to be engaged in our own lives, rather than theirs.

◇◇◇◇◇◇◇◇◇◇◇◇◇◇◇◇◇◇◇◇◇◇◇

Chapter 19 Endnotes

1   Marjorie Shostak, *Nisa: The Life and Words of a !Kung Woman*, 112.

2   Mahatma Gandhi, *The Collected Works of Mahatma Gandhi, Volume XII* (Indian Opinion, 1913), 158.

Part V

How Children Learn

*A young father called me for advice on how to
teach his toddler to understand "No."*

 *Chapter 20*

Their Learning Reality

The title of this book section, *How Children Learn,* is a misnomer. Yet we need a familiar place to start the topic. From there, we progress into how children teach themselves. When we see our children learning through constant observation and exploration— i.e., teaching themselves—we see them as empowered; initiating and guiding their own education.

When we view children as learners, we naturally ask, "What are they going to learn, and how?" We want to be helpful by creating a learning environment, providing material for learning, and directing a learning process. Only in doing so we wind up doing it for them, and they end up being passive receptors.

In order to develop as individuals, be self-motivated, and be emotionally healthy social beings, children need to be responsible for their own lives. If every tomorrow is going to be an adventure and every challenge is going to unveil a new horizon, they need to exercise their natural adaptive ability and their natural curiosity for the unconventional. This needs to happen from the earliest age, and continually through their growing years.

How can we best honor and support the self-teaching process? How can we facilitate without interfering? By providing them a safe environment—though not *too* safe—then stepping back and chilling out. That done, it usually doesn't take long for any adults with lingering doubts to discover that children are designed to teach themselves. And, that they're quite good at it. The following story illustrates what this type of facilitation can look like.

A Parent Learns from His Child

Recently Moe, a young father, called me for advice on how to teach his toddler to understand *No.*

"She's rambunctious," said Moe. "She ends up pulling things off the table on top of herself, playing in the toilet, and burning herself on the wood stove."

Moe was getting advice from well-meaning friends and family members that amounted to either corporal punishment or putting her behind bars. He didn't feel comfortable with either approach, and yet he couldn't come up with another option that would allow her to learn without danger.

"The *Native Way* of teaching children is to let them teach themselves," I explained. "That's what their curiosity is all about—to bring them the experiences that shape their relationship with their world."

"That sounds great," he replied, "but at the rate my girl's going, she's not going to live long enough to have *any* relationship with her world."

"You need to become your child."

"What?"

"Become your child. If you were her, you'd probably be able to see that she's only doing what comes naturally. What could be wrong with that?"

"She'll kill herself; that's all."

"And you need to keep her from doing that. In doing so, you're coming from the assumption that she has to change, and you have to protect her, right?"

"I guess so."

"Perhaps there is another option. If you were able to become your child and see the world from her vantage point—crawl where she crawls, explore with her fingers, I would wager that the way you feel about your daughter and relate to her will change dramatically."

The next day, Moe called back: "Wow!" was the first word out of his mouth. "I did what you suggested, and what an eye-opener—I felt like I was in a giant's world. I looked up and all I saw was the underside of the table. The giants were sitting at the table, moving and clanging things around on top of it. I wanted to know what they were up to; it sounded a lot more interesting than what was happening on my side of the table.

"And that's not all. The giants would walk around, take things out of the cupboards, and set them down on the counter tops. I wanted to see what those things were. I tried and tried, but I couldn't. I tried to reach, I tried to climb up there, but I got pulled down and scolded. The more my curiosity was denied, the more frustrated I got and the harder I tried. I screamed."

"Didn't you have your own world, your own things?"

"Sure, I had the floor, and I had my toys. I liked them, and they would preoccupy me for a while, but they didn't satisfy my curiosity. I knew there was a bigger world, and why couldn't I be part of it? It's not that I was neglected, 'cuz I had all sorts of neat things on my floor world, and the giants would sometimes come down and play with me, but their world, their toys, were pretty much off-limits for me."

I then described for Moe a typical Native household, which is conspicuous for its lack of chairs, tables, and counters. Rather than a giant world juxtaposed upon a diminutive world, everybody lives on the same level and everything is in plain sight. Children are naturally involved in household activities, so their curiosity is spontaneously satisfied. Feeling secure and content, they are more self-involved, less demanding, and seldom agitated.

"Yeah, the agitation is what really got to me," said Moe. "After I realized why my daughter got so agitated, I wondered what I could do about it. My first impulse was to get rid of the table and chairs and join her on the floor. I wondered if we could just eat our meals and do our other activities on the floor, and be a family that's really together."

"Well, that seems to make good sense," I replied. "Awareness is the first step in change."

What about Dangerous Lessons?

"I still haven't figured out what to do about my daughter and the wood stove," Moe continued. "I imagined being her, watching me feed the stove, adjust the draft, and take out the ashes and then basking in its warmth, so I can easily see why she'd be fascinated with it. Like everything else, she wants to touch it and play with it. How can I let her explore without getting burned?"

I replied: "As Julius Caesar said, 'Experience is the teacher of all things.'[1] Let me share with you the example of how my boy Wabineshi learned respect for fire. We heat entirely with wood and we have a freestanding wood stove right in the middle of our living room. When Wabineshi started to crawl, his mother was concerned about him getting burned, so she suggested we put a fence around the stove."

"Did you?"

"Well, putting up a protective barrier is a common response of people who no longer live in direct relationship with the natural realm. But our ancestors—including toddlers—have lived around open hearths for probably 400,000 years and thrived. The children of cliff-dwelling peoples and treetop village jungle peoples have the natural ability to move safely around heights. The same is true with those who dwell by water. Babies instinctively hold their breaths under water, and the youngest of children learn to swim so quickly and easily that one would think they were intended to be water rather than land creatures. However, these natural abilities need to be exercised at an early age. The older children get, the harder it is for them to gain proficiency."

"But what about fire?"

"The same is true of fire. Notice how it repels the young of all other animals, while young humans are drawn to it, as though there was something magical about it ... and there is. Have you ever seen a child who hasn't been fascinated by a candle flame or a campfire, or who wants to play with matches and make fire? Relationship with fire is imprinted in our genetic memory. Modern humans were able to evolve because of our relationship with fire. It opened doorways for us, allowing us to cook food, make more complex tools, and inhabit previously unpeopled environments."

"That's all fascinating, but how does it keep a child from getting burned?"

"Okay, back to how Wabineshi learned respect for fire. He liked to watch me feed the wood stove because he could see the fire. Having his attention, I would reach toward the stove as though I was going to touch it, and pull my hand away with an exaggerated motion while saying 'Hot!' He got the biggest kick out of that, and soon he wanted to try it himself.

"When the stove was warm but not hot enough to burn him, I would pick him up and bring him over to the stove. The closer he came, the more animated he got. I couldn't get him more than an arm's length from the wood stove and he was already laughing, throwing up his hands, and saying 'Hot, hot!' He was so pleased

with himself! (And I was so pleased with him—*hot* was one of his first words.)

"Each time we'd get a little closer before he'd throw up his hands, until he got near enough that he might touch it. At that point it was time for the message to hit home. I touched the stove and recoiled, saying 'Hot!' while shaking my hand and painting an exaggerated look of pain on my face.

"His changed expression told me he had immediately caught on. This time when we approached the wood stove, his look was serious. He tentatively reached out and touched the stove. Feeling the bite of the heat, he not only pulled back his hand, but he arched his whole body back from the stove. With a bewildered look on his face he looked at me, and I said, 'Hot.'"

"Did he know hot from then on?"

"To imprint the experience, we went through the routine a couple more times. After that, I would test him every now and then. The closer we got to the stove, the tenser he would get. At the last minute he would arch his back, pull back and say 'Hot,' then look at me with a big smile. From that time on we didn't have to worry about him around the wood stove. When it was hot, he could feel the radiant heat and he knew not to go any closer."

Following our conversation, Moe did well in supporting his daughter to teach herself respect for fire. Both she and Wabineshi did just what children are designed to do—teach themselves by experience.

Learn It the First Time

There is a saying *Near is my shirt, but nearer is my skin.*[2] The closer learning is to the skin (as in the fire example above) the more meaningful the learning. However, when the immediate physical consequence is removed from the experience by replacing it with a verbal explanation or scolding, the child is left confused. Words do not correlate directly to the danger, and the direct–experience learning potential is lost.

To this day, direct experience is the learning method of nearly all children living close to the Earth. They retain their learning experiences through repetition. The Awabakal Aborigines of Southeast Australia call this way of learning *wi-ye-a*,[3] and *aina uudelleen* is the term used by the Saami, the reindeer people of Arctic Scandinavia.

Dangerous lessons usually need to be experienced but once, which Native Hawaiians expressed in this way: *O ka huhū 'ino ka mea e ola 'ole ai—The fish whose mouth has been pierced by the hook will never again take another.*[4] Germans have a similar proverb: *He who has burnt his mouth always blows on his soup.*[5]

A Parent's Dilemma

"I want my children to learn by experience," stated a parent, "but I'm afraid they'll hurt themselves. What can I do?"

"Confucius said, 'Experience is the bitterest way to learn,'"[6] I replied. "Pain is a natural and sometimes necessary part of the learning process, as a pain-based memory is solidly imprinted and not easily forgotten."

Of course this does not mean that we allow our children to place themselves in situations of mortal danger in order to learn. Just as with the fire example, when a lesson holds the potential for severe injury, the child can be guided by her caretaker to experience the soft edge of memory-imprinting pain without causing serious harm.

If a child does not experience some pain while learning not to touch metaphorically hot objects, she runs the risk of someday getting severely burned. Fortunately, the risk of being seriously hurt from normal experiential learning is slight.

Yet the slight risk must be taken, as the cost of avoiding it could be much higher. The longer a lesson goes unlearned, the greater the chance of injury to the child, and the greater the chance the injury will be severe. Being curious creatures, we humans—especially as children—like to keep pushing our edge, to see how far we can go. The longer there are no immediate consequences to temper our curiosity, the more dangerous pushing our edge becomes.

Chapter in a Page

When we view children as learners, we naturally ask, "What are they going to learn, and how?" We want to be helpful by creating a learning environment, providing material for learning, and directing a learning process. Only in doing so we often wind up doing it for them, and they end up being passive receptors.

In order to develop as individuals, be self-motivated, and be emotionally healthy social beings, children need to be responsible for their own lives. If every tomorrow is going to be an adventure and every challenge is going to unveil a new horizon, they need to exercise their natural adaptive ability and their natural curiosity for the unconventional. This needs to happen from the earliest age, and continually through their growing years.

How can we best honor and support the self-teaching process? How can we facilitate without interfering? By providing them a safe environment—though not *too* safe—then stepping back and chilling out.

Of course this does not mean that we allow our children to place themselves in situations of mortal danger in order to learn. When a lesson holds the potential for severe injury, the child can be guided by her caretaker to experience the soft edge of memory-imprinting pain without causing serious harm. If a child does not experience some pain while learning not to touch metaphorically hot objects, she runs the risk of someday getting severely burned.

Fortunately, the risk of being seriously hurt from normal experiential learning is slight. Yet the slight risk must be taken, as the cost of avoiding it could be much higher.

◇◇◇◇◇◇◇◇◇◇◇◇◇◇◇◇◇◇◇◇◇◇◇◇

Chapter 20 Endnotes

1   Stuart Berg Flexner, *Wise Words and Wives' Tales: The Origins, Meanings and Time-Honored Wisdom of Proverbs and Folk Sayings, Olde and New.* (Avon Books, 1993), 2.

2   Nathan Bailey, *Divers Proverbs* (Yale University Press, 1721), 52.

3   L.E. Threlkeld, *Australian Grammar* (Sydney: Stephen and Stokes, 1834), 102.

4   Mary Kawena Pukui, *'Olelo No'eau: Hawaiian Proverbs & Poetical Sayings*, 262.

5   Dwight Edwards Marvin, *The Antiquity of Proverbs* (The Knickerbocker Press, 1922), 53.

6   Rev. James Wood, *Dictionary of Quotations from Ancient and Modern, English and Foreign Sources* 34.

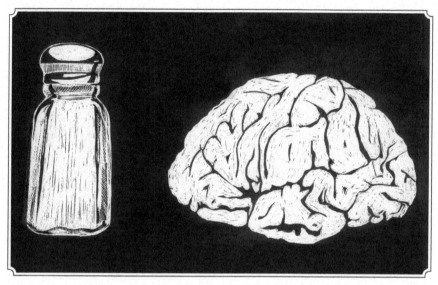

Do not offer salt or brains—children do not need criticism or advice.

 *Chapter 21*

The Ways They Teach Themselves

There is an old folk saying: *Do not offer salt or brains*.[1] No matter how well intended, and no matter whether positive or negative, regular outside input weakens children. Rather than becoming self-empowered and self-knowing, they learn to follow others and do their bidding. Unless they rebel, they usually spend their lives conforming and pleasing.

Is there an alternative? Another proverb tells us that *Who hears, forgets; who sees, remembers; and who does, learns*.[2] A child's natural way of teaching herself—the Blossoming way—is through example, experience, stories, dreams, and clan knowledge. Because stories and clan knowledge are forms of example and dreams are another type of personal experience, we could summarize all the ways of learning as *experience* and *example*. Experience is personal; example comes from others.

Teaching vs. Learning

If a child learning in the Blossoming way were asked how she learned through experience and example, she would probably have to deliberate for a while to come up with an answer. They are internal methods, which function organically and spontaneously, as opposed to external teaching methods, which are structured and often forced.

Teaching usually happens at the convenience of the teacher. Nisa, whom we have heard from several times now, once commented that "If you force a child to go gathering with you, she cries and makes it impossible to accomplish anything. If you leave her behind, she won't cry and you can come home with a lot."[3] In situations like this, children gain a lot as well, as they spend the day immersed in the Children's Culture, where !Kung San children become well-equipped for adult life through the skills they learn through play.[4]

Because of this very personal and un-methodical way of learning, people of Native cultures are generally not considered to be good teachers from the perspective of mainstream Western culture. Not having learned in a formal, step-by-step manner, they find it hard to teach in that way. In fact, formalized teaching would be considered a silly concept for those who consider learning to be intrinsic to living. It is natural to grow into things, then let them grow within you. Among the !Kung San, there is little formal teaching. Example and experience provide virtually all of the children's education.[5]

Modern people, on the other hand, have little opportunity to teach themselves. Their parenting methods and mainstream teaching institutions tend to be based largely on the *I have the answers; don't bother asking questions* approach. What children often hear from that is, "They say they know what's best for me, so it doesn't much matter who I am or what I have to say based on my perspective." In such a setting, children are trained to be students: to be given knowledge and proficiency rather than to gain them.

Do It Now

The older a contemporary child becomes, the harder it is for him to teach himself. As much as we like to think we are intellectual beings in control of our destinies, in practice we are creatures of habit and pattern. *Old habits die hard*, so it takes diligence and consistency on the part of caregivers to support children in reawakening their sense of wonder and lust for adventure. Yet no matter what it takes, don't put it off. The sooner the passive-learning habit is broken, the sooner engaged, embodied learning can begin.

To Err Is Divine

A "saint" of a child—one who never does anything wrong and always does what he is told— is merely a trained animal. A child grows wise because he is foolish; he becomes graceful when he is klutzy; he develops cleverness from being dull. Praise the child who stumbles and blunders: he has found the Master Teacher!

An urban child typically learns his limits and capabilities from adults telling him "Don't go out on the street," or "You can't go over to the neighbors." Is he learning his limits and capabilities, or is he being taught to rely on what others say is best for him?

In a natural setting a child learns by his own wits or lack thereof. He trips, gets wet and cold, goes hungry, and destroys. As the Irish say, *Youth doesn't mind where it sets its foot.*[6] The Native child seldom hears "Don't." Instead, he is encouraged with an implied or spoken "Do," then he is seemingly ignored.

The do-it-yourself learning approach works so well for a child living in the Native Way because he lives in a personalized world. His home is the outdoors and he has few personal possessions. He has little to bind him, little to covet or protect, and there is little for adults to have to worry about him upsetting, breaking, or infringing upon. This gives him endless opportunity to learn from unfettered personal experience, along with the experience of all the human and nonhuman relations he lives with.

By contrast, the typical modern child grows up indoors in a human-constructed and oriented environment, filled with human-made and owned things. Control is the name of the game: your things and mine, your space and mine, your time and mine. So as not to infringe on others' property rights and boundaries, the child is taught early on what is proper to touch and not touch and where it is proper to go and not go. He learns what other humans expect of him rather than what works and does not work for him and the Circle.

Conflict arises within the child between personal yearnings and the expectations of others, which usually results in control issues. The child is pressured to accept subservience to adults and adult supervision. He might react by refusing to eat or dress, breaking toys, throwing tantrums, or abusing other children. When he is older, he may rebel from authority or seek escapes through addictive behaviors with drugs, alcohol, sports, academics and/or video games. He ends up being less independent and far less self-directed than his Native counterpart. He could sink into depression, and like more and more of his peers, entertain suicide. Once an adult, he is likely to crave approval and recognition, which may well turn him into an enabler, or he'll cope by becoming a lifelong victim. All because he was denied his Nature experience.

Here is a story of how experiential learning, along with adult support, can work. The setting is a tepee camp on the Great Plains in the 1800s, and the storyteller is Chief Standing Bear, an Oglala Lakota:

One day I accidentally started a small riot in camp when one of my blunt tipped arrows bounced off the ground and struck the pony in the tender part of the jaw. The pony was loaded with bundles of household goods on his back and had been peacefully grazing when he was suddenly startled by the blow from the arrow. He immediately began lunging about which caused the load to fall off, scattering things all over the ground. This further frightened the animal, and he started to run. Other animals became frightened at the commotion and began to run also.

Soon the entire camp was in a state of excitement ... Women ran here and there, men shouted; there was disorder everywhere. I expected to be scolded for my carelessness, but not a word was ever said to me, though I knew that my folks were fully aware that I was to blame for this uproar. I learned a good lesson that day, for deep within I resolved never to be so careless again. Little as I was, perhaps six or seven years of age, I realized that I had done something which I must not do again. To this day I look back upon my childhood and say with pride that, in all the days spent with my mother and father, never did I feel the sting and humiliation of a blow from their hands.[7]

Trust vs. Experience

One living the Native Way validates given information with her own experience. A person living the Modern Way usually accepts information based upon trust or belief in external information, simply because her way of life does not allow her much direct experience. She has largely substituted outside authority for her own experience. In this way unsubstantiated information can end up being passed on from person to person.

I have seen writers and workshop presenters pick up information in books or from classes, and then use it untried in their book or class. This can result in inaccurate information being passed on from one disconnected source to another, each time getting further and further away from personal experiential validation. In my profession as an outdoor skills instructor, I too often see misinformation being passed down from teacher to a student, who then becomes the teacher and does the same, all because the "knowledge" was transmitted rather than gained from personal experience.

When we attempt to pass belief-based information on to our children, expecting them to believe it, oftentimes they ask "Why?" To believe blindly is not natural—it is a learned behavior. In order for children to accept belief-based information as valid, they have to trust in the source. If they don't, they seek personal validation. Young children, trusting close adults, accept that Santa Claus and all-knowing parents are real. When experience tells them otherwise, they not only lose faith in Santa Claus, but they lose trust in their parents.

It doesn't have to be that way. Native people know better than to rely solely upon belief. Instead they trust in their experience-based knowledge, they are self-secure and self-reliant. They have special terms for their cherished earned knowledge; the Saami, or Laplanders, call it *kokea*. To gain this experience, the !Korana used to say *Sanã xamku-xa sana /ko-s xu—You leave your child with the lions.*[8]

Can Children Teach Themselves Values?

Why is it that there are people who go to church, even though they do not believe in the precepts of the religion? I've even met agnostics and atheists who attend church; some tell me it is for social or business reasons, while others say it is for their children. These parents feel isolated; the nuclear family is not enough to create the culture they feel their children need. Church is a coun-terbalance to the secular, materialist, "I"-oriented world. They want their children to gain a sense that something exists greater than themselves, to know that loving, sharing community is pos-sible, and to be instilled with personal moral values. Even though many of these parents feel hypocritical, they justify their actions by their children. My impression is that these families, though a minority, are numerous enough to help fill the pews in this age of declining faith.

I wonder if they would continue to attend after they read one of the recent studies showing that all people have an innate sense of ethics. The moral values of pagans, animists, atheists, mono-theists, churchgoers, and non-churchgoers were compared, and all turned out to have a highly developed moral code.[9] Along with brain function research, animal studies and observations of Native peoples are helping us understand our innate moral-ity. The core of morality appears to be *empathy*: the awareness that others feel hurt in the same way we do, and that others tend to return favors or pleasure received. This empathy-based morality is not uniquely human, as it is possessed by many of our animal kin.[10]

Although morality is genetically programmed, it—like the ability to walk or talk—needs practice to become functional. Example shows the way and experience hones the skill. The Children's Culture plays a vital role in determining how morality is expressed and employed.

Michael Schulman, author of *Bringing up a Moral Child*, gives this helpful example to illustrate this point:

> If a four-year-old was at first asked not to eat in the living room, they would accept it as a rule to follow and then if the parents later changed their minds and said that it was now okay to have food in the living room, the child would easily comply. However, if Dad says it's alright to push her brother off the couch, she is likely to respond with something like, "No, a dad shouldn't say that."

The eating issue is merely a social convention, to which the child can adapt, but not so with the pushing issue, because it is a matter of morality, which is genetically fixed.[11]

Just Don't Do It

How does a parent learn not to fix, rescue, or enable when she wants her child to be successful, do things right, and not get hurt? The answer is by ceasing and desisting. It's really that simple. The Kalahari Sandawe (a band related to the !Kung San) express it this way: *//o-i ?ie ta-sen-ts'i /ikaa—You carried a child who is running.*[12] For examples to follow, observe a cat or dog raising her young, watch videos of wild animals with their little ones, and watch documentary films of cultures still living in the Native Way.

Our goal as natural parents is not to coddle our children and keep them dependent on us, but to let them do as much for themselves as they can, and as soon as they are able. Our role in their lives is temporary, as it must be if they are to blossom into the people they are intended to be. As the old saying states, *There are no birds of this year in last year's nests.*[13] From the dawn of our species and on through tens of thousands of generations, children have largely raised themselves in the company of other children  and their non-human relations. Let us return to that tradition, and we will again love our children to life.

Chapter in a Page

No matter how well intended, and no matter whether positive or negative, regular outside input, criticism, or advice weakens children. Rather than becoming self-empowered and self-knowing, they learn to follow others and do their bidding. Unless they rebel, they usually spend their lives conforming and pleasing.

A child's natural way of teaching herself—the Blossoming way—is through example, experience, stories, dreams, and clan knowledge. Because stories and clan knowledge are forms of example and dreams are another type of personal experience, we could summarize all the ways of learning as *experience* and *example*. Experience is personal; example comes from others.

Our goal as natural parents is not to coddle our children and keep them dependent on us, but to let them do as much for themselves as they can, and as soon as they are able. The role we play in their lives is temporary, as it must be if they are to Blossom into the people they are intended to be. From the dawn of our species and on through tens of thousands of generations, children have largely raised themselves, in the company of other children and their non-human relations. Let us return to that tradition and we will again love our children to life.

◇◇◇◇◇◇◇◇◇◇◇◇◇◇◇◇◇◇◇◇◇

Chapter 21 Endnotes

1 Teodor Flonta, *A Dictionary of English and Romance Languages Equivalent Proverbs* (DeProverbio.com, 2001), 416.

2 Xunzi, *Xunzi: The Complete Text*, trans. Eric L. Hutton (New Jersey: Princeton University Press, 2014), 64.

3 Marjorie Shostak, *Nisa: The Life and Words of a !Kung Woman*, 96.

4 Ibid, 96-97.

5 Ibid.

6 Gennady Uchitel, *Don't Judge a Book By Its Cover* (Lulu Enterprises Incorporated, 2009), 48.

7 Luther Standing Bear, *My Indian Boyhood* (University of Nebraska Press, 1988), 90-92.

8 Menán du Plessis, *Kora: A Lost Khoisan Language English*, 246.

9 J. Kiley Hamlin, "The Origins of Human Morality: Complex Sociomoral Evaluations by Preverbal Infants," *Research and Perspectives in Neurosciences* 21 (2014): 165-88.

10 Frans de Waal, *Our Inner Ape* (Riverhead Books, 2006), 183-84.

11 Michael Schulman, *Bringing Up a Moral Child* (Main Street Books, 1994), 101.

12 Gerard M. Dalgish, "Subject Identification Strategies and Free Word Order: The Case of Sandawe," *Studies in African Linguistics* 10, no. 3 (1979), 292, https://journals.linguisticsociety.org/elanguage/sal/article/download/1062/1062-1629-2-PB.pdf.

13 Thomas Fuller, *Gnomologia* (B. Barker, 1732), 210.

*There is no more need to teach a child how to do
something than there is to teach an Eagle to fly.*

 **Chapter 22**

Experience: The Master Teacher

To truly know a thing, one must live it completely. When the body has learned, so has the heart, the inner parts of your being.[1]
Chea Hetaka, (Indigenous to the Brazilian Amazon)

Most people consider experience and example to be two different learning processes. However, learning by example can also be seen as learning from experience, because it is the observation of another's experience. In this sense, a person's experience is not just his, but the observer's as well. Thus, all learning is by experience. Like the facets of a crystal, stories, example, experience, dreams, and clan knowledge are all aspects of the same self-teaching process. This meshing of example and experience can be more easily seen when we step aside from our egos and cease for a moment to distinguish between self and other. Such an awakened state of empathy is hard to achieve, and even harder to maintain, for those of us who live in I-focused cultures. And yet if we are to know and support our children, we would do well to make the effort, because this state of relationship is the one in which our children naturally dwell.

The Best Teachers

The two most reliable and trusted teachers I have ever met work very closely together. You may have heard of them: they go by the names of *Trial* and *Error*. Neither can do much alone, but together they are dynamite! Fortunately, they are nearly always available, so invite them often. In fact, they'll move right in if you let them. Don't worry—they'll more than earn their keep with their miracle program: Experience. You will soon find them to be the only teachers you'll ever need.

Three Facets of Experience

1. Stories

Wherever people gather, whether it be around campfire, table, or bed, stories are likely to be told. Common to all cultures and times, they are the most cherished and accustomed means of sharing memories and aspirations. Stories are unique in that they create worlds with characters and situations where the listener can join in—and even become a character—and then learn through experience. This distinctive feature is why the ceremonies, celebrations, and other activities in so many traditions are story-centered (See Chapter 15).

Dance and song are popular forms of stories. When they accompany one another, as they often do, they work together as the voice and gesture of the storyteller. When dance and song are group activities, all participants are storytellers.

Both dance and song are ancient forms of storytelling. Song is used by virtually all birds and mammals, and by many reptiles, amphibians, and insects. Dance is employed by even more creatures, particularly the voiceless. Fish, spiders, and bees dance to tell their stories. Dance is often augmented by the shape and color of skin, scales, or plumage, and by props such as sticks, feathers, or leaves.

Before we humans evolved symbolic language, we probably relied heavily on song to share our experiences. The elements of song that helped to tell the story: scale, melody, volume, and rhythm, were replaced by symbolic language. For example, a song might increase in tempo to convey excitement, whereas in symbolic language the storyteller would merely have to say, "I was excited." Like song, dance in its many forms—pantomime, body language, sign language, and signals—was used extensively before the advent of symbolic language.

The ancient roots of dance and song are shown in our children, especially the youngest. Before they are able to use language, they naturally communicate by dancing and singing. Language needs to be learned; the ability to dance and sing is imprinted in their DNA. Even after they are able to express themselves via language, their storytelling remains rich in body movement, with their voices taking on song-like character.

Dance has acquired new meaning in the contemporary culture of Indians. Where once dance was a major part of the culture, it is now the mainstay. Traditional dance gatherings called powwows have become the most vibrant force in cultural preservation. Imagine a combination family reunion, parish picnic, cultural fair, craft show, and ceremonial event, and you'll have some idea as to why powwows are well attended by Natives of virtually all ages and persuasions.

With the popularity of powwows, there is usually one every week that is not too far away. Some families travel the powwow circuit, so their children virtually grow up in powwows. Demonstrating their innate ability to dance, children can be found dancing in the circle with older people even though they may be just learning to walk. Their participation is a giving and receiving: They dance their stories to their people, and they dance the traditional ways of their people into themselves

(For an in-depth exploration of stories, see *The Power of Story: Where Stories Come from and Why We Tell Them* in my book *Whispers of the Ancients*.)

2. Example

The power of example was impressed upon me in my youth with the words of a Blackfoot elder: "We become what we surround ourselves with." As I walked and meditated upon those words, I came by a saloon on the edge of the reservation. The front door was open and I could see the place was filled with young Natives. A couple of them saw me and kindly invited me to join them. I respectfully refused. They then asked me for money to buy more beer. I needed to meditate no more.

We have basic instincts to guide us, and at the same time we have much to learn in terms of how to use that guidance. If we do not gain these skills, our instinctual voice is either distorted or ignored. As social beings, we are exposed to these skills as we see them practiced around us, i.e., by example.

Example is so powerful that it can shape a basic instinct such as hunger into a vehicle for sharing and celebration, or for hoarding and killing. From a child's very first impressions, example begins to shape how she expresses her instincts. The more rich and balanced the cultural cradle in which we lay our newborn, the more rich and balanced a person he becomes.

Change First, Baby Second

I consider example to be such a vital part of a child's world that whenever I counsel anyone considering or about to have children, I help them see the importance of encircling themselves in healthy, functional surroundings before having the child. For these reasons:

- We are creatures of habit; change takes time.
- Changes in lifestyle and location are easier to make when not engrossed with a newborn.

For more on this topic, go back to Part III of this book.

Following are words on example from those who were raised in rich and balanced cultures. We can adapt their ways to help create the cultural cradle we would like to surround our children with. Because these are the ways of our ancestors, no matter what our ancestry or place of origin, you are bound to feel these voices resonate deep within:

"I tried to be like my mother, and like another woman ... I carried my doll on my back just as mothers carry their babies;

and besides this I had a little tepee that I pitched whenever my aunt pitched hers. It was made exactly like my aunt's, had the same number of poles, only of course my tepee was very small."[2] *—Pretty-shield, Crow, 1800s*

"You see, as a Cree man, you usually don't tell your son, 'Go split some wood for me.' You go out and do it yourself. You let your kids watch you. We call it *shadowing*, and this spring I'll be starting it with my five-year-old son. When I take him out trapping with me, I'm not going to tell him what to do, just let him observe so he can see what it's all about. In this way, he'll learn how to work and to love the land. As we take more trips together, the land will become a part of him."[3] *—Robbie Niquanicappo, Cree, 1900s*

"The old Lakota was wise. He knew that man's heart, away from Nature, becomes hard; he knew that lack of respect for growing, living things soon led to lack of respect for humans, too. So he kept his children close to Nature's softening influence ..."[4] In talking to children, the old Lakota would place a hand on the ground and explain: 'We sit in the lap of our Mother. From her we, and all other living things, come. We shall soon pass, but the place where we now rest will last forever.' So we, too, learn to sit or lie on the ground and become conscious of life about us in its multitude of forms."[5] *—Chief Standing Bear, Oglala Lakota, 1800s*

"We [children] had rigged travois to some dogs, and while we girls traveled the deep trail, pretending that our play-village was on the move, the boys kept out on the ridges, playing that they were our wolves [scouts]. They would signal to each other and to us as the men do when they are the wolves for the grownups. We were having a fine time."[6] *—Pretty-shield, Crow, 1800s*

"We taught our children by both example and instruction, but with emphasis on example, because all learning is a dead language to one who gets it second hand."[7] *–Ohiyesa, Santee Dakota, 1800s*

Sadly, many of our indigenous forebears found it extremely hard to sustain their intrinsic Balance, their genetic roadmap. Even for those who intend to stay on course, example is so powerful that it usually prevails. Hawaiian Elder Kaili'ohe Kame'ekua had this to say about how the power of example destroyed her culture: "The young wanted to do things the *ha'ole* [foreigner] way. Many parents felt shamed by their children, so they discontinued old ways. It was not so much the missionaries that changed things on Moloka'i, as the younger generations."[8]

The younger generations: This is where we need to focus. We can blame the missionaries, the culture, our parents, but that is all history. This is the *now*, and we can take responsibility for our lives by heeding the following words from Robert Fulghum: "Don't worry that [children] never listen to you; worry that they are always watching you."[9]

Blah Blah Blah ...

Children spell second-hand teachings, s-e-r-m-o-n, whether they come from preachers or parents. When children are given a "sermon," what they hear is not its content but that it is good and proper to sermonize. They, in turn, are likely to carry on the family tradition and preach to their children. *As the old cock crows, the young cock learns,*[10] say the Irish. I am sure that any child would rather spell sermon, e-x-a-m-p-l-e, as the best sermons are *lived,* not preached.

James Baldwin said, "Children have never been very good at listening to their elders, but they have never failed to imitate them."[11] Example works both ways, which gives us the opportunity to use it to our children's advantage. Once we recognize that we do have that choice, we can make a significant difference in our children's lives.

3. Dreams

Young children often make little distinction between Dreamtime and awake-time. Both are real to them: They describe their experiences in each state with similar emotional attachment, and they retain lucid memories of events occurring in each state. In both Dreamtime and awake-time, teachings play into their evolving sense of self and relationship beyond the self.

In most contemporary societies, children soon learn that the dreamworld is not real. "Don't worry; it was just a dream," is the response they commonly get from parents and older children when they express concern for something they dreamt. Little or no attention is paid to dreams, and the rational-materialist values that dominate awake-time life contradict dream-time's unbounded relationship-based world.

Is this part of the normal evolution of a child? Of the Native peoples I have come to know, or those whom I have researched, I have yet to come across any who do not consider Dreamtime and awake-time to be as related to each other as inhaling is to exhaling. The Achuar people of the Ecuadorian Amazon wake up together in the predawn and share their dreams;[12] various Siberian Natives need dreams to see because in awake-time they are near-blind in the darkness of their long winters; the Iroquois consider it a crime to deny personal dream guidance.[13]

In general, Natives see Dreamtime as a gateway to the ethereal realm, and dreams themselves as guidance from that realm. The guidance is usually personal, or it can apply to the clan, as with the Achuar. The Diegueño of Southern California receive diagnoses and cures for illnesses.[14] Like the New Guinea peoples I'm familiar with, Natives generally see their dreamworld experience as of equal value to their awake-world experience, if not more. They relate their dream messages to the here-and-now and apply them on a daily basis.

Considering that the gift of dreams appears to be universally valued by natural living people, dream interpretation is in all probability an innate human practice. It then has likely been with us since the dim reaches of our existence as a species.

What does this mean for our children? If dreams are not recognized and given a place of honor in our families, our children are denied a significant part of who they are. They have no opportunity to gain experience in a parallel world. The one source of guidance that is uniquely and personally crafted for them—and not filtered through anyone else's beliefs or perspectives—is denied them.

Fortunately, the dream experience is easily restored. Here are some suggestions to get you started:

- Share dreams in the morning, similar to story time before bed.
- Do this immediately upon waking, when dreams are fresh and before the distractions of the day's activities.
- Don't take dreams literally—most are metaphorical: Objects are symbolic, and characters represent aspects of self.
- Listen to others' dreams with openness, and accept their dream messages without interpretation or judgment.

In closing, Kaili'ohe Kame'ekua left us with the following warm, inspiring portrayal of a Hawaiian child's relationship with dreams. Her words could have been spoken by one of your or my clansfolk from the time when our people lived in the *Native Way*. Through these words, Kaili'ohe Kame'ekua lives on as a kind-eyed elder guiding us back to what it is to be human:

"Everyone in the *'ohana* [clan] had a high degree of dream understanding. From the time a child began to talk, his dreams were discussed with him. His dreams showed him errors, and how to correct them. He learned of things past and things future, or body conditions that needed correcting, and warning signals of illness."[15]

Chapter in a Page

Most people consider experience and example to be two different learning processes. However, learning by example can also be seen as learning from experience, because it is the observation of another's experience. In this sense, a person's experience is not just his, but the observer's as well.

There are three core facets of experience that deserve special attention: stories, example, and dreams. Wherever people gather, whether it be around campfire, table, or bed, stories are likely to be told. Common to all cultures and times, they are the most cherished and accustomed means of sharing memories and aspirations.

Meanwhile, the power of example was impressed upon me in my youth with the words of a Blackfoot elder: "We become what we surround ourselves with." Example is also power-ful—so powerful that it can shape a basic instinct such as hunger into a vehicle for sharing and celebration, or for hoarding and killing, depending on how one is taught to per-ceive it. The richer and more balanced the cultural cradle in which we lay our new-born, the richer and more bal-anced a person he becomes.

D r e a m s form part of

this cradle, as they give substance and context to a person's nocturnal world. Young children often make little distinction between Dreamtime and awake-time. Both are real to them: They describe their experiences in each state with similar emotional attachment, and they retain lucid memories of events occurring in each state.

In general, Natives see dreams as a form of guidance, either for the person or the clan, and are honored as a significant part of who one is. Encourage your children to share their dreams in the morning, similar to sharing stories before going to sleep; listen with openness, and encourage your children to find meaning in them.

◇◇◇◇◇◇◇◇◇◇◇◇◇◇◇◇◇◇◇◇◇◇

Chapter 22 Endnotes

1   Kay Cordell Whitaker, *The Reluctant Shaman* (San Francisco: Harper, 1991), 24.

2   Frank Bird Linderman, *Pretty-shield, Medicine Woman of the Crows*, 10.

3   Shirley Jones, *Simply Living: The Spirit of the Indigenous People* (New World Library, 2011), 40.

4   Kent Nerburn, *The Wisdom of the Native Americans*, 40.

5   Ibid, 15.

6   Frank Bird Linderman, *Pretty-shield, Medicine Woman of the Crows*, 42.

7   Kent Nerburn, *The Wisdom of the Native Americans*, 98.

8   Pali Lee and Koko Willis, *Tales From the Night Rainbow*, 21.

9   Robert Fulghum, *It Was On Fire When I Lay Down On It* (Ivy Books, 1991), 102.

10 Harold V. Cordry, *The Multicultural Dictionary of Proverbs* (McFarland, 2015), 81.

11 James Baldwin, *Nobody Knows My Name* (Vintage, 1992), 61-62.

12 Andy Isaacson, "Amazon Awakening," *The New York Times*, last modified 13 October 2010, accessed 20 July 2020, https://www.nytimes.com/2010/10/17/travel/17Ecuador.html.

13 Anthony F. C. Wallace, "Dreams and the Wishes of the Soul: A Type of Psychoanalytic Theory Among the Seventeenth Century Iroquois," *American Anthropologist* 60, no. 2 (1958): 235.

14 Gertrude Toffelmier and Katharine Luomala, "Dreams and Dream Interpretation of the Diegueño Indians of Southern California," *Journal of California and Great Basin Anthropology* 26, no. 2 (2006): 215–28.

15 Pali Lee and Koko Willis, *Tales From the Night Rainbow*, 25.

*Clan memory is generational: the young need to hear the song
of the old ones in order to echo them with their chirp.*

 *Chapter 23*

Clan Knowledge: The Forgotten Source

One child's experience goes only so far. Every day she comes across new opportunities and challenges, and often she is ill-equipped to handle them. However, a friend or family member may have experience in that area and can share it with her. This is clan knowledge.

The clan's cumulative knowledge that is passed down from one generation to the other is known as *clan memory*. Each member holds a portion of the clan memory, so everyone is valued for their contribution. Over time an individual's clan memory grows, thus elders are particularly esteemed for all they carry. Because Elders have clan memories that span generations, along with them being living links to Elders of the past, Elders bring continuity to clan life.

All as One

No man [woman, child] is an island,[1] says the familiar adage. We are clanspeople, adept at celebrating our individuality and at the same time coming together and functioning as one. The strength of a clan circle lies in the uniqueness of each member. Imagine the time in our past when we were nomadic forager-hunters: If we all had the same ability and reasoned in the same way—let's say we were all good net makers—we would have nothing unique and helpful to contribute to the clan, and we would all perish. However, if one of us was perceptive and able to scout—be the eyes of the clan—another was a good crafter—the hands of the clan—someone else was intuitive and sensitive to feelings—the heart of the clan—and so on, the clan would be a complete organism and thrive.

We find ourselves in a culture that stresses individuality: the me generation, personal abundance, self-reliance, personal space, a man and his castle. Sure, we are still family people; but the modern, isolated, nuclear family is a far cry from the extended families of our past, with their Shared Parenting, Children's Culture, and caring, nurturing relationships among individuals.

Our children are designed to tap into the experience of others— clan knowledge—to complement their own experience-gained knowledge. Without adequate clan knowledge, children face tremendous pressure to meet their own experiential needs. Some adapt and do all right; others suffer from failure complexes such as low self-esteem, withdrawal, and antisocial behavior. Without functioning elders in their lives to pass on clan memory, many children eventually turn to gangs, cults, and various disciplines (academic, martial arts, diet, sports).

This may sound dire, and for a clan-less child, it is. Some of you know this from firsthand experience, and some of you know from the experience of your children. And yet there is a way—both for us and our children. In Germany they say, *Wie die Alten sungen, so zwitschern die Jungen—The young ones chirped as the old ones sang.*[2] Renewing clan memory brings the return of the clan ways. Clan memory is generational: The young need to hear the song of the old ones in order to echo them with their chirp. Wandjuk Marika, an Australian Aborigine who grew up in the early 1900s, left us with this vivid example of one way the clan memory is passed on:

> "When I was a young boy, my father who was a very
> important man in Arnhem Land, started to teach me the
> beliefs and ways of my people, the Rirratjinu, the songs and
> dances and ceremonies and he also passed on to me his skill

at playing the ... didjeridu. My father knew all the designs or the stories of our ancestors and he showed me how to paint these. In this way I learned from my father all the important things I needed to know about life, about our history, our customs, and our ceremonies."[3]

Return of the Clan

Most of us who wish to renew the clan ways tends to draw from what we already know—our clan knowledge. Coming from a sensible civilization, we see this as a sensible approach. Unfortunately, such attempts inevitably fail. Clan is built on the relationship continuum that spans from the ancestors to the unborn. If we were to first honor and embrace this way of relationship, we would be well on our way to renewing clan ways.

Here are some steps for renewing clan memory, which makes the gaining and sharing of clan knowledge again possible for your children and you:

- Allow that anything you know, believe, and read about Native Lifeway could be false.
- Read books written by Native People who have actually lived the Circle Way.
- Spend most of your time with people who are one or more generations older and younger than you.
- Redefine your idea of family so that others might join and you might join others.
- Arrange for your children to regularly be in the presence of older adults and elders.
- Seek the advice of Elders and toddlers.

Chapter in a Page

One child's experience goes only so far. Every day she comes across new opportunities and challenges, and often she is ill-equipped to handle them. However, a friend or family member may have experience in that area and can share it with her. This is clan knowledge.

Cumulative knowledge that is passed down from one generation to the other is known as clan memory. Each member holds a portion of the clan memory, so everyone is valued for their contribution. Over time an individual's clan memory grows, thus elders are particularly esteemed for all they carry.

The strength of a clan circle lies in the unique-ness of each member. Just as a human body has various, diverse organs that support the functioning of the whole, so a clan relies on a diverse set of abili- i - ties, skills, and contributions for its healthy functioning.

We now find ourselves in a culture that stresses individuality: the me generation, personal abundance, self-reliance, personal space, a man and his castle. While individuality matters, the degree of individuality we now experience comes at the expense of clan, Shared Parenting, the Children's Culture, and caring, nurturing relationships between individuals.

Most people who wish to renew the clan ways focus on clan knowledge: They come together with a group of peers and set about gathering relevant information. Because they come from a sensible civilization, they see this as a sensible approach. If clan were knowledge, it could work; however, clan is relationship, so their attempts inevitably fail. Clan memory is built on relation-ship—the continuum that spans from the ancestors to the unborn. Those who first honor this relationship find they have the format for clan knowledge.

◇◇◇◇◇◇◇◇◇◇◇◇◇◇◇◇◇◇◇◇◇◇

Chapter 23 Endnotes

1   John Donne, *The Works of John Donne, vol. III* (London: John W. Parker, 1839), 574-75.

2   John Stoddart, *Glossology: Or, The Historical Relations of Languages* (R. Griffin, 1858), 252.

3   Wandjuk Marika and Jennifer Isaacs, *Wandjuk Marika: Life Story*, 36.

Knowing fire was sacred. I realized that breaking the connection between fire and an individual would be an act of disrespect.

 *Chapter 24*

The Role of Adults

As previously mentioned, children of the Yupik, the Natives of the Bering Sea area, learn the ways of their people in the qasgiq, the men's lodge, and the ena, the women's lodge. They are built underground, with a central fire pit and a subterranean entryway to keep in the warmth. Located right next to each other, they are sometimes connected by a tunnel. In the summer the people are on the move foraging, along with hunting seals and salmon, so the qasgiq and ena are used primarily in the wintertime.

Along with dances, ceremonies, and festivals being held in the ena and qasgiq, boys stay with the men in the qasgiq to learn how to make tools and kayaks, along with the skills of the hunt. Girls live with the women in the ena, where they are guided in making clothing and cooking. For a period of about a month, the girls and boys trade places, so they can learn each-others' skills.[1]

Teaching vs. Guiding

How does the Yupik way fit with children teaching themselves? Our image of the typical teacher is not the best fit for the Native adult who is working with a child. A Native plays more the role of a guide or facilitator. Her words are few and well-chosen, and she is careful not to get in the way of a child's enthusiasm and yen to experiment. Knowing that some day she will not be there for the child and he will be on his own, she values and encourages his self-motivation.

To encourage that, she gives the child just enough to go on to find his own way, so that he can learn in his own time and way. This way he teaches himself, rather than copying his teacher. The knowledge he gains is his: It fits with his particular abilities and the way his mind functions, he understands why it works and what didn't work. He is able to adapt his skill to a variety of materials and situations.

A Yupik child could be shown how to build a kayak: what wood to use for the frame, which skin works best for the covering, and how to assemble it. He could make one boat, and another, then another, and he might get quite good at it. However, he would not know how to build kayaks. Why? Because he gained knowledge, but it wasn't his—it was his teacher's. If it were an emergency and he needed to rely upon his wits and resources to make a kayak, he would not have the experience to do it. He did not experiment with various woods so that he would know their strengths and weaknesses; he did not learn how to process different skins to make them work; he did not experiment with various assembly techniques so he could see which best work in less-than-ideal conditions with makeshift tools.

Young Warrior Training

Rather than the hierarchical teacher-student system, a traditional Guardian (the more accurate term for Warrior, from Native perspective) training camp has peer learning, with the older and more experienced being an example for the younger. The older Guardians draw from experience and clan memory, which becomes the example for the young. You'll find more on this topic in my book *Like a Shadow: The Life and Training of a Guardian Warrior.*

The Student as Seeker

In the same way the Native adult is not a typical teacher, the Native child is not a typical student. He is more of a seeker, searching for knowledge and striving to gain experience in ways that are relevant to him. Unlike the student, he has a close relationship with his guide, as she works with only as many as she can give one-on-one attention. It takes much more involvement to help birth what is already within the seeker than to merely offer what you know.

With the guide crafting her input to fit the seeker's current need, the relationship constantly changes. This keeps it interesting and challenging for both. Their ongoing sharing helps the seeker learn communication and relationship skills along with the subject at hand.

To keep the learning process seeker-centered, the guide deliberately maintains a low-key presence. Employing her expertise, power of persuasion, or charisma would focus the attention on her. This often causes the seeker to feel incomplete and inadequate next to her, so he becomes dependent upon her. Rather than developing self-knowing and self-confidence, he feels the need to keep coming back to her.

A codependent relationship results, where he sanctifies her because he thinks he can never match her feats or attain her wisdom, and her ego thirsts for his constant attention and adulation. The upshot is that they both lose: He has no motivation and direction without her, and she serves her ego rather than gaining fulfillment serving her people. (You'll find more on codependency in Chapters 9 and 32.)

In my early days with Native guides, I often felt that I was being played with (and at times perhaps I was). However, the more I listened, the more I realized it was me—I just could not understand. I expected a lot of verbal guidance; they shared more by example and story. I had many questions; their way was to allow things to come in their own time and manner. I felt uncomfortable with silence and tried to fill it with ... well, anything; they drank in silence, seeming as though they were always either listening for something, or to something beyond my range. (And they deftly used silence for punctuation!) I expected my specific desires to be addressed; they suggested that my agenda might not be what I was intended to learn.

I found I was first intended to learn humility, for without it I was self-absorbed and could not listen. In humility I found honor and respect, which breached the language barrier—I could begin to understand what my guides meant when they spoke words like those of Chief Standing Bear: "Children ... were never allowed to pass between the fire and an older person or a visitor."[2] Knowing fire was sacred. I realized that breaking the connection between fire and an individual would be an act of disrespect.

One reason children show such respect for visitors is their valued role as guides: They bring stories of far-off places and new ways of seeing and doing things. The Lakota greeting, *Cante wasteya nape ciyuzapelo—With a good heart I take your hand,* shows how warmly guests are received. They are always welcomed, given the place of honor and the best of everything, and served right after elders at meals. In honoring, the children are honored, and in humility they find pride.

Bringing It All Together

The last stage of learning is sharing with others what has been gained. The process of pulling a teaching together into presentable form clarifies and imprints it. Native Hawaiians have a saying for this: *Ho'olale i ka 'ai a ka u'i,* which means *Show what youth can do.*[3]

At Ogden Community School in Thunder Bay, Ontario, teachers and administrators decided to step back and give fifty-eight fifth and sixth graders a chance to *show what they could do.* The students wanted to produce a play based on the traditional legend, *How*

Bear-Heart-Woman Brought Truth Back to the People.[4] The students, asking for adult help only when needed, constructed the sets and designed the costumes themselves, and they directed the play. Principal Denise Baxter said that having full ownership of the creative process helped the students "transform ... into the characters, and they were believable as the Crane, and believable as the Ravens."

Ann Boo, the fifth grade teacher, added that, "To actually be acting those things in the play makes it even more relevant to them. They really are able to connect. If we had kept doing that play for another week or so, those kids would be just crazy, because every time they did it, they put more depth into it, and really understood what they were trying to get out of the characters that they were portraying. I was choked up watching them because it was really fantastic—a huge moment for me. I learned things that I can do with the kids, and I can do it with less fear."

The children fully embodied the knowledge learned from the creative process as they became the characters. The effect on their community (many of the students were Native) was tremendous. After the performance, one of the Elders in the audience stood up and spoke: "We always say to our children, 'Listen to your Elders,' and that is good. But we have not been as strong as we should. We have communities that are hurting: There is alcohol, drugs, and abuse happening in some of our communities. We are out of Balance, like the play says. Perhaps it is now time for the Elders to listen to the children."

Chapter in a Page

The Native adult is not a typical teacher, and the Native child is not a typical student. He is more of a seeker, searching for knowledge and striving to gain experience in ways that are relevant to him. The teacher works with only as many as she can give one-on-one attention; it takes much more involvement to help birth what is already within the seeker than to merely offer what you know.

With the guide crafting her input to fit the seeker's current need, the relationship constantly changes. This keeps it interesting and challenging for both. Their ongoing sharing helps the seeker learn communication and relationship skills along with the subject at hand. To keep the learning process seeker-centered, the guide deliberately maintains a low-key presence. Employing her expertise, power of persuasion, or charisma would focus the attention on her.

In my early days with Native guides, I often felt that I was being played with (and at times perhaps I was). However, the more I listened, the more I realized it was me—I just could not understand. I expected a lot of verbal guidance; they shared more by example and story. I had many questions; their way was to allow things to come in their own time and manner. I felt uncomfortable with silence and tried to fill it with ... well, anything. I expected my specific desires to be addressed; they suggested that my agenda might not be what I was intended to learn.

I found that I was first intended to learn humility, for without it I was self-absorbed and could not listen. In humility I found honor and respect, which breached the language barrier. This same approach to learning, teaching, and listening can help us connect with our children and encourage their Blossoming.

◇◇◇◇◇◇◇◇◇◇◇◇◇◇◇◇◇◇◇◇◇◇

Chapter 24 Endnotes

1   Liam Frink, *A Tale of Three Villages: Indigenous-Colonial Interactions in Southwestern Alaska* (University of Arizona Press, 2016), 44-46.

2   Kent Nerburn, *The Wisdom of the Native Americans*, 14.

3   Mary Kawena Pukui, *'Olelo No'eau: Hawaiian Proverbs & Poetical Sayings*, 117.

4   Tamarack Song and Moses (Amik) Beaver, *Whispers of the Ancients: Native Tales for Teaching and Healing in Our Time* (University of Michigan Press, 2010), 58-65.

Part VI

The Serious Business of Play

Through play, children are educated.

 *Chapter 25*

Play Laid Bare

What would our children do all day if they quit school and we quit parenting them? Probably the same thing they now do before school, between school, after school, and often during school: play. All weekend and all summer, they play. As much as they can get away with —in fact, nearly all their waking time—they play. To the consternation of some parents, they sometimes want to play even while eating (not to mention that the play often involves their food!). Can play be anything but seriously important to children when they devote their entire lives to it?

Never-Ending and Never Far Away

Not even travesty or weather extremes can keep them from playing. I've seen footage of children in war-torn areas playing in bomb craters between raids, and at funerals I watch children often gravitate toward each other and play if not kept in tow. Chief Standing Bear says this of his childhood in the 1800s on the harsh Northern Plains: "The winters were long and extremely cold. As far as we could see, the world seemed covered with snow and rivers were frozen hard. But we played just the same. We were strong and enjoyed all seasons equally well."[1]

And yet children are hardly the only ones to take their play seriously. Pretty-shield, the Crow medicine woman who has already shared so much of her wisdom with us in this book, said in her elder years, "I have never lost my love for play."[2] and the classic Greek philosopher Heraclitus is quoted as saying that man is most nearly himself when he achieves the seriousness of a child at play.[3] There are few adults who do not struggle with the temptation to play rather than stay focused. What better way to escape drudgery than turning it into a game? And then there is the big carrot—the promise of retirement's endless play—that helps keep noses to the grindstone for half a lifetime. We have not only cities (Anaheim, Orlando, Las Vegas, Monte Carlo) but states and entire countries (Hawaii, the Bahamas, Fiji) devoted largely to play. We are talking serious business! And it is universal. If anything unites people of any age and all ages, it is play. Games of nearly endless variety are and have long been favored leisure time activities, as well as being popular at social gatherings.

Not just humans, but many other animals, thrive on play. Most of the time I spent with wolves was in play, and who hasn't known a dog who can't seem to get enough playtime? Dolphins, otters, bears, cats, and many other animals, play even as adults. Bonobos, also known as Pygmy Chimpanzees, are our closest relatives. For their young, much like ours, play is a big part of growing up. Perhaps as a reflection of the fact that Bonobos and humans have a common ancestor and share 98.7 percent of our essential genetic material,[4] their young and ours play many of the same games. Similar to Blind Man's Bluff, captive Bonobos cover their eyes with their hands and chase each other.[5] In another game, one of them tries to remain King of the Mountain atop a rock or mound while his playmates push and tug to dethrone him.[6]

Animals with rational minds need to accumulate databases in order to function, and play provides the data. It seems to me that the more rationally intelligent and socially-oriented the species, the more time its members spend playing, probably because they have more data capacity and require more data to function. Animals relying on instinct are born with their database, so they have little or no need to play.

Because play is so necessary for thinking animals, it has built-in positive reinforcement: fun. In much the same way that orgasm encourages procreation, fun is a motivation for play-based data collection.

Play Is School

When I ask parents what they think is the most important part of a child's upbringing, the most common responses are: family, education, instilling values, and parental guidance. When I ask the same question of children, most of those who have not yet been tamed respond quickly with "Play!" It would appear that parents have different goals for their children than they do for themselves. Does this make play the antithesis of family, education, and values?

For some it would seem so, considering how much energy children put into devoting their lives to play, while some adults are working just as hard to keep them from playing. Imagine what might be possible if these two tremendous forces could work together ... and they can. In fact, they naturally do, and they probably always have—until we domesticated ourselves and separated the fun world of the child from the serious world of the adult. If Standing Bear's traditional Oglala Lakota upbringing is indicative of Native childrearing in general, his statement, "Play hours of our boyhood were really a preparation for the tasks and duties of man-hood,"[7] shows there is no natural conflict between the two.

Even for those parents who believe in focusing on the 3Rs (reading, writing, and 'rithmetic), play is a more effective and efficient way of learning them than is the traditional classroom. In a recent Chinese study, one group of children was taught by the standard repetition-review method and two groups learned via self-motivated play and example. The latter groups significantly outperformed the former.[8]

Make a Child's Day

If you would like to see your child's jaw drop to the floor, tell her you just learned—and now believe—that play is a better way to learn than school. And then again, you might just get a "Duh, no kidding, Mom."

This bears repeating: Not only is there no conflict between play and education, and not only *is* play education, but play out-educates school. Much of the reason for this—and a big reason to seriously consider play to be education (i.e., unschooling)—is the impressive suite of attendant benefits:

- Organizational skills
- Communication skills
- Physical and intellectual exercise
- Recognizing and honoring personal passion

Yes, these abilities are also developed with a traditional education; however, they are often either not emphasized or they are taught separately. These abilities are an integral part of play, which means children develop them as an integral part of life.

Chapter in a Page

What would our children do all day if they quit school and we quit parenting them? Probably the same thing they now do before school, between school, after school, and often during school: play. Not even travesty or weather extremes can keep them from playing. I've seen footage of children in war-torn areas playing in bomb craters between raids, and at funerals I watch children often gravitate toward each other and play if not kept in tow.

Humans and other animals thrive on play. Most of the time I spent with wolves was in play, and who hasn't known a dog who can't seem to get enough playtime? Dolphins, otters, bears, cats, and many other animals play even as adults. Animals with rational minds need to accumulate databases in order to function, and play provides the data. Because play is so necessary for thinking animals, it has built-in positive reinforcement: fun. In much the same way that orgasm encourages procreation, fun is a motivation for play-based data collection.

When I ask parents what they think is the most important part of a child's upbringing, the most common responses are: family, education, instilling values, and parental guidance. When I ask the same question of children, most of those who have not yet been tamed respond quickly with "Play!"

Does this make play the antithesis of family, education, and values? Not necessarily. Play *is* education in the sense that it develops organizational skills, communication skills, physical abilities, reasoning abilities, and more, that are necessary to be fully functioning adults and community members.

◇◇◇◇◇◇◇◇◇◇◇◇◇◇◇◇◇◇◇◇

Chapter 25 Endnotes

1 Luther Standing Bear, *My Indian Boyhood*, 139.

2 Frank Bird Linderman, *Pretty-shield, Medicine Woman of the Crows*, 10.

3 Andy Zubko, *Treasury of Spiritual Wisdom* (Motilal Banarsidass Publishers, 2003), 58.

4 Ann Gibbins, "Bonobos Join Chimps as Closest Human Relatives," *Science*, last modified 13 June 2012, accessed 21 July 2020, https://www.sciencemag.org/news/2012/06/bonobos-join-chimps-closest-human-relatives#:~:text=%22This%20will%20allow%20us%20to,them%20our%20closest%20living%20relatives.

5 Kristina Cawthon Lang, "Primate Factsheets: Bonobo (Pan paniscus)," *Primate Info Net*, last modified 1 December 2010, accessed 21 July 2020, http://pin.primate.wisc.edu/factsheets/entry/bonobo/behav.

6 "Bonobo (Pan paniscus)," *San Diego Zoo Animals and Plants*, accessed 21 July 2020, https://animals.sandiegozoo.org/animals/bonobo.

7 Luther Standing Bear, *My Indian Boyhood*, 24.

8 Sum Kwing Cheung and Catherine McBride, "Effectiveness of Parent-Child Number Board Game Playing in Promoting Chinese Kindergarteners' Numeracy Skills and Mathematics Interest," *Early Education and Development* 28, no. 5 (2016): 572-89.

The child focuses on the commercial toy and goes no further. He ends up cloning the imagination of the toymaker rather than expanding his own.

 *Chapter 26*

Like a Kid with*out* a New Toy

If only all toys and games were created equal. The reality is that something as seemingly benign and pleasurable as a toy or game could have the power to yank a child out of the now, sap her passion, and rob her of her individuality.

At the same time, games and toys are vital components of play. They hold the potential to bridge the chasm between work and play, and to transform even traditional schools into learning playgrounds. And toys and games are for life: They possess the magic to Blossom our children into playful adults. This chapter helps us to creatively—and enjoyably—practice much of what we have gained about the Blossoming Way up to this point.

What Money Can't Buy

In Native cultures, children typically invent their own toys. This is more than a cultural phenomenon: All children have the innate capacity to envision and associate. Association is the key skill that is short-circuited and goes undeveloped when we provide children with toys. We see association demonstrated when a child picks a large leaf, saying, "This is a plate," then finds a couple of sticks for a fork and a knife, and proceeds to set the table. If he was given a toy dish set, he would have no need to associate or envision, and this is how these two key components of imagination go undeveloped and unexercised.

My grandson is not yet two years old, yet he has his own kitchen, complete with range, oven, cabinets, utensils, and a selection of raw ingredients. His oven is a cast-away computer box, his countertop and cutting board is a low table, and his utensils are various items pilfered from the family kitchen. He makes noodles, vegetables, and other delectables to steam and bake out of Play-Doh. All of this came about from his wanting to help in the kitchen as soon as he was big enough to make his way there on his own power.

His parents had considered getting him a play kitchen set, only they couldn't afford it at the time—and what a gift that was to their child! Not knowing that a kitchen set was an option, he put his imagination to work and created his own kitchen.

By age three, a child's interactive patterns are pretty much set for life, and this lucky boy was inadvertently given the opportunity to develop his imaginative powers. Today it's a play kitchen, and who knows what it will be in twenty or thirty years. One thing is certain: We don't have to be concerned about what could have been.

The Building Blocks to Raising a No-Toy Child

Would you like your child to be imaginative and inventive? Would you like her to be self-entertaining and interact easily with other children? The good news is that your child already is all of these things. And in order to allow her to Blossom and get the exercise she needs to develop and mature, all you have to do is two things:

1. Don't provide her with any toys
2. Get out of the way

Your child will then take over, doing what she is genetically programmed to do:

1. Observe what is going on in the world around her
2. Imitate what she observes by creating her own version of it

Using her innate metaphorical and imaginative abilities, she then finds items that are like those she has observed to use as props in her reenactment. This crucial stage in her development is short-circuited when she is provided with ready-made props. Instead of encouraging the development of her abilities of association and metaphor, we encourage them to atrophy. It is sad to think that most of us assume we are supporting our children's development by giving them a rich array of toys, whereas in actuality we are creating unimaginative consumers.

On Toys and Imagination

A reason for competitiveness over toys that I seldom hear discussed is that *attachment to toys is a direct result of an underdeveloped imagination.* I think it's important to bring this point into the conversation, as it's often a factor when there is tension over toys, no matter what other circumstances might be involved.

I talk with many parents about this sibling rivalry around toys and its root causes, and most of the time the parents come to grasp what's going on. Yet, for some reason, the topic of toys is sacred turf on which they are reluctant to tread. Some say it is because they have fond memories of their childhood toys. Others say that it would be impossible to convince indulging grandparents to get on the no-toy bandwagon.

However, when these people are able to get into their deeper feelings, they usually admit to the fear that they would somehow be depriving their children by not providing toys for them. Even though these parents understand the intrinsic harmfulness of toys, the feelings associated with long-standing traditions are slow to change.

Here are some ideas to help incorporate the no-toy concept into scenarios where toy-giving is inevitable, such as holidays, birthdays, and visits from relatives and friends:

- Building blocks for the imagination, such as Lego pieces not in a set
- Art and craft supplies, without instructions

- Kid-size hammers, saws, scrap wood, and nails
- Brightly colored fabric of various sizes and textures, along with fasteners
- Stones, sticks, shells, pinecones, bones ...
- Baskets, pails, trowels, old kitchenware items, and anything else that can be used in a multitude of ways
- Cardboard boxes of all sizes

When Life Becomes Her Plaything

To rephrase, the core concept behind the suggestions listed above is to have the physical item be a component, symbol, or metaphor, rather than the primary focus of play. The item is then used by the child as a catalyst or adjunct to expressing something within. Otherwise, the item is the product of someone else's creative expression, which tends to override the child's.

Once your child becomes creatively engaged with her playthings, it's likely that she will be drawn toward finding and crafting her own. She might go out on treasure hunts with her friends, and she'll start asking you if she can use this or that item for something she has in mind. You can help by taking her to thrift shops and yard sales, and by traipsing over the beaches and fields and woods with her—with a backpack, of course.

Going hand-in-hand with the materials is the skill to use them. Here is where the Children's Culture comes into full play, with older children helping younger ones learn how to craft and use tools. Caregivers might participate in building a fort or making a labyrinth, and Elders can share the finer points of such crafts as needlepoint, woodcarving, painting, and any number of other crafts and skills. The important point is to feed interest, and our job is done, as our children are fully equipped to take it from there.

Chapter in a Page

Games and toys are vital components of play. In Native cultures, children typically invent their own toys through envisioning and association. These skills often become short-circuited and undeveloped when we provide children with ready-made toys.

We see association demonstrated when a child picks a large leaf, saying, "This is a plate," then finds a couple of sticks for a fork and a knife, and proceeds to set the table. If he was given a toy dish set, he would have no need to associate or envision, and this is how these two key components of imagination go undeveloped and unexercised.

Would you like your child to be imaginative and inventive? Would you like her to be self-entertaining and interact easily with other children? The good news is that your child already is all of these things. By not providing toys, we encourage her to use her innate metaphorical and imaginative abilities. It is sad to think that most of us assume we are supporting our children's development by giving them a rich array of toys, whereas in actuality we are creating unimaginative consumers.

Here is where the Children's Culture comes into full play, with older children helping younger ones learn how to craft and use tools. Caregivers might participate in building a fort or making a labyrinth, and Elders can share the finer points of such crafts as needlepoint, wood carving, painting, and any number of other crafts and skills. The important point is to feed interest, and our job is done, as our children are fully equipped to take it from there. We let all of life itself, rather than prepackaged plastic toys, become their plaything.

When a young Wolf or Lion plays, she is training for her adult life.

 *Chapter 27*

Play Is for Life

Unfortunately, early childhood is the only time we modern people are allowed freeform and unconstrained play. Our young children can play out their fantasies, play at being the people they admire, and have play bring them fulfillment and peace. It's okay for them to listen to voices we can't hear and speak to beings we can't see. It's all fine—until it's time for them to grow up.

The Price of Growing up

Why grow up if it means giving up the beauty of youth? No matter what our age, are we not still children of the Earth Mother? The great spiritual masters implore us to be childlike: "Be ye as little children,"[1] spoke Jesus; *"Become like a little child anew,"* said Lao Tzu;[2] *and* Osho stated that "Now you will never become old … You will always remain fresh, young, a child, innocent."[3]

Perhaps we are intended to be children all our lives. After all, the childlike qualities of inquisitiveness, spontaneity, and trust would serve us well no matter what our age. When we retain these qualities, we do not take on the classic adult attitude of having arrived, but rather we continue to grow and discover until our last breath.

As with children, we "adults" are naturally designed to learn through play. Doesn't everyone yearn to do what is fun? Does anyone really want to grow up so completely as to give up the playfulness of youth? Only after years of conditioning and the breaking of our fervent and unbounded spirits could we be willing to accept adulthood on the stoic terms upon which it is presented to us.

Unfortunately, modern life leaves us adults with little time for fun, even if we had the childlike inclination. Nor do we expect to have as much fun as children, because early on in our lives we were indoctrinated with the twin beliefs that:

- Learning occurs separately from play, therefore learning is not necessarily fun, but more like work.

- Play is not a necessity, but a luxury, to be indulged in only after learning and work are finished.

The Dominant Twin

Every child knows that school is work. If not, she would call her school involvements *school play* rather than *school work*, and what she brings home from school to finish she would call *home play* rather than *homework*. Every adult says he *goes to work* rather than *goes to play*. There is no confusion: Too much play at school and the child fails; too much play on the job and the adult gets fired.

Herein lies the fundamental flaw of the twin beliefs: Above all, people need play. Being a production-oriented society, we cannot afford to let play get in the way of profit, so we have extracted play from the major activities of our lives and marginalized it. Perhaps the fundamental role of Prozac, alcohol, and television is to help us get by in lieu of play. They do a pretty good job of pacifying us, even though they're not able to provide fun and experiential knowledge of play. And they usually don't interfere with the important matters of life: work and school.

If we understood play, we wouldn't even be tempted to ask our children to "Buckle down and get serious about life." If we trusted in play and allowed it to progress, we would see that it gets increasingly more sophisticated as children get older.

Just as with school, the lessons learned and information gained from play also get increasingly more sophisticated. If we allowed play, i.e., the freedom to learn in an unstructured, enjoyable way, our children would gladly seek out knowledge and would retain their natural inquisitiveness. We would have healthy children: open, trusting, in the moment, and seemingly without a care in the world. In other words, they would be playful.

Play to Be Human

The above definition of healthy children can be used to describe adults living the Native Way. In fact, missionaries and explorers commonly refer to them as being *childlike*.[4] In historical times, more derogatory terms such as *irresponsible* and *naïve* were applied to Natives by those who judged them as inferior, even subhuman, because of their childlike qualities.[5] More accurately, Natives are humanlike rather than childlike, because their characteristics are intrinsic to humans regardless of age. In the natural realm, everything exists for a reason. We evolved to be "irresponsible" and "naïve" so we could remain aware, attuned, and adaptable—critical survival characteristics. They keep us in our bliss: in the now, connected with our feelings, and immersed in the Hoop of Life.

Not coincidentally, these characteristics also make us good game players—except for the game of surviving in modern society.

> *I know we've come a long way,*
> *We're changing day to day,*
> *But tell me, where do the children play?*
> – Cat Stevens[6]

What served us so well on our evolutionary journey now only distracts us from focusing, carrying on repetitive tasks, and doing the bidding of others. We are expected to adopt these new survival traits whether or not they are compatible with who we are. Being the antithesis of awareness, attunement, and adaptability, they are the core reason work and play do not mix. Play is for life, not work.

Chapter in a Page

Early childhood is often the only time we modern people are allowed freeform and unconstrained play. Our young children can play out their fantasies, play at being the people they admire, and have play bring them fulfillment and peace. It's okay for them to listen to voices we can't hear and speak to beings we can't see. It's all fine—until it's time for them to grow up.

Yet the childlike qualities of inquisitiveness, spontaneity, and trust would serve us well no matter what our age. When we retain these qualities, we do not take on the classic adult attitude of having arrived, but rather we continue to grow and discover until our last breath.

As with children, we "adults" are naturally designed to learn through play—to learn in an unstructured, enjoyable way. Doesn't everyone yearn to do what is fun? Only after years of conditioning and the breaking of our fervent and unbounded spirits could we be willing to accept adulthood on the stoic terms upon which it is presented to us.

Being a production-oriented society, we cannot afford to let play get in the way of profit, so we have extracted play from the major activities of our lives and marginalized it. Perhaps the fundamental role of Prozac, alcohol, and television is to help us get by in lieu of play. They do a pretty good job of pacifying us, even though they're not able to provide fun and experiential knowledge of play.

Part of our task in raising healthy children is to reconnect with our own innate yearning for play as adults. Play is what keeps us in our bliss: in the now, connected with our feelings, and immersed in the Hoop of Life.

◇◇◇◇◇◇◇◇◇◇◇◇◇◇◇◇◇◇◇◇◇◇

Chapter 27 Endnotes

1   "Matthew 18:2-4," *New International Version* (Biblica, 2011), https://www. biblegateway.com/passage/?search=Matthew+18%3A2-4&version=NIV.

2   Lao Tzu, "Chapter 28" in *Tao Te Ching* (Harper Perennial Modern Classics, 2006), 38.

3   Osho, *The Way of the White Cloud* (Rajneesh Foundation, 1975), 123.

4   Hayes Peter Mauro, *Messianic Fulfillments: Staging Indigenous Salvation in America* (University of Nebraska Press, 2019), 60.

5   Ibid, 38.

6   From the 1970 Cat Stevens song, *Where Do the Children Play?*

What if Grasshopper and Ant got together and made a game of food gathering?

 *Chapter 28*

We Can Help Restore Play

Not so long ago on a breezy summer day, Grasshopper was dancing blissfully about in the waving grasses. When Bluebird lit on an overhead branch and gave out a lilting melody, Grasshopper lent rhythm with his raspy voice. Glancing down, he caught sight of Ant, who was completely preoccupied with storing away food for the coming cold.

"Hey, neighbor," Grasshopper called out, "come and join us, so that we can celebrate this beautiful day together!"

"Maybe later," Ant replied. "I have a lot of work to do before the ground freezes, and maybe you two ought to consider doing the same."

"Ha! The sun shines and my feet say 'dance,'" Grasshopper quipped back. "What's your rush, anyway? There is so much food just laying around for the taking; and as hot as it is, winter must be a long way off."

With a shake of her head, Ant dismissed the pair of songsters and went off to gather more food.

One bone-chilling morning when the frost lay thick on the brown and brittle grasses, Grasshopper crawled up to Ant's door. "I am starving," the summer-prancer whimpered. "Please pity your feeble neighbor and share some of the bounty you have stored away."

"I have food laid up for only one reason," replied Ant matter-of-factly. "You chose to play, and what did it bring you? And where is your (ahem) 'industrious' friend Bluebird when you need him? Now if you'll excuse me, my breakfast is waiting."[1]

A Time and Place for Play?

The well-known Aesop's Fable I just told is a classic metaphor for the work ethic our children are weaned on. When they hear "Not now: I have to go to work," they learn early-on that work is more valuable to their parents than play. Because children relate to people through play, when it is devalued, they can feel devalued as well. Have you ever said anything like the following to your children?

"You can play after you get your work done."

"Don't play at the table."

"Play is for after, not during, school."

Every time they hear messages like these, they hear Ant's admonition to Grasshopper. Many of our children feel guilt and shame for wanting to play rather than study or do chores. Their sense of self-worth plummets as they struggle to live up to their parents' expectations.

I know parents who would prefer to let their children play. However, they fear the judgment of others, or they see themselves as having to face the hard realities of modern life. "We have to support our families," some of them say, "so don't we have to place work first?" Others say, "Our children live in the real world, so we should prepare them for what it's really like."

The Germans have a saying: *You can do anything with children if only you play with them.*[2] We function on a big assumption: that work and play are mutually exclusive. What if Grasshopper and Ant got the whole neighborhood together and made a social game of food gathering? If school were play, the conflict between play and school would disappear. If there were no meaningless rules at the dinner table, eating might be more fun. If work were approached playfully, it wouldn't occur to children to distinguish between the two (remember Tom Sawyer and the fence painting?).

Play Therapy

To help our children, along with our own child within, through the guilt and confusion surrounding play, I would suggest enrolling your family in play therapy. Don't worry; it doesn't take expensive weekly sessions with a psychiatrist. Play therapy is simply play. Because we respond so positively to play (remember: We are designed to play), just doing it can heal the wounds of play deprivation.

There's one catch: It has to be done regularly and always. Imagine that: someone suggesting you go play your life away. AND that you give your children free license to play, play, play! Sound too challenging—even impossible? Here are some suggestions to help make it happen:

- Adopt a playful approach to life. The saying *Life is just a game* then takes on new meaning.

- Avoid giving mixed messages. We can't tell our child to be who she is and then deny her reality by saying, "That's not funny," or deny her nature by saying, "Quit playing around."

- Find humor in all things. Instead of saying, "Get serious," practice saying, "Get amused."

- Watch your language! WORK is a four-letter word, so avoid it just like all other profanities. Instead of "I'm going to work," how about, "I'm going to spend the day with some friends."

- If it's not fun, either don't do it or make it fun. Even funerals can be a good time—just ask the Irish.

- Fake it to make it. One of the best ways to heal is by acting healed. If we can go through the motions of having fun, the feeling is almost sure to follow.

And Don't Forget to Quit Working

I'm not suggesting you quit your job, or anything else you do, only that you quit turning it into work. Try changing a diaper with your arms crossed over each other, or while singing a song, and you may find that work is just an attitude. Imagine what might happen if you approached your whole life in that way.

I've found that young children usually rebound quickly, while the older ones—adults included—take time to rediscover their fun-loving selves. Since we adults can be deeply wounded and tend to be more conditioned to suppress our playfulness than our offspring, we need to practice the above points diligently. As a reminder, write or print out a few attractive copies and hang them in conspicuous places, such as your kitchen, workshop, office, car, or wherever else they'll regularly catch your eye.

Yet It's Not All Fun and Games

Play is far from being all smiles and thrills. Frolic and games can be rough, challenging, and frustrating. There are bound to be tears and bruises, anger and envy. Some of us are tempted to protect and rescue our children (as well as ourselves). Before we do that, we would serve them well by remembering that their struggles hardly mean they are not having fun. How often have you heard, "I can do it myself," when you've tried to help? She is trying to tell you, "Challenge is opportunity. I don't care if I can't do it as fast or well as you. I'm enjoying learning, and I expect the process to be painful and irritating at times. I wouldn't have it any other way." Our primary responsibility is to step back and keep a watchful eye, so, as the Germans would say, *they do not tickle the nose of a sleeping bear.*[3]

Speaking of bears, here in the words of Standing Bear is an explanation of how play can hurt and be fun: "We grew hardy and the more we could stand the better we liked it. Although we scarcely ever fought among ourselves, still we played quite rough with one another. We often tried to see how much the other fellow would stand and we were anxious to take all the rough handling we got. None of us wanted to be quitters. We wanted to be courageous and good-tempered. We pelted each other, we wrestled, we kicked and hit each other, but all in fun. Of course, we got hurt sometimes as do all boys, but we grew so hardy in body that we did not really mind. I have had the tears come to my eyes, but I would remember my father's words, 'Son, be brave; never give up.'"[4]

My favorite guiding motto is *Humor in all things*. If I didn't see humor in paradox, I'd be struggling right now to find the fun in writing so seriously about—of all things—play. I have another motto: *We are not rational creatures*; so if something resonates with my heart, I don't worry so much if it doesn't click with my head. Life is intended to be fun, and fun is the heart's elixir (not that the head couldn't benefit as well), so let's play on!

Chapter in a Page

Many of our children feel guilt and shame for wanting to play rather than study or do chores. Their sense of self-worth plummets as they struggle to live up to their parents' expectations. I also know parents who would prefer to let their children play, but who fear the judgment of others, or they see themselves as having to face the hard realities of modern life. "We have to support our families," some of them say, "so don't we have to place work first?" Others say, "Our children live in the real world, so we should prepare them for what it's really like."

We function on a big assumption: that work and play are mutually exclusive. Yet this is actually a modern cultural phenomenon. Because it is so pervasive and ingrained in us, I would suggest enrolling your family in play therapy to begin to unlearn it. Don't worry; it doesn't take expensive weekly sessions with a psychiatrist. Play therapy is simply play, after all. Because we respond so positively to play, just doing it can heal the wounds of play deprivation.

There's one catch: It has to be done regularly and always. I've found that young children usually rebound quickly, while the older ones—adults included—take time to rediscover their fun-loving selves. Since we adults can be deeply wounded and tend to be more conditioned to suppress our playfulness than our offspring, we need to practice this diligently.

◇◇◇◇◇◇◇◇◇◇◇◇◇◇◇◇◇◇◇◇◇◇

Chapter 28 Endnotes

1 Ben Edwin Perry, *Babrius and Phaedrus* (Cambridge, MA: Harvard University Press, 1965), 487.

2 Willyn Webb, *Solutioning: Solutio-Focused Intervention for Counselors* (Taylor and Francis, 2013), 254.

3 Martin H. Manser, Rosalind Fergusson, and David Pickering, *The Facts on File Dictionary of Proverbs* (Facts on File, 2007), 100.

4 Luther Standing Bear, *My Indian Boyhood*, 37-38.

Part VII

Be a Blossoming-Supportive Parent

Children naturally view the flowers, grasses, trees,
birds, fish, and ethereal essences as people.

 *Chapter 29*

Know by Becoming

"Knowledge was inherent in all things," said Chief Standing Bear. "The world was a library."[1] Yet a library card is needed, and here is how a client of mine got his when he asked, "How can I know how to best treat my child?"

I began our exploration with: "Imagine yourself Becoming the child." To parent in the Blossoming Way is to leave the assumed knowledge of our parenting role behind and come to know and trust the inherent knowledge of the child. To truly embrace knowledge, one becomes that which holds the knowledge. If I want to know swimming, I become a swimmer; if I want to know children, I become a child.

There is a child in each of us screaming to be allowed to Blossom—a child who has been denied the blessings of nourishment without boundaries and the beauty of following his Heartvoice uninhibited. She waits ... fearful, unfulfilled, for the day when she might come out into the light to complete the childhood she was denied. And there is a child standing before us, who looks up with pleading eyes for nourishment without boundaries and the sanction to follow his Heartvoice. When we become our child within, we become kin with our biological child. We can understand and empathize; we can share stories and adventures. This is the heart and soul of parenting the Blossoming Way.

How to Become

I. Remember Who We Are

How can we as mothers and fathers, and as wounded children ourselves, renew the time-honored ways of respectful nurturing? A child knows what works and what does not work; so if we were to again become children, we would know. Theories and techniques can't hold a candle to knowing. With understanding, these parenting constructs appear to have been invented by people who sadly lost the ability to become children.

We are each born with the skill to step outside ourselves and transform into something other than ourselves. Children practice it regularly, yet by adulthood most of us have forgotten how. I call it *Becoming*. When we see children Becoming, we sometimes call it *make-believe* and pass it off as no more than a childhood pastime. For the child it is anything but pretend: A part of him has left his ego behind and entered another consciousness. He is actually practicing a hereditary know-your-prey survival skill that would serve him well if he were living in the Native Way.

It would serve our own modern children well if they retained this skill. Imagine what one could learn if one truly knew his mentor. Consider his ability to communicate according to each considered situation. And imagine how that person might parent if he truly knew his child: how she thinks and feels, what motivates and scares her, why she smiles or frowns.

I remember the day my son Wabineshi, then about five years old, became a cat. We were visiting friends who had a cat named Henry. While we adults were catching each other up on news, our friend motioned for us to look over toward a sunny spot on the floor where Henry, posed like the Sphinx, had positioned himself at just the right angle to absorb as much sunlight as possible. Right next to him was Wabineshi, the mirror image of Henry and just as absorbed in the bliss of the moment.

The person who practices Becoming is naturally heart-centered, which, as we learned earlier in the book, is the state where mind, intuition, feelings, senses, and ancestral memories come together to balance and guide the person. Because this state threatens the ego's control, the ego frequently resists allowing him to Become. When a person functions from his *Heart-of-Hearts*, his ego serves rather than controls him.

You have probably heard the familiar saying, *If you want to know a person, walk a mile in his moccasins.*[2] With Becoming, you skip the moccasins and walk in the person.

We can renew our ability to Become. It is the skill that does the most to give us the knowledge and insight we need to provide our children guidance and example, rather than rearing them. Perhaps the best thing we can do to assure our children do not forget how to *Become* is to remember how to do it ourselves. Only in knowing our children can we allow them to grow into their true selves, instead of having them end up products of our own wants and fears.

II. Embrace the Essence

By Becoming, we suppress our Self: the awareness that we are an entity separate from everything else. In the state of Becoming, we dwell fully in the moment, completely immersed in the life around us. We become fluid, able to pour ourselves into whatever might be around us, or to evaporate into the air and drift through the treetops. We no longer have friends or foes; we no longer feel joyful or oppressed; the compulsion to teach or change leaves us. The experience of Becoming brings us to the realization that real change only comes from the transformation of the self.

One of the sheer beauties of Becoming is how we come to know another life when we are able to feel beyond feeling and see with eyes not distracted by the seen. It is in the depths of these normally unreachable areas that a Wolf goes to know her mate and the trees in a grove find their kinship with one another. Any focus on conscious sharing would only get in the way. For example: A feeling like a faint escaping odor from the day's stew, gives little or no help in really knowing someone because:

- It can change faster than a shifting breeze.

- Reflection from our own knowledge, biases, and sensory input distracts from the deeper self.

- The way in which it is expressed can be misleading and subject to misinterpretation.

III. Prepare

Intrinsic to the skill of Becoming is being in communion with Life. My Ojibwe elders call this life with a capital "l," *Bimadisiwin*,[3] which you may already know as the Circle, Hoop, or *Web of Life*. To dwell in Bimadisiwin, is to leave enmity and empathy behind. Many think of empathy as the antidote to enmity, whereas they are both forms of separateness. Whether we are empathetic (bridging a gap) or adversarial (creating a gap), our approach to the situation or person comes from *separateness consciousness*.

It is within this state of separation that we humans look out at the rest of life, as reflected in the commonly used terms *man* and *Nature* (as though we are not Nature) and *humans* and *animals* (as though we are not animals). The Judeo-Christian Bible states that when God created us, He said, "Be fruitful and multiply, and fill the earth and subdue it; and have dominion over the fish of the sea and over the birds of the air and over every living thing that moves upon the earth."[4]

In the state of Bimadisiwin, we view life as *Nakanagana*, an Ojibwe term meaning *All My Relations*.[5] The birds, fish, grasses, flowers, trees, and ethereal essences are naturally viewed as people. From this place of interconnection we can Become quite easily. (To help know the non-human people as Nakanagana, practice the shadowing exercises in Appendix B at the back of the book).

As a preparation for Becoming, these exercises can be particularly helpful because Becoming is a progressed form of shadowing.

IV. Practice

The fact that Becoming is an innate ability that spontaneously manifests itself makes it hard to come up with a precise process to jump-start it. After years of living with wolves and other animals, I have identified three steps that precede my own personal experience of Becoming. I describe the steps that bring one to the threshold of Becoming as *Coming to Oneness*, after the Buddhist principle that we come from Oneness and strive to return to Oneness.

1. **Find a comfortable place**, free of distraction.

2. **Let your attention be fully absorbed** by something outside yourself, to the point where you sense, feel, and think like the focus of your attention.

3. **Draw what you wish to become** into this expanded consciousness.

You may need to repeat this process over and over until it finally clicks and shakes your Becoming ability out of its dormancy.

Some people mistake the journey of the Coming to Oneness process for the actual Becoming because of the growing awareness they feel as they open up their consciousness to all around them.

It has been so long since they experienced Becoming that they forgot what it was like. You'll know you have completed the steps of Coming to Oneness when you find that you have lost track of yourself having been fully immersed in what lies beyond. You'll have Become.

Is It Meditation?

Because of their similarities, the practice of Coming to Oneness and the practice of meditation are often compared. In Eastern meditation the intent is to practice a mode of consciousness that helps the individual quiet the mind and turn inward in order to be self-aware, whereas Coming to Oneness enlivens the mind and carries the person beyond himself; becoming more aware of the life and energies around her.

As an example of how it works, consider that you are writing a letter to someone you are struggling with and you want to anticipate how she might react to it. You Become her by the process of Coming to Oneness, which allows your consciousness to be absorbed into hers. It gives you a feel for her current state of mind and the circumstances in her life. You are then able to read the letter as though you are her and experience it as she would. You would then be able to consider if the message you intended to send to her is the message that she is going to receive.

Communication is entirely successful only if the intent of the sharing is retained throughout the communication experience. This is the basis of *Communication Theory,* which states that "the meaning of the message one person transmits is never exactly the same as the meaning another person interprets."[6]

A personal example that I have experienced was when my mate, Lety, was having a particularly rough time with something and I wanted to be fully attuned to her reality. We joined hands and together Came to Oneness. With my fears, prejudices, and preconceptions thus dropped, she flowed into me and I adopted her inner world, complete with biases and blind spots. Releasing her hands, I looked through her eyes and touched life with her feelings. I Became her, which brought me to a place of instant empathy with her. Sensing that I had caringly embraced her reality, she was then able to drop her defenses and relax into our sharing.

Sometimes Becoming can be practiced with the other person present, as in the example with Lety, and at other times the person could get in the way, as in the letter example. Because her presence could trigger my reactiveness, I might not be in a sufficiently open and trusting place to Become her in her presence. The reverse was true with Lety, as her presence helped me Become her because of our level of mutual trust and caring.

V. The Result

Our children change when we change. We are unable to make positive changes to anything when we distance ourselves from our own negative traits (such as compulsions, addictions, or parenting practices) by judging them as being acceptable, insidious, or any other label. We further distance ourselves from others (including our children) when we label them as well.

Instead, when we Become others, they also Become us. No longer can they be classified as anything without us recognizing our externalization and self-judgment. At this point, something miraculous happens: We lose our taste for judging our children's behaviors.

I remember a time when my son Wabineshi, who was three years old at the time, came up to me with a troubled look on his face. I asked him what was wrong, and he wouldn't answer. I got frustrated with him, as he was already speaking very well. Was he being stubborn, I wondered, or was he trying to irritate me? Fortunately, I quickly realized what I was doing and Became him, which right away helped me hear what he was saying beyond words.

With judgment no longer separating us from our children, we can now sincerely honor their thoughts, feelings, needs, and wants. Oddly, this places us in a predicament: We have no more reason to control-style parent our children. Most of us had felt the need to do this because we were unable to really listen—most likely because we were unaware of what prevented us from truly connecting. How rewarding it is to embrace the beautiful beings that have been around us all along and bask in their Blossoming.

Chapter in a Page

There is a child in each of us yearning to Blossom. And there is a child standing before us, who looks up with pleading eyes for nourishment without boundaries and the sanction to follow his *Heartvoice*. When we become our child within, we become kin with our biological child. We can understand and empathize; we can share stories and adventures. This is the heart and soul of parenting the Blossoming Way.

We do this by practicing what I call *Becoming*. We are each born with the skill to step outside ourselves and transform into something other than ourselves. Children practice it regularly, and we sometimes call it *make-believe*. Although for the child it is anything but pretend: A part of him has left his ego behind and entered another consciousness.

He is actually practicing a hereditary know-your-prey survival skill that would serve him well if he were living in the Native Way. In this state, we dwell fully in the moment, completely immersed in the life around us. Without the filter of the rational mind, we are fully connected to the Now.

Intrinsic to the skill of Becoming is being in communion with Life. My Ojibwe elders call this life with a capital "l", *Bimadisiwin*, which you may already know as the Circle, Hoop, or Web of Life. In the state of Bimadisiwin, we view life as *Nakanagana*, an Ojibwe term meaning *All My Relations.* The birds, fish, grasses, flowers, trees, and ethereal essences are naturally viewed as people. From this place of interconnection, we can Become quite easily. When we practice speaking, moving, and living from this place of connection, we create space for ourselves and our children to Blossom.

◇◇◇◇◇◇◇◇◇◇◇◇◇◇◇◇◇◇◇◇

Chapter 29 Endnotes

1   Kent Nerburn, *The Wisdom of the Native Americans*, 13.

2   "Walk a Mile in His Moccasins," *AAANativeArts.com*, accessed 29 July 2020, https://www.aaanativearts.com/walk-mile-in-his-moccasins.

3   Frederic Baraga, *A Dictionary of the Ojibway Language* (Minnesota Historical Society Press, 1992), 80.

4   "Genesis 1:27-29," *21ˢᵗ Century King James Version* (Deuel Enterprises, 1994), https://www.biblegateway.com/passage/?search=Genesis%20 1:27-29&version=KJ21.

5   Dolleen Tisawii'ashii Manning, "Mnidoo-Worlding: Merleau-Ponty and Anishinaabe Philosophical Translations," (2017), 201.

6   William Gudykunst and Young Yun Kim, *Communicating With Strangers* McGraw-Hill Humanities, 2002), 7.

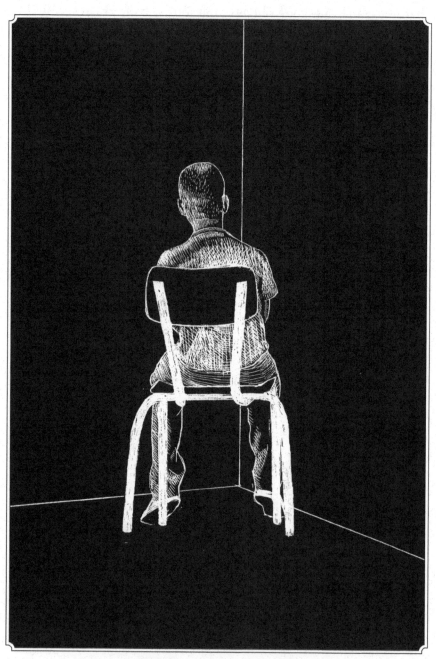

*Plain and simple, time-outs are the junior
equivalent of solitary confinement.*

 *Chapter 30*

The Parenting War

When we cannot empathize with our children and compassionately embrace their stories, we usually end up practicing *Control-Style Parenting* by default. It's a parenting style that can be best described as a war, as there are power struggles, retribution (commonly known as *punishment*), and classic battles (such as *The Terrible Twos* and *Teenage Rebellion*).

"But it's not like that all the time," some parents retort to me. Neither is war. Battles are short-lived and constitute only a small part of wartime. War is mainly strategizing, propagandizing, positioning, and negotiating.

Many of us are wartime survivors, yet we don't realize it. And many of us are waging war right now—with our children, and perhaps our partners as well. Do any of the following comparisons describe your parenting or relational dynamics?

Wartime Tactics	Family Parallels
Declaration of war	I'm right; you're wrong
Strategy	Playing one parent against another
Espionage	Mistrust, spying, gossip
Propaganda	Bribes, misinformation
Torture	Punishment, grounding, restricted privileges

Combat	Arguments, power struggles
Defensive line	Boundaries
Cease-fire	Timeouts
Martial law	What I say goes
Defeat	Victimization
Pacification	Enabling, rewards
Insurgency	Rebelliousness, tantrums
Guerrilla warfare	When mom and dad aren't around ...

It takes a war to control a child when everything inside him strives to be free-roaming and self-guiding. Being this far into the book, you have probably realized that parenting becomes war only because we make it so. Rather than being responsive and engaged with our child, we end up being reactive, which inevitably triggers reactiveness.

As our instinctual inclination is *not* to be reactive, we have to be trained (or train ourselves) through great effort and pain to become so. And our children, in turn, naturally go through great effort and pain to resist. The result: conflicting values, opposing sides, entrenched positions, pitched battles; in short, war.

We are products of conquering cultures that have figured out how to continue waging war surreptitiously after guns are laid down and treaties are signed. We see it in our attitudes and policies toward indigenous people, minorities, and other histori-cally oppressed groups (such as women). Many modern parenting "experts" advocate the same cleverly disguised wartime meth-ods for pacifying our children. The methods are clever because doublespeak makes the pacification sound progressive and altruistic, and disguised-yet-unyielding pressure is exerted from all sides.

Very few parents intend to mistreat their children. Parents usually see their actions as merely helping their children align with social norms. Doing so, parents reason, is protecting their children from negative outcomes such as social isolation and underachievement.

The following section is an exposé of one of the most effective and seemingly benign child pacification methods in our culture to date. Subsequently, we'll reacquaint ourselves with a method for which we are already naturally programmed. It takes minimal energy, creates little stress, and brings such fulfillment and joy that the contrast with what we so benevolently call parenting is shocking.

Training Humans

The *reward-punishment* system is a commonly employed tactic for getting children to do what adults want them to do. It is based on the *Behaviorist Theory of Reinforcement*,[1] which is the sociological equivalent of Newton's Third Law of Motion: *For every action there is an equal and opposite reaction*.

Not surprisingly, behaviorist theory evolved in the late nineteenth and early twentieth centuries, along with the evolution of modern physics. The behaviorist argument is based on the theory that animals can be conditioned to act in certain ways in response to the use of reward and punishment, and since we humans are animals, the same must be true of us.

Behaviorist researchers seem to have overlooked a critical bit of information: Conditioning does not consider the deeper impacts on the animal conditioned. Animals respond to much more than reward-punishment. It appears behaviorists were primarily interested in their test animals' performance, as there is no mention of the deprived, needy, neurotic creatures behaviorist training produces.

Sadly, these results correlate directly with many modern child-drearing practices, the products of which are also increasingly deprived, needy, unbalanced, and unsocialized, as evidenced by volumes of social research on ever-increasing childhood violence, psychological problems, and wider social ills.

Positive Research

Some of the most well-regarded animal trainers—those who *know* their animals—do not use reward-punishment. As an example, Marian and Keller Breland, both former colleagues of B.F. Skinner, the father of operant conditioning, noted better results from positive reinforcement.[2] The approach has been supported and furthered by subsequent growth in the cognitive sciences, along with a wider understanding of how critical it is to consider more than just base responses to stimulus.

Behaviorist training requires maintaining distance (primarily emotional, but also physical) from the subjects, for them to respond to the training. Imagine you are a child given all the nurturing you need and desire without strings attached. Consider the level of motivation you would have to perform for a reward when you already have everything you need. Consider next your feelings if arbitrary punishment came from the same hand that had so caringly and unconditionally given you nourishment?

Naturally, you would be baffled; this is why behaviorists must maintain distance. Many of us have witnessed or experienced the distant, authoritative father, or the schoolteacher who insists on being called *Mr.* or *Ms.* and has a policy of not befriending students.

Once when hitchhiking, I was picked up by a man with a dog in the back of his pick-up truck. "Hop up with the dog," he said. A few miles later, he pulled off the road and sternly admonished me for the attention I was giving his dog, saying I would spoil him and make him untrainable. From the dog's (or child's) perspective, this imposed distance boils down to one thing: deprivation.

Behavioral conditioning appears in many guises and goes by many names: positive-negative reinforcement, praise-shame, reward-punishment, indulgence-denial, self-control/self-abuse, selflessness-selfishness, on and off the wagon, affirmation-self-deprecation, and attention-withdrawal are a sampling. For our school-age children it's pass-fail and win-lose, and later it's pro-motion-prison and finally, heaven/Nirvana-hell/reincarnation.

The Battle of the Terrible Twos

Randy was a single mother and first-time parent of two-year-old Ben. Feeling unfulfilled in life and not having a nourishing upbringing to draw upon, she found herself ill-equipped for mothering. When Randy was overwhelmed or frustrated during meals, and when she deemed Ben's behavior inappropriate, he was refused nursing. Unable to communicate effectively at such times, she relied on "No" and "I want you to ..." statements, and lecturing to him as though he were an adult. Nursing time was no longer relaxed and spontaneous, but charged. Unsure he'd be permitted to nurse, Ben would become forceful, insistent, and sometimes whiny. This triggered Randy, who would reject him, and they'd have a blowup.

The deprivation and rejection caused Ben to place a greater-than-normal emphasis on nursing. He wanted to nurse more often than normal; he turned to nursing for comfort when he might otherwise have used something else; and he was slow to try new foods and incorporate more solid food in his diet.

"What can I do with this child?" she asked me in desperation.

"For starters, it might be better to ask what you can do with yourself," I suggested. "Your child is fine—he's only following his nature. If you two can align your energies, you'll do beautifully together. If your energies keep clashing, your troubles have just begun, not to mention his. I see you punishing him for his natural inclinations and manipulating to get him in alignment with the way you think he ought to be."

For Randy, reward and punishment substituted for meaningful relationship. Unable to communicate, she felt the need to control. The resulting energy clash drained her, forcing her to distance herself from Ben. Struggling with anxiety and depression, she found it difficult to be present, to listen, and to empathize.

Feeling inadequate as a mother, she used treats in an effort to express her caring and assuage her guilt. Not having been able to see beyond her own suppressed childhood and resultant reactive behaviors and expectations, Randy insisted that Ben adapt to her rather than creating an environment of growth for them both. As many lifelong patterns are established by age three, Randy had about one year to change her legacy, or Ben would end up its unwitting perpetuator.

My assessment was that Ben suffered from separation anxiety as a result of his mother's intentional distancing and difficulty adapting to Ben's needs. I explained to Randy that he could be a prime candidate for developing an addictive relationship with food, as well as struggling with insecurities in his human relationships.

For perspective, I explained to Randy that in our aboriginal past, separation anxiety was likely a rarity. Living in close-knit clans, we would have been engaged in deep caring and trusting relationships on a regular basis. In our modern culture, with its isolated nuclear family structure, the type of emotionally nurturing relationships we once took for granted are a rarity. Now, separation anxiety often gets reinforced even after a child is weaned.

Once Randy realized that her power was in trusting herself—and Ben—rather than trying to control the relationship, she was able to begin making changes. Ben, being so young and yet in touch with his Original Instructions, rebounded quickly. Soon, Randy's life as a mother became infinitely easier and more enjoyable. "I just had to break the control pattern," she told me.

It sounds so deceptively simple, yet it is a pattern of countless past generations that we are working to break as we relearn to know and trust our natures. However difficult the road, breaking this pattern is a legacy we can pass on to our future generations. Randy chose to step forward with her newfound awareness, by trusting in herself and her son, and their relationship—along with their personal lives—have improved beyond recognition.

Simple Yet Ineffective

Reward-punishment is easy: It fits into a busy life, anybody can do it—parents, teachers, daycare providers—and it requires no growth or healing. The behaviorist theory behind it explains behaviors simply and rationally, with 1-2-3 bolt-on solutions. Formula parenting. As a result, reward-punishment childrearing has swept the Western world. The only problem is that it doesn't work.

Examples of Reward and Punishment

To illustrate several core problems with reward-punishment models, let's look at a variation that most of us are familiar with: *praise-isolation*. I'll break down each component separately:

Praise

We hear and use a common form of praise, called *accolades*, all the time: *That's a good boy, You did a good job, Way to go!* While these are not intended negatively, they can translate to an assessment of the validity of the person, as well as valuing certain accomplishments over others. Over time, praise tends to become rote and meaningless, similar to the overuse of the word *No*.

To put it bluntly, there is not much real difference between *That's a good boy* and *That's a good dog* other than not patting our boy on the head and throwing him a treat. Like the dog, we are training our children to do things for extrinsic rewards and approval, not for the intrinsic joy of the action.

Rather than doing things for approval, most of us would like our children to develop their own values and be freethinking individuals who are sensitive to their surroundings. When a child is trained, he is being taught to look for the reward; asking himself, "What's in it for me?" One outcome of this type of upbringing could be generational increases in egocentrism and materialism.

Acknowledgment without Reward

Many know how to flatter; few know how to praise,[3] states a Greek proverb. To take the reward out of the recognition, just say, "You did it!" instead of "You did well." This validates an action without it being assessed as either good or bad.

Isolation

Timeouts remove and isolate a child who is exhibiting behavior deemed improper by those in power. The isolation area might be a mat, chair, room, or outside. A long-term timeout is known as a grounding. Some overseers use a formula for duration, such as one minute for every year of age.[4] There are two commonly used methods:

- Isolation: explain why his behavior was unacceptable, and then have the child go alone to the timeout area.

- Coaching: talk with the child in the timeout area to help him see why his behavior was unacceptable and what he might do that would be deemed acceptable in the future.

- Timeouts have grown increasingly popular since the 1970s, to the point where three out of four parents now use the method.[5] As gently as we might word and execute a timeout, the child still hears, "If you don't exhibit behavior acceptable to me, I don't want you in my presence." Or worse, they interpret the timeout as it being *them*, and not just their behavior, that is unacceptable.

A Chilling Parallel

Timeouts are the junior equivalent of solitary confinement. It may not be coincidental that the timeout is the most popular child disciplining technique in the United States, and that the U.S. leads the Civilized world in incarcerations.[6]

As with all reward/punishment techniques, we see the rejection and emotional manipulation of the parent leading to fear of abandonment on the part of the child. In addition to the fear is the often-resulting anger and resentment, which can lead to vengeful behavior. Regardless of his reaction, he learns that manipulation and withholding are proper ways to resolve conflict. And the pattern takes root in another generation.

Chapter in a Page

When we cannot empathize with our children and compassionately embrace their stories, we usually end up practicing *Control-Style Parenting* by default. It's a parenting style that can be best described as a war, as there are power struggles, retribution (commonly known as *punishment*), and classic battles (such as *The Terrible Twos* and *Teenage Rebellion*). It takes a war to control a child when everything inside him strives to be free-roaming and self-guiding.

Yet parenting becomes war only because we make it so. Rather than being responsive and engaged with our child, we end up being reactive, which inevitably triggers reactiveness. The skills and perspective gained from this book help us learn to choose differently.

Nowadays we describe ourselves as members of "Civilized" cultures. Yet we are actually products of conquering cultures that have figured out how to continue waging war surreptitiously after guns are laid down and treaties are signed. We see it in our attitudes and policies toward indigenous people, minorities, and other historically oppressed groups (such as women).

Many modern parenting "experts" advocate the same cleverly disguised wartime methods for pacifying our children—for example, the reward-punishment system of parenting, or its praise-isolation variant. Sadly, most of these techniques rely on rejection and emotional manipulation, which often leads to our children feeling fears of abandonment, anger, and resentment. Regardless of their reactions, they learn that manipulation and withholding are proper ways to resolve conflict. And the pattern takes root in another generation.

◇◇◇◇◇◇◇◇◇◇◇◇◇◇◇◇◇◇◇◇◇◇◇◇

Chapter 30 Endnotes

1   Wolfram Schultz, "Neuronal Reward and Decision Signals: From Theories to Data," *Physiological Reviews* 95, no. 3 (2015): 853-951.

2   K. Breland and M. Breland, "The Misbehavior of Organisms," *American Psychologist* 16, no. 11 (1961): 681-84.

3   Tryon Edwards, *A Dictionary of Thoughts* (F.B. Dickerson Company, 1908), 431.

4 "Effective Discipline for Children," *Paediatric Child Health* 9, no. 1 (January 2004): 37–41

5 Andrew Riley, et al., "A Survey of Parents' Perceptions and Use of Time-Out Compared to Empirical Evidence," *Behavior and Mental Health* 17, no. 2 (March 2017): 168–75.

6 Roy Walmsley, "World Prison Population List," *ICPS*, last modified 21 November 2013, accessed 2 August 2020, https://www.prisonstudies.org/sites/default/files/resources/downloads/wppl_10.pdf.

What a food craving feels like to an emotionally starved child.

 *Chapter 31*

What Food Cravings Tell

The frustrated father of a five-year-old recently called me wanting some guidance for his son, who was continually eating sweets. It didn't matter whether it was fruit, baked goods, or candy; as long as it was sugary-sweet, it was fair game.

"I've tried everything," he said, "from giving him all the fruit he wants to switching up when he gets fruit to making sure he gets enough of the non-sweet foods he likes, but still he's into the sweets whenever he can get his hands on them."

First, I assured this father that he's not alone. I've known many children who have what seems to be an out-of-control craving for sweets. Next, I told him that there may be a simple answer, but there's usually not. "Let's start with perspective," I suggested, "and we'll see what resonates with you." I listed the four typical causes of sweets cravings:

- Nutrient deficiency
- Unfulfilled emotional needs
- The desire to fit in (we become what surrounds us)
- Patterned behavior

"All of the above," the father replied. "I can see how each of them play a role."

Unraveling the Mystery

We discussed each of the bullet points, and it turned out that his son didn't have much variety in his diet when he first started to eat solid foods. The parents went out of their way to feed him what he preferred for fear he wouldn't otherwise be eating enough. "This could have caused some early nutrient deficiency," I suggested. "We evolved a sweet tooth to make sure we get enough vitamin C and bioflavonoids, which we cannot manufacture and we need on a regular basis. So if he wasn't getting quality fruit and greens, he could have started to crave them, which kicked his sweet tooth into high gear.

"How about his emotional climate when he was younger?" I asked.

"His mother and I had some turbulent times," Dad confessed. "And we still do."

"It's common for kids, and adults as well, to get a feeling of fullness with food as a substitute for emotional fulfillment, and that comfort food is most commonly some form of carbohydrate, which gives us a quick sugar buzz." I replied, "What kind of neighborhood do you live in?"

"A friendly one," he replied. "There are several families with kids, and we all get along really well. The kids play together, and they go over to each other's houses, and that's part of the problem. They give the kids candy, and I asked them not to give my kid any, but they usually do it anyway."

"That brings up the next point," I added. "Your boy wants to do what the other kids are doing. It's only natural. And if he has a craving besides, well, young children are creatures of the moment. And that brings us to the last point, patterned behavior, which is usually the result of the first three points. We humans are creatures of habit and pattern, so once your boy becomes accustomed to fulfilling his emotional needs with sweets, he's on automatic pilot. When he feels lonely or sad, he'll go right for a banana, or to the neighbors for a piece of candy."

"I see it all the time," said Dad. "What can I do about it?" he asked, in a desperate tone.

In the continuing discussion with the father, I addressed topics that are covered elsewhere in this book. Yet they are worth revisiting here, as they relate directly to food cravings.

"The answer is simple," I replied, "yet it's anything but easy. You've heard the saying that it takes a village to raise a child, but even that's not enough. It takes a clan. Even if you're surrounded by friendly and open neighbors, your child is still primarily being raised in an isolated nuclear relationship with one mother and one father putting him to bed, greeting him when he wakes up, and providing for most of his needs and wants during the day. That's not nearly enough.

"Even if you were the ideal couple and did everything right, giving him all the nurturance you could, it is still giving him just one adult male and one adult female role model. Children need more than that. A variety of close adults give them different perspectives and ways of doing things in their early formative years: before age three. A child doesn't always resonate with Mom or Dad at critical times, and vise-versa.

"Yet if that's all there is and there's no one else to turn to, this can be the start of unfulfilled emotional needs for the child, and oftentimes feelings of frustration, resentment, and inadequacy for the parents. That's in the best of circumstances. In a less than ideal relationship, which most are, the issue of inadequacy is compounded by the strife between Mom and Dad and the resulting lack of presence for the child."

"Then what's the answer?" the dad asked. "This is my present situation. What can I do?"

"Shared housing would help," I replied. "Or joining a community, or extended family if you two have brothers or sisters or parents you're compatible with. Anything that brings multiple adults in your child's life on a regular basis would be helpful."

And Equally Important

"Yet as crucially important as that is," I added, "it's only half of what's needed. Your son yearns to be part of the Children's Culture, where he goes to bed and wakes up with other kids. Literally. Where he's eating, sleeping, playing, crying, laughing, everything that kids do, with other kids of varying ages. No peer groups.

"Then, so much of what you see manifesting in your child that's dysfunctional takes care of itself. You can spend time and play with your child all you want, yet you can't begin to substitute for the Children's Culture.

"It's essential that there be older children to care for the younger ones and set the example for them, and younger children learn through experience how to interact with a variety of children of varying ages. A continually changing dynamic environment is created for a child when he is sometimes the younger one, and sometimes the older one. Playgroups are no real substitute for that, nor are structured environments such as daycare and preschool. It has to be a free-flowing pack of kids—under the watchful eyes of adults, of course—yet left largely to their own devices."

For more on the essential topics of Shared Parenting and the Children's Culture—and especially on how to create them—please go to Parts III and IV of this book. I cannot emphasize enough how vitally important an extended-family environment with varied-age children is for your child to be emotionally grounded and reach her full potential. When she has her core social needs met, you see an adventurous, self-reliant child who is truly happy.

Chapter in a Page

The four typical causes of sweets cravings are:

- Nutrient deficiency
- Unfulfilled emotional needs

- The desire to fit in (we become what surrounds us)

- Patterned behavior

Children with sweet cravings often didn't have much variety in their diets when they first started with solid foods. That could lead to a vitamin C deficiency, which kicks the sweet tooth into high gear. Other children who are struggling with emotional stress frequently turn to comfort food, which is nearly always some form of carbohydrate. Its quick sugar buzz provides an easy escape.

It all comes back to the need for Child-Friendly Parenting. Even if you're surrounded by friendly and open neighbors, your child is still primarily being raised in an isolated nuclear relationship. That's simply not adequate.

You may be the ideal couple, giving him all the nurturance you can, yet it is still just one adult male and one adult female role model. Children need a variety of close adults, to give them different perspectives and ways of doing things in their formative years (before age three).

Children also yearn to be part of the Children's Culture, where they go to bed and wake up with other kids. Where they are eating, sleeping, and playing with other kids of varying ages. Play groups, daycare, and preschool are no real substitute. It has to be a free-flowing pack of kids—under the watchful eyes of adults, of course—yet left largely to their own devices. Then kids get their core social needs met, which results in adventurous, self-reliant, and truly happy children.

Whatever the degree or form it takes, chronic clinginess is suffering. In all likelihood the child is emotionally deprived, which leaves him insecure and struggling with fear of abandonment.

 *Chapter 32*

Clinginess Clarified

If we haven't experienced it personally, we've witnessed it: a child who becomes the shadow of mom, dad, or an older sibling. The child can't seem to get enough of his caretaker, and can't seem to do anything without being held or having the caretaker's direct involvement. In its milder form, it's often seen as love and devotion, and in its more extreme form, it's typically called *clinginess*.

Let's first establish the fact that clinginess is a normal early childhood trait in all primates, including humans. Infants and very young children cling to their mothers for the following mutually beneficial reasons:

- Transport, protection, warmth, and nursing
- A secure base from which to venture forth and explore the world
- An emotional recharge
- A safe haven when feeling fear or vulnerability

We are not concerned with the temporary or periodic clinginess related to the above-listed reasons, but rather *chronic clinginess*, which is characterized by the child insisting or manipulating to be continually held, and/or to keep the caretaker continually engaged with him. Under no circumstances does the child let the caretaker go, and any effort in that direction typically results in a pained emotional outburst from the child.

Pain Disguised as Love

Whatever the degree or form it takes, *chronic clinginess is suffering*. In all likelihood the child is emotionally deprived, which leaves him insecure and struggling with fear of abandonment. He has a desperate need to relieve his pain by filling the emotional void and obtaining the sense of security he needs. He strives to do so in the only way he can—by turning to his primary caretaker.

In order for us to help this child, it is imperative that we first recognize that his chronic clinginess is not him. It is just an external manifestation of his pain. If we approach him as someone who is suffering, we are much better able to empathize with him than if we see him as being insufficient in some way or having developed a bad habit.

There are two ways we typically deal with pain:
- Treat the symptom.
- Find the source and alleviate it.

Working with the clinginess itself is seldom successful in the long term. Some symptom-focused approaches, such as establishing regular routines, shielding, and talking to the child to prepare him in advance for a threatening situation, appear to help because they reduce the clinginess. However, when we step back and take a look at the child's overall behavior, we usually see that he has just replaced his unacceptable clinginess with another behavior that meets his needs that is less offensive to his caregivers.

Unbeknownst to his caregivers, what they may have really accomplished is to plant the seeds of addiction and establish exploitative relationship patterns. (You'll find full coverage of these topics in Chapters 30 and 33 of this book.)

Another issue to address is that circumstances aren't always as they seem. The pain can start with the caregiver, who often subconsciously encourages clinginess as a way to mitigate the ache of loneliness and failed relationships.

Four Steps Away from Clinginess

Here is a supportive approach to help a clinging child transition from codependent-based to interdependent-based relationships.

1. **Support the child where he's at.** Above all, we do not want to shame or criticize him. We want to reassure him without invalidating his feelings (see Chapter 19). And we want to refrain from trying to explain what is going on in his relationship with us. An insecure child is in no place to venture forth on the frontier of his relationship dynamics. It is essential that our actions provide the child with a strong sense of security, as the more grounded he feels emotionally, the less he needs physical contact with his primary caregiver in order to feel safe.

2. **Involve additional trusting adults.** Here we lay the foundation for the child to expand beyond the one or two relationships he has come to rely upon almost exclusively. These people should be adults and older children he already knows well and has good relationships with. Have patience, as this step takes some time to fully enact. Some children can take a long time to accept new people into their innermost circle, yet this is the way it has to be. The child's clinging behavior was a long time in developing, and it takes time to change it. As well, his primary caretakers invested a lot to establish the behavior (even though it may have been inadvertently), and they now have to invest a lot to transform it.

3. **Spread out the attention.** Once a child is accustomed to having some of her emotional needs met by other people, have them become more and more available to the child when he reaches out. It's important to gradually incorporate new caregivers, while at the same time the primary caregiver becomes less and less available, until a balance is achieved amongst all caregivers. In that way, feelings of abandonment are not triggered in the child.

4. **Address the roots of the clinging relationship.** Here is where the greatest work begins—and the greatest reward. A very young child considers himself to be a part of his mother. He feels as she does. If she is stressed, depressed, or threatened, he responds as though he is stressed, depressed, or threatened (more on this in Chapter 9). His typical spontaneous response is to find comfort and security by clinging. Fortunately, the reverse is true as well: When mom is calm and her stress level lowers, his sense of security increases, with a corresponding reduction in clinginess.

Step 4 Cannot Be Compromised

If we wish to make a significant and lasting change in our clinging child's life, we must take Step 4 to heart. The reason is that our actions in raising our children can have a very different effect than we intend. Children learn primarily by example, so if we do one thing and say another in front of our child, we only end up teaching him how to be a hypocrite—along with passing on the skills that lay the groundwork for unhealthy future relationships.

The Stark Reality

... is that most of the chronically clingy young children I've known end up hardwired for codependent relationships later in life—no matter what their parents did or did not do for them. It started early, first with siblings and playmates, then with teachers, boyfriends and girlfriends, and on to business and intimate partners in adult life.

We are treading on thin ice here, because—again—it's easy to focus on our children, and in doing so miss the reason so many of our children become codependent. I can ask myself, "Am I raising my child to be codependent?" only I won't get a helpful answer, because it's like asking a bird if she's raising her chicks to fly.

I would suggest instead that we ask ourselves these questions:

"Is hanging on to my child easier for me than letting him be a free spirit?"

"Do I have the support I need to allow him to be who he is?"

"What am I getting out of his clinginess?"

"Am I threatened by his growing independence?"

If we can answer those questions honestly and follow through with what they tell us, we stand a good chance of bucking the tide of our family's codependency legacy. We are then able to grace our children with a wondrous gift: the opportunity to Blossom into who they are, rather than into someone who needs to think and feel through someone else's filter.

A point of clarity: *Codependency* affects everyone. No person or profession is immune to codependent-tainted relationships. It manifests not only with caregivers making choices that are not in the best interest of their children, but also where we least expect it, such as with therapists making choices not in the best interest of their clients.

For further help with this all-important step toward our children's Blossoming, you may want to seek the guidance of a qualified mental health practitioner.

Now, to set yourself on a solid course toward lasting change, I would like to suggest that you repeat these affirmations regularly during your work with codependency:

- The clinginess, which is codependency, starts and ends with me.

- No matter how it looks or feels, I am clinging to my child as much as he is clinging to me.

- I take full responsibility for my relationship with my child by asking, "How am I encouraging my child to be clingy?"

- I am thankful that what I learn in my personal growth process automatically reflects in my relationship with my child—and in his emotional health.

Chapter in a Page

Infants and very young children cling to their mothers for transportation, protection, warmth, and nursing. Sometimes this behavior becomes chronic, and it is then commonly referred to as *clinginess*. It is characterized by the child insisting or manipulating to be continually held and/or engaged with the caretaker.

Whatever the degree or form it takes, *chronic clinginess is suffering*. In all likelihood the child is emotionally deprived, which leaves him insecure and struggling with fear of abandonment. He has a desperate need to relieve his pain by filling the emotional void and obtaining the sense of security he needs. He strives to do so in the only way he can — by turning to his primary caretaker.

In order for us to help this child, it is imperative that we first recognize that his chronic clinginess is an external manifestation of his pain, not just a "bad habit." From there, we can best address clinginess using the following four steps:

- **First, reassure the child** without invalidating his feelings. Doing so provides a strong sense of security for his journey ahead.

- **Second, involve additional trusting adults,** laying the foundation for the child to expand beyond the one or two relationships he has come to rely upon almost exclusively.

- **Third, dedicate more attention** to the child, and do it gradually, to have these additional adults meet some of his needs.

- **Lastly, address the roots of the clinging relationship** by reflecting on our own emotional wellness, knowing that our children's emotional states often stem from our own.

I call it the Cute Doll Syndrome... *Parents dress and groom their children to resemble mini adults, the opposite gender, or to look the way they wish they looked when they were younger, thinner, and perhaps more courageous.*

 *Chapter 33*

Compliments: Help or Harm?

Would you agree that complimenting your child is a healthy, esteem-building way of encouraging her? Nearly everyone does. This may be why so many parents react as though I was some kind of wild-eyed radical when I express that my experience has been that most compliments given to children are to manipulate and domesticate. Considering the culture at large, manipulative complimenting is our most common motivating tool. It is used to:

1. Modify behavior
2. Gain favor
3. Direct development
4. Express agreement or disagreement

Compliments are sugarcoated manipulations, which is why we eat them up even though the complimenter has an ulterior motive. The sweet glaze makes compliments one of the more palatable versions of the reward-punishment system that pervades our culture. Just like grades, money, awards and titles, advertising, and so many other reward-punishment methods, compliments create children and adults who do things to seek approval rather than to follow their hearts.

In essence, compliments and criticisms are the same form of expression, as both are another person's opinion of an individual. For example, "You smell like garlic," could be taken as either a compliment or a criticism. With a smile and a sweet tone of voice, a criticism can be made to resemble a compliment, so that it can be delivered without reaction. This is one reason compliments are so often and easily used to manipulate.

Even at Story Hour

At a library program my son and I attended, we parents were given a poster: *100 Ways to Compliment a Child.* It would have been more accurately titled *100 Ways to Give Hidden Messages,* because most of the praises were designed to be warm fuzzy persuasions. Here are representative examples of those "praises," with their hidden messages:

- **Domesticating**: *You're growing up. You're responsible.*
- **Self-esteem Building**: *I knew you could do it. There's nobody like you.*
- **Controlling**: *You make me laugh. You belong.*
- **Corrective**: *I like the way you did that. Now you've got it.*
- **Judgmental**: *You learned it right. That was an exceptional performance.*

Marshall Rosenberg, founder of Non-Violent Communication, said that in NVC they "consider praise and compliments [to be] a violent form of communication. Because they are part of the language of domination, it is one passing judgment on another."[1] Dust the sugar off the compliments and what do we find underneath? We are likely telling our child what we like and don't like about her or her activities. Because we are the life providers for our children, our input carries much more weight than that of their peers. A child soon learns that, in order to draw attention from adults and win their favor, she must do what draws compliments from them.

The disparity between adults and children that fosters this lopsided relationship is one of the major drawbacks of our child–adult culture. When children grow up in their own culture (see Chapter 16), they feel quite free to speak their truths with each other, whether or not they be met with agreement. Another child's truth is accepted, the differences are soon forgotten, and their merry lives go on.

The Compliment-Scarred Child

A typical child's first memories are compliments:

> "Daddy is so proud of you—you pooped in your diaper this time."

> "Good baby; you slept through the whole night without waking mommy."

> "Smile for grandma ... Oh, what a charmer you are!"

> "That's my little man; you didn't cry through the whole service."

Here is an opportunity to take a peek under the sweetness: Strip these compliments down and see what you have. For example, the second one would be *You're good because you didn't wake me.* Notice the fulfillment of the adult expectation—*you didn't wake me*, which earned the reward—*you're good.* Implied is that if the child did not meet the expectation, she would not be considered good, and possibly even bad. What she is likely to interpret is, "I am not cherished just because I *am*, but because of how I please."

When a child regularly solicits compliments, it is quite certain she has been conditioned by their use. How often have we seen the toddler working her audience for smiles and compliments, and a couple of years later, running up to someone saying, "Watch what I can do!" In an extreme case, a child even begs for compliments. The mildly conditioned child says, "Look at this picture I did; do you like it?" whereas the heavily-conditioned child says, "I did this picture; it's really good, isn't it!"

These children have been trained to seek validation outside themselves, to find value in what they do from others, and to gain happiness from pleasing others. They are children who have been manipulated and domesticated via compliments.

The Cute Doll Syndrome

I recently saw a mother primping her young son to look and act the way she preferred. Over the years I've seen this sad symptom of the isolated nuclear parenting relationship so much that I've wanted to know how it originates. I call it the *Cute Doll Syndrome*. Here are the classic symptoms:

- Parents dress and groom their children to resemble mini adults, the opposite gender, or to look the way they wish they looked when they were younger, thinner, and perhaps more courageous.

- They have their child take the classes, adopt the hobbies and interests, play the sports, and make the friends that they like.

- They tend to see only their child's good qualities, and they defend the child—often vigorously—against any threats to their image of the child.

These parents risk raising a child who does not know herself. Sometimes they continue to control the child's life, even after college graduation and marriage. I've even watched parents continue the pattern with their grandchildren, often with the complicity of the grandchildren's parents. However, such cases are the minority. Here are the more likely scenarios for the victim of Cute Doll Syndrome:

1. **A pleaser:** At an early age the child learns to please his parents in order to gain recognition and approval, and to have his emotional needs met. He carries this into his adulthood, getting involved in codependent relationships and losing himself in them.

2. **A rebel:** Adolescent hormones, coupled with the discovery of a world beyond the construction of his parents, lead him on a wild orgy of sloughing off what is not him and often

gobbling up anything and everything that just might help him find himself.

3. **A recluse:** Dispirited, not knowing who he is or isn't, he buries himself in a profession, a hobby, or in a dark corner of his room. He has a high likelihood of becoming an alcoholic or drug addict, and his type's suicide rate is high.

If compliments are so hurtful, why do we use them?

It is most likely because our parents used them on us. Since we learn by example, and since we are creatures of habit, it is so easy for us, without thinking, to continue the family legacy. On top of that, modern culture as a whole seems completely immersed in the use of compliments. We see it all over in our schools, industry, religion, the media, and virtually any other institution you care to name. The use of compliments seldom comes into question, as they are effective, they just plain feel good, and it is hard to see beyond the short-term gain to the long-term cost.

Chapter in a Page

Would you agree that complimenting your child is a healthy, esteem-building way of encouraging her? Nearly everyone does. Yet it is also a tool to manipulate and domesticate our children. While compliments may seem sweet, they are just a version of the reward-punishment system that pervades our culture.

Just like grades, money, awards and titles, advertising, etc., compliments create children and adults who do things to seek external approval rather than to follow their hearts. Children raised with compliments have been trained to seek validation outside themselves, to find value in what they do from others, and to gain happiness from pleasing others. They are children who have been manipulated and domesticated via compliments.

Closely related is what I call the *Cute Doll Syndrome*. Here are the classic symptoms:

- Parents dress and groom their children to resemble mini adults, the opposite gender, or to look the way they wish they looked when they were younger, thinner, and perhaps more courageous.

- They have their child take the classes, adopt the hobbies and interests, play the sports, and make the friends that they like. They tend to see only their child's good qualities, and they defend the child—often vigorously—against any threats to their image of the child.

These parents risk raising a child who does not know herself. Sometimes they continue to control the child's life, even after college graduation and marriage. Raising children to Blossom means honoring them as unique individuals, capable of growing and thriving without our criticism, judgments, compliments, or plans, no matter how well intentioned.

◇◇◇◇◇◇◇◇◇◇◇◇◇◇◇◇◇◇◇◇◇◇

Chapter 33 Endnotes

1   William Stierle, "Marshall Rosenberg's Non Violent Communication NVC," *Yogi Times*, accessed 2 August 2020, https://www.yogitimes.com/marshall-rosenberg-nvc-non-violent-communication.

As social beings, humans thrive on recognition from their own kind.
When a child does not receive spontaneous acknowledgments from
those close to him, he either acts out in order to gain attention,
or he withdraws. Either way, his sense of self is eroded.

 *Chapter 34*

The Power of Acknowledgment

Are any compliments sincere? Certainly they are not inherently evil, and often they come from the heart. They are like a knife, which can be a valuable tool during meal preparation, even though the same knife could be used to cause harm to another. If someone was haunted by the experience of being stabbed, they may have to avoid being around knives for a while. The same is true of a child who has been raised with compliments: It is important that *all* complimenting be avoided to break the approval-seeking pattern so that he can be given the opportunity to reconnect with who he is.

However, the child still needs *acknowledgment*. As social beings, humans thrive on recognition from their own kind. When a child does not receive spontaneous acknowledgments from those close to him, he either acts out in order to gain attention, or he withdraws. Either way, his sense of self is eroded.

The conundrum with eliminating compliments is that we may also eliminate acknowledgments—the proverbial throwing out the baby with the bathwater. Fortunately for us, there is an acknowledgment disguised in every compliment. All we have to do is strip off the expectation and reward and we have a self-affirming acknowledgment. This makes changing our complimenting pattern so much easier, because rather than having to discontinue one behavior and replace it with another, we merely have to fine-tune the behavior. For example, if we take "Good baby, you pooped in your diaper this time," and toss out the reward, *good baby*, and the judgment, *this time*, we are left with the core acknowledgment, "You pooped in your diaper!" This gives the child all the benefits of a compliment, including positive reinforcement and self-affirmation, with none of the harm.

What Else Can I Use?

If I say to my child, "You finished your picture; it's beautiful!" is that all I mean, or am I also subversively encouraging her to do more artwork? In addition, my compliment could be a double manipulation: I think it's important for my child to finish something, and I approve of what he finished.

To genuinely recognize the accomplishment, I can *acknowledge* rather than compliment. The difference? Leave out the rating— beautiful, great, best, etc.—and strip the compliment down to its core acknowledgment by simply stating, "You painted a picture!"

Couldn't a Compliment Be My Truth?

What if I genuinely see the picture as beautiful? Wouldn't stating that then be speaking my Truth? Our role as parents is to act as guides, supporting our child's process, rather than assessing how she is doing. One goal of *Truthspeaking* is to communicate the voice of our hearts with clarity, in a language our audience can understand. The question to then ask is: What is it that I want to stress as my children's guide? If I rate this picture as beautiful, what do I then do if I don't find the next picture beautiful?

Now you are being supportive and encouraging: You are reinforcing your child's choice to do what he wants and when and how he wants to do it. Along with that, you are clearing the path for him to do it again. And you are doing it without being manipulative. Compliments enslave; acknowledgments empower. Compliments create clones; acknowledgments create individuals.

Acknowledgments are naturally supportive of who the child is, and at the same time they have more to give. A child can be nourished by an acknowledgment—not by what is said but by how it is presented. When he feels interest and caring in your voice, he listens with his heart as well as his mind, and his trust in relationship grows stronger.

Because of this qualitative aspect of acknowledgments, they do not have to be verbal. Oftentimes a smile, a nod, or a touch, conveys more than words. The important thing to remember is that acknowledgments, even if delivered awkwardly, are vital to your child's psycho-emotional health and development.

My mother kept every gift I made for her, regardless of its beauty. It was the effort and feeling that I had put into it that made it precious to her. The fact that she cherished my gift for what it represented to her was much more meaningful to me than an art critique.

To summarize, compliments are subjective, whereas acknowledgments are merely observations. If I compliment someone, it is really about me—what I think and feel—whereas if I were to acknowledge the person, it would be about him, because I would merely be reflecting what he has said or done.

Now go back to the compliments listed under *The Compliment-Scarred Child* above and see if you can identify how each compliment coerces the child to do what the parent considers worthwhile, in the time and way the parent would like it done.

Another Option

Those living in the Native Way can appear to be people of few words. This is because of their reliance on Direct Communication. The time and closeness of their lifeway allows them to know each child's natural rhythms and body language, so they can nourish and guide their children with little need for acknowledgments or manipulative compliments. If a parent senses when her child is going to take a dump, she can help him so that he doesn't soil his clothes. We can do the same, by awakening to our intrinsic selves and adopting natural ways of relationship.

Tools for the Transition

Since we have already acknowledged when we compliment, all that is left to do is clean up the compliment to bring out the hidden acknowledgment. Along with that, we are already in the habit of acknowledging, though we may not recognize it as such because it is nonverbal. Every time we hold someone's hand, give a hug, or offer tea, we are acknowledging.

How often have you found yourself fishing around for just the right words in order to pay a compliment? You won't have that problem with acknowledgments, because they are just simple statements of fact. All we have to do is catch a compliment before we voice it and turn it into an acknowledgment. For most of us, the main challenge is catching the compliment in time. Being creatures of habit, we do many things without thinking about them. Here are some suggestions to help catch ourselves and break the compliment habit:

- **Post *No Compliment Zone* signs** in house, car, yard, office, and wherever else they could be helpful.

- **Ask friends and family members** to point out when you compliment.

- **Practice on yourself** by acknowledging, rather than complimenting, your own discoveries and accomplishments.

- **Team up with a friend** and take turns describing each other. Convert anything that sounds complimentary to an acknowledgment.

Four Steps to Acknowledgement

1. Cease all complimenting.
2. Acknowledge often.
3. Be objective.
4. Speak with heart.

Success Is Failure

There may be nothing more harmful in raising children than praising their successes and consoling them when they fail. Success, as it is typically construed in our culture, ultimately leads to failure. I should say, the focus on success as it is construed in our culture, ultimately leads to failure. When we create competitive situations for our children and put pressure on our children to excel in those situations, we create competitive, self-centered children who often compromise themselves and exploit others in order to advance. Many of them end up feeling chronically unfulfilled and struggle with depression as they continually strive to prove themselves. Consoling them when they fail, as our culture typically defines failure, is just as bad as praising them for their successes.

Frustration over failure is an uncommon response with children who are allowed to grow and learn without parental pressure to achieve. Watch a toddler learning a new skill such as walking. She makes many attempts before she is able to take her first step; and as she progresses, she stumbles and falls many, many times. However, if left to her own devices, she thinks nothing of it. She just gets up and continues going.

Notice I didn't say she gets up and *tries* again. As soon as I use the word *try*, I am telling my child that she has not accomplished something. Rather than her naturally taking her stumble in stride and integrating what she learned from it, I am having her focus on the fact that she failed, and I want her to do better next time.

In her learning process, the falling is more important than the steps she takes, as it is the falling that teaches her how to walk. However, if we console her for the falling and reward her for the walking, we plant the seeds of success and failure. She learns at a very early age what mistakes are and that she is a good girl when she accomplishes what others consider to be of value, and she is a failure when she does not achieve that. She gets lost in the equation and her learning process gets subverted. It is just as important to learn how to fall as it is to learn how to walk, as there is much more falling in life than walking. She ends up not adequately developing the skills for falling, and this carries over to all the forms of falling one experiences in life.

Our children end up becoming people-pleasers and conformists, at least on the surface. They often hide resentments and end up acting out and becoming rebellious. Many of these children transition through the problem child phase and learn how to survive by essentially giving people what they want. In their childhood friendships, in their relationships with their parents, and ultimately in their intimate relationships, they engage in codependent behaviors with others. They end up leading lives that may appear peaceful on the surface, yet they are largely unfulfilling. There is always something better that they have not yet achieved.

To make it worse, their desire to achieve is hollow, as they know deep down that they are not really working for themselves, but for the approval of others. They work desperately to avoid failure; and when that is not possible, they typically deny and suppress it, or escape it with diversions or mood alterants.

The next time your child fails, smile. The next time you want to praise him for succeeding, bite your tongue. He could care less if he is taking three steps today and he could only take two yesterday. He is on a journey, and his goal is in the walking, not the achieving. Rather than "What a good boy, you took two steps today!" or "Oh, you poor boy, you fell," let's be a benign loving presence and allow our children to have their experiences in their world, in their way.

Chapter in a Page

It is important to distinguish acknowledgment from compliments. While compliments can be corrosive to our children's long-term growth and wellness, our children still need acknowledgment. As social beings, humans thrive on recognition from their own kind. When a child does not receive spontaneous acknowledgments from those close to him, he either acts out in order to gain attention, or he withdraws. Either way, his sense of self is eroded.

The conundrum with eliminating compliments is that we may also eliminate acknowledgments—the proverbial throwing out the baby with the bathwater. Fortunately for us, there is an acknowledgment disguised in every compliment. All we have to do is strip off the expectation and reward and we have a self-affirming acknowledgment. This makes changing our complimenting pattern so much easier, because rather than having to discontinue one behavior and replace it with another, we merely have to fine-tune the behavior.

Compliments tend to be really about me—what I think and feel—whereas if I were to acknowledge the person, it would be about him, because I would merely be reflecting what he has said or done. For example, if I say to my child, "You finished your picture; it's beautiful!" is that all I mean, or am I also subversively encouraging her to do more artwork? Instead, I might simply leave out the rating (beautiful, great, best, etc.) and say, "You painted a picture!" When he feels interest and caring in your voice, he listens with his heart as well as his mind, and his trust in relationship grows stronger.

Part VIII

Are You a Childhood-Deprived Parent?

At some time in our family history, our ancestors began depriving their children of the childhood normally intended for them.

 **Chapter 35**

Patterns to the Past

The Saami People of Scandinavia have a saying: *The memories of youth make for long, long thoughts.*[1] Some parents I counsel reflect those words when they say, "If only I could go back to my childhood and regain what I have lost."

I nod in agreement. They initially came to see me because they were frustrated about their children, and they came to realize that it was really about them.

The only way I know of to prevent the creation of another generation of childhood-deprived parents is for parents to return to their own childhoods. Even though we are now grown, the children we once were are still very much with us and affecting our adult lives. Our self-esteem and depth of character are wholly dependent on our child-self's level of contentment and security.

The first step in healing is awareness. We begin to break the family pattern by consciously acknowledging that our children's psychological and emotional well-being—both now and later as adults—is dependent upon our own. When we recognize the power we hold over our children's future, along with how our nuclear families lack the checks and balances of a greater circle, we can begin to see the tremendous responsibility—and opportunity—we have for change.

We Can Go Back

As complex and confusing as our adult dysfunctional behaviors might seem, they are invariably the same behaviors we developed as children. In other words, our behaviors are a clear reflection of how we were raised. Hawaiians state it this way: *Hewa kumu waiho i keiki—Faults of the source are left to the children.*[2]

Now as parents, we can see our relationship with our children as a reflection of our relationship with our child-self. That's why we can so easily slide into the familiar groove of our childhood and replicate our upbringing for our children. In doing so, we create another generation of childhood-deprived parents.

It all started at some time in our family history when our ancestors began removing childhood from the world of their children. At times it was done out of necessity, such as in wartime or periods of economic or environmental crisis. At other times, it was in response to cultural pressure or belief systems. Currently, babysitting, daycare, nursery schools, summer camps, structured community, school, and church activities—and even playgrounds—are the agents of childhood attrition.

It's not that our parents weren't well intentioned, as they believed they were supporting and nourishing us. Those institutionalized activities were their way of giving love and attention. However, the activities created a deprived environment because they did not provide us with adequate nourishment and support. We, like all children, needed a developmental climate of spontaneity, diversity, and challenge, made secure by the familiar, caring presence of older and younger siblings, parents, and extended family.

The result has been that within each of us lives an incompletely developed and wounded child. It shows when we lack resonance with our children. No matter how well adjusted or successful an adult we might appear to be, we often feel inadequate as parents because we don't know how to handle what comes up with our children. They are so different than we think they *ought* to be. *This is because we are childhood-deprived parents.*

Like a Child at Play

In this chapter, we explore how our devotedness to our children is hurtful to both them and us when we lovingly distance ourselves from them by structuring and institutionalizing their childhoods. Let us remember that our deprivation is not our parents' fault, and it is not our fault that we have continued the pattern of deprivation. Both we and our parents are the products of a society with a broken Children's Culture and a commitment to driving children to meet the expectations of others rather than seeking their own fulfillment.

This book as a whole is a guide for that to change, by inviting us back to the time of childhood when our lifelong patterns and behaviors were being set. It then gives us the format to nourish and heal our child within. It *is* possible to re-become our *inner child* and complete that critical developmental phase in our life in a way that is healthy and nourishing.

We can work on our relationship with our child-self right along with our relationship with our children. The healthy patterns we create reflect not only in the relationships with our child-self and children, but in all of our relationships, whether they be professional, familial, or intimate.

Won-nai-ki-lo-a is the Australian Awabakal Aborigine term for being childlike.[3] When we give ourselves permission to be won-nai-ki-lo-a, we spontaneously become able to commune with our child-self.

Changing Course

Early on in this book, I told you that it was only ostensibly about raising children, as it was just as much—if not more—about applying what we are learning to our own child-selves. We explored the need to go back to the roots of our turmoil, in order to heal from it. The Wise Ones encourage us to become again as children, as they have the innate capacity for spontaneous healing. Our Original Instructions tell us the same thing, as being childlike is our natural and intended state of being.

The adults I have worked with on childhood trauma are nearly all childhood-deprived. Yet even if we are wounded and repressed, our child-self is still alive—and where there is life, there is hope.

While writing this book, I reconnected with a still-struggling couple who were inadvertently imprinting their turmoil onto their child. After I helped them see what they were doing, they asked what they could do differently. I advised immediate, strong action, which I share here with you:

- **Honor the Self.** The greatest gift is the gift of self. Even more harmful than selfishness (indulgence in self) is the denial of self. It dishonors our unique reason for being and robs our family of an engaged member who provides strength and support for the other members. Children growing up in an environment that honors the self recognize the value of honoring themselves.

- **Speak Your Truth.** The family, as our fundamental social unit, needs to be a place where its members can feel safe to express themselves, regardless of circumstance. Chronic suppression of thoughts and feelings so often leads to interpersonal turmoil, along with physical and mental imbalances.

- **Find Your True Clan.** Along with honoring the self goes honoring our primary social unit as an extension of self. That can prove difficult when extended family members have values different than ours, yet expect us to abide by them. We can honor our family of birth with respectful listening, while at the same time abiding by our family of heart.

- **Overcome the Fear of Flying.** Above all, we must not paralyze ourselves by continuing to plod on through life as best we can. Venturing forth can be frightening, yet sticking with the status quo is nearly always more so. New knowledge brings growth and change only when we have the courage to put it to practice—and the good sense to get help when we struggle.

My hope is that the recommendations above convey the necessity of renewing our relationship with our child-selves and continuing their healing. You can find additional support in my book *Becoming You: 3 Steps to Emotional Freedom and What Keeps You from It*. Our reawakening is a momentous gift to ourselves, our children, and our children's children.

How Children Guide Us to Our Lost Childhood

Those of us with arrested childhoods often wind up being nihilistic adults. Being self-absorbed and self-protective, we find it hard to trust. We place the burden on our intimate relationships to have our personal and social needs met. With so much invested in such a small circle of people, we can grow overly possessive and isolationist, even becoming obsessed with the relationships.

Conversely, when we have healthy relationships with our child-selves, we tend to be open and sharing—an approach to life my Elders call *The Gifting Way*. In the process of opening to our child-self, we usually grow more comfortable with children, as well as with people in general. We tend to ease up on our socially prescribed role as parents and begin relating to children as fellow people. They are then free to become our guides on the journey to our lost childhoods. At the same time, they are the Ancient Ones returning to us and bringing us the ageless wisdom that has successfully guided untold generations of our young.

Though we may not have been able to mature into ourselves in our growing years, children give us a second chance to do so. Through them and with them, we can regain our squelched spontaneity, inquisitiveness and intuitive abilities. These beautiful qualities still exist within each of us and can be quite easily restored, as they are our birthright and only need to be dusted off and exercised.

No matter what our chronological age may be, within us we are children of all ages. In the process of parenting ourselves and our children in The Blossoming Way, we heal the string of generations, both past and future, so that our lineage can walk on in Balance, and leave a legacy of Balance.

In the course of reawakening, as set forth in this book, we can look forward to three fundamental qualities that are likely to manifest in our children—and our child within:

1. **Contentment**. Children who are bathed in nurturing presence and have their true needs immediately tended to seldom get frustrated or needy. Neither are they prone to acting out or crying. The primary reason may be that their flexible brains make them highly sensitive to the stress hormone, cortisol, and the love hormone, oxytocin. Children are thus able to respond quickly to nurturing or threatening input. When it is consistently nurturing, a "problem child's" reactive behaviors can be reduced and even eliminated.[4]

2. **Creativity**. When children are fully nurtured and allowed to be themselves, the life energy they once had to devote to

maintaining autonomy and a sense of safety is freed up for its originally intended use: creativity. All of a sudden, a child becomes content with—and may even prefer—simple toys that can be used in a multitude of ways. I've seen well-balanced children prefer the box to the toy it contained. (more on this topic in Chapter 26.)

3. **Security.** With our fragmented lives, security is something many of us find difficult to provide our children, at least to the degree needed. We already covered a number of practices that give children security, such as Shared Parenting, the Children's Culture, and babywearing. Sleeping with our child (known as *bedsharing, co-sleeping,* or *the family bed*), which is commonly practiced around the world,[5, 6] is another self-confidence builder.[7]

When we begin to witness or experience these three qualities, we know that our children are responding to our efforts. And we again know what it is to be a child. Then—not from this book, but from the very fiber of our beings—we know how to guide children in their Blossoming.

Chapter in a Page

As complex and confusing as our adult dysfunctional behaviors might seem, they are invariably the same behaviors we developed as children. In other words, our behaviors are a clear reflection of how we were raised. Yet our deprivation is not our parents' fault, and it is not our fault that we have continued the pattern of deprivation. Both we and our parents are the products of a society with a broken Children's Culture and a commitment to driving children to meet the expectations of others rather than seek their own fulfillment. The first step in healing is awareness. We begin to break the family pattern by consciously acknowledging that our children's psychological and emotional well-being—both now and later as adults—is dependent upon our own.

Here is what I advise to engage in this healing process:

- **Honor the Self.** Even more harmful than selfishness (indulgence in self) is the denial of self. It dishonors our unique reason for being and robs our family of an engaged member who provides strength and support for the other members.

- **Speak Your Truth.** The family, as our fundamental social unit, needs to be a place where its members can feel safe to express themselves, regardless of circumstance.

- **Find Your True Clan.** Along with honoring the self goes honoring our primary social unit as an extension of self, whether that means our family of birth or our family of heart.

- **Overcome the Fear of Flying.** Above all, we must not paralyze ourselves by continuing to plod on through life as best we can. Venturing forth can be frightening, yet sticking with the status quo is nearly always more so.

◇◇◇◇◇◇◇◇◇◇◇◇◇◇◇◇◇◇◇◇◇

Chapter 35 Endnotes

1   ?

2   Mary Kawena Pukui, *'Olelo No'eau: Hawaiian Proverbs & Poetical Sayings*, 105.

3   L.E. Threlkeld, *An Australian Grammar* (Stephens and Stokes, 1834), 17.

4   James, Oliver, *Love Bombing: Reset Your Child's Emotional Thermostat* (Routledge, 2012), 2.

5   Marissa Diener, "Gift from the Gods: A Balinese Guide to Early Child Rearing," in *A World of Babies: Imagined Childcare Guides for Seven Societies*, eds. J. DeLoache and A. Gottlieb (Cambridge University Press, 2000), 91-116.

6   Gilda A. Morelli, et al., "Cultural Variation in Infants' Sleeping Arrangements: Questions of Independence," *Developmental Psychology* 28, no. 4 (1992): 604-13.

7   Darcia F. Narvaez, "Understanding and Helping Toddler Sleep," *Pschol-ogy Today*, last modified 24 March 2013, accessed 22 November 2020, https://www.psychologytoday.com/us/blog/moral-landscapes/201303/understanding-and-helping-toddler-sleep.

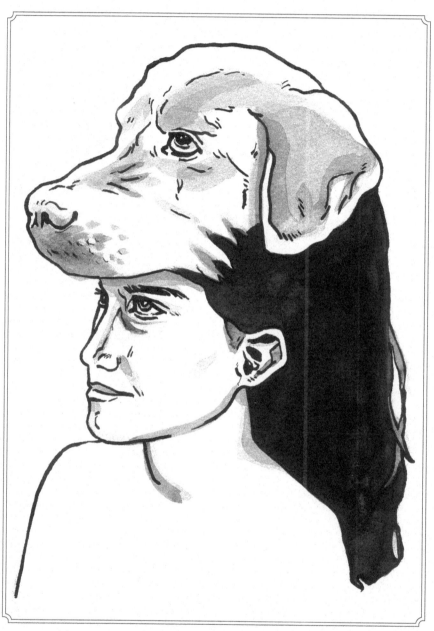

*For some adults, their Dogs come first: they
play the role of surrogate children.*

 **Chapter 36**

Should Children Come First?

"I've given up so much for my children."

"My kids come first in my life—I'd do anything for them."

"I live for my kids."

These are typical of the statements I hear from many parents I have talked with and counseled. They believe their foremost purpose in life is to nurture and sacrifice for their children. These parents describe how fulfilled they feel when they are involved with their children. When their children are happy, they are happy.

Other parents tell me how confused they are about how their relationships should be with their children. Some of these parents were raised in households where they, as children, came first. Now that they are independent adults, they look back and see their parents with no lives of their own.

Still other parents feel isolated being home all the time with their offspring. Many of them struggle with feelings of guilt because their relationship with their children does not completely fulfill them, and they think it ought to.

The Questions Raised

From single parents looking for direction to couples arguing between themselves (or with their parents and friends) on the best way to raise their children, their questions usually follow along these lines:

- Should my kids be my first priority?
- Is it right to base our decisions on what our kids want?

- I was told that I should place my children before my mate; is that the right thing to do?

- If we don't always place our children before ourselves, are we bad parents?

Still other parents ask these questions in retrospect, after their children have left home. These parents often start off complaining about facing day after aimless day, as though they had lost their reason for living. Or they find themselves depressed without knowing exactly why.

The idea of our identity and life purpose shifting to that of a parent the moment we have kids is widely accepted in our culture. The reasons are varied and complex. Here are the ones I most often run across:

- The isolation of the nuclear family from the greater culture

- Parents attempting to compensate for their own compromised childhoods

- Fear of inadequacy due to the lack of parenting experience

- People searching for meaning in their lives

- A belief, often religiously based, that parents are ordained to serve their children

- Individuals looking for an escape from chronic depression

The Imbalance

Our children, especially in their first two years, depend entirely upon us, either directly or indirectly. They demand nearly constant attention. In the nuclear family system, we are not only their primary caretakers; we are their world. They have such a vested interest in their relationship with us that any slight disparity, such as mom leaving the room for a moment, could trigger an emotional outburst.

Realizing this need for constant connection—especially when we are parenting alone or as a lone couple—we may be tempted to invest fully in the relationship with our child. If we do so, we pay the cost: our own needs and interests, and our other relationships, including the one with our partner.

This rings especially true if we felt unfulfilled before the coming of our child. All of a sudden, we have something all-encompassing to fill the void. We feel fulfilled, and we have a new sense of purpose in life. The people close to us give us positive reinforcement, as they see us newly happy and dedicated to our child's well-being.

If only cultural acceptance and the sanction of our friends and family made placing children first in our lives a natural and healthy practice. If only the fact that it perpetuates itself from one generation to the next gave it validity. If only "My children are all I have" was true.

The truth is that many of us are unaware that it is not only possible to raise our children *and* maintain a rich personal life, but that it is by far the best thing for both child and parent.

I have found that the core issue for nearly every one of us who believes a child comes at our expense has lost touch with the natural process of finding Balance with the Circle of Life before attempting to reproduce. As a result, the quest to find ourselves and our life's purpose is answered solely in the role of parent.

One of the most unfortunate fallouts of leading child-first lives is that we lose touch with the fact that the child is not really ours. We are merely entrusted by the Great Mother and Father to care for *their* child. We are asked by them to guide the child so that he may continue to live in Balance as he grows into adulthood. Being placed in the center of another person's life is nowhere near Balance.

The Cost

Those who had child-centric upbringings generally leave their families with the expectation that they are going to be the be-all and end-all of other people's lives. Hence the *Cinderella Complex*[1]—the unconscious desire to be taken care of by others—and the *Knight in Shining Armor Syndrome*—the belief that helping others is our reason for existence.

Here is a story to illustrate the personal cost of a child-centric life:

> *Long ago when we lived in little villages, it was the tradition to send our young to a neighboring community, where they would learn a trade by apprenticing to a craftsperson. The children would spend several years in training, during which they served both their master and their host community. After completing their apprenticeships, they would return to their village, capable of supporting themselves and their future families, and of making a positive contribution to their village.*
>
> *One such child went to serve with a Basketmaker who was known for her exceptional craftsmanship. The Basketmaker was young herself, and she had just moved to the community, so she wanted to do well by her first apprentice and make a good impression upon her new neighbors.*
>
> *So intent was she on providing for the child that she dropped nearly everything in order to shelter, feed, and clothe him, and to educate him in the arts and sciences. It came to the point where she had very little time to practice their craft anymore. Over time, she lost sight of why her apprentice initially came to her.*

When we choose to devote our lives to our children, we risk ending up as did the Basketmaker: losing ourselves, along with the reason our children came to us. Just as the Basketmaker quit her craft because of her preoccupation with providing for the child, we risk sidelining the most precious parts of ourselves—and depriving our children of that.

If we do not nourish ourselves, and if we are not intrinsically content and self-fulfilled, what example and teachings do we have for our children? Is our emptiness and lack of life-direction the model we want our children to emulate? Are we not intended to be more than our children's nannies?

Chapter in a Page

Our children, especially in their first two years, depend entirely upon us, either directly or indirectly. In the nuclear family system, we are not only their primary caretakers; we are their world. Realizing this need for constant connection—especially when we are parenting alone or as a lone couple—we may be tempted to invest fully in the relationship with our child. If we do so, we pay the cost: our own needs and interests, and our other relationships, including the one with our partner. The truth is that many of us are unaware that it is not only possible to raise our children *and* maintain a rich personal life, but that it is by far the best thing for both child and parent.

One of the most unfortunate fallouts of leading child-first lives is that we lose touch with the fact that the child is not really ours. We are merely entrusted by the Great Mother and Father to care for *their* child. We are asked by them to guide the child so that he may continue to live in Balance as he grows into adulthood. Being placed in the center of another person's life is nowhere near Balance. If we do not nourish ourselves, and if we are not intrinsically content and self-fulfilled, what example and teachings do we have for our children? Is our emptiness and lack of life-direction the model we want our children to emulate? Are we not intended to be more than our children's nannies?

◇◇◇◇◇◇◇◇◇◇◇◇◇◇◇◇◇◇◇◇◇◇◇

Chapter 36 Endnotes

1 Colette Dowling, *The Cinderella Complex: Women's Hidden Fear of Independence* (Pocket Books, 1990).

Young children naturally include the animals in their Hoop of Relations.

 *Chapter 37*

Healing the Hoop of Relations

I am encouraged by the fact that I hear many parents and future parents questioning the *putting our children first* way they were raised, as curiosity creates a doorway to change. And change is crucial, for this reason: Who we are and how we choose to fulfill our lives lays the blueprint for who our children become and how they are going to find fulfillment.

There would likely be no issue if we were living indigenously. We would naturally understand from living the Circle Way that allowing ourselves to live fully allows others to do the same, and vice versa. Further, we would know that how we raise our children is not a matter of choice or priority, but of honoring the many in relationship within the Circle.

The Hoops in Order

We humans have an intrinsic way of relationship that naturally honors and supports the roles of parent and child. Imagine all the people we know surrounding us in circles, with our most intimate relationships in the circles closest to us, and our more distant relationships in the outer circles. These are what the Blackfoot elders described to me as the *Hoops of Relations*. Everyone we are in relationship with dwells within these hoops, as in the following:

The Central Hoop is home to our most intimate of relationships, which is with what is variously called our guardian angel, spirit guide, power animal, or *dodem*. Many

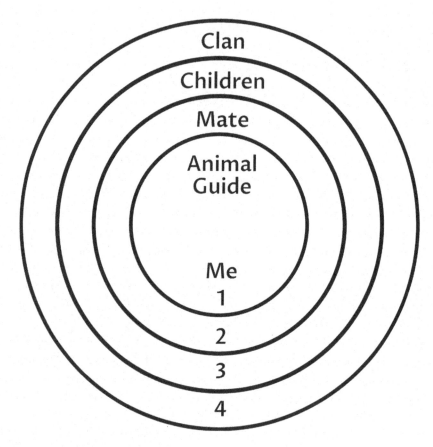

Chart 7: Hoop of Relations

indigenous people see this relationship being so close that the two join at birth, share the same spirit, and travel together throughout life.

The Second Hoop is for our most intimate relationship with another person. It could be our mate or an inseparable lifelong friend.

The Third Hoop is the dwelling place of our children, and others with whom we have a deep and consistent connection, such as siblings, godchildren, nieces and nephews, aunts and uncles.

The Outer Hoop holds a special place as Guardian, encircling all the other relationships in our life and giving them context, comfort, and protection. For most of us, close friends, supportive communities of various kinds, and extended family play the role of clan that defines the outer hoop.

What It Means

Seeing how we are related to others can help us gain the perspective to sort out and prioritize our relationships. The Blackfoot elders explained that when we honor our innermost relationship (self/animal guide) first, our other relationships, in descending order of importance from self to clan, are naturally honored.

To better illustrate why it is imperative that we honor our inner relationships before our outer, let us look at a tree. Imagine the roots as the first circle of our Hoop of Relations. If that relationship is strong, it can support and nourish our second circle, the trunk; from it grows the stout branches—our third circle. They bring forth the luscious leaves of the fourth circle—our clan, which shades and nourishes the entire Hoop.

An important thing to remember is that *this cause-and-effect relationship works only one way: from the inside out.* We cannot prioritize our clan relationship and expect it to improve our relationship with our children.

The Hoops Out of Order

When a couple is gifted with the opportunity to bring a child into the world and they are in Balance with the Hoop of Relations, they dedicate themselves to nurturing that life. They know that, come fun or frustration, they are caretakers.

At the same time, they are mates. For those whose relationship with their children takes precedence over that with their mate, it is only a matter of time before their mated relationship crumbles before them. They run a similar risk if they attempt to caretake a child outside the context of the Fourth Hoop.

It is never too late to bring our Hoop of Relations back into Balance. Otherwise, it's only a handful of years before we see our imbalances playing out in our children's lives and relationships. The reason it happens is that we have attempted to rearrange the Hoops, by putting our children's circle where our mate's belongs, and vice versa. As if that isn't damaging enough, some of us try to bring our children into the Central Hoop (which was the topic of the last chapter). That leaves no space for us, as we have learned, as it strips us of our self-identity and life direction, and ultimately distorts all of our circle relationships.

Any switching around of the Hoops creates distortion, as we have to compress a large Hoop in order to fit it into a small-Hoop space, and we must somehow stretch a small Hoop in order to attempt to fill a large-Hoop space.

How Distortion Plays Out

I recently counseled a longtime acquaintance named Rich, who got himself entangled in a Distorted Hoop of Relations with the child-first parenting model. He and his wife had fallen out of relationship years ago, yet for the sake of their two children, they decided to maintain a semblance of family by continuing to live under the same roof, only in different bedrooms. Following is the essence of our session.

Rich: "Recently I had an interview for a job I really wanted—my dream job—but it's five hours away and I'd have to live there. However, my sons don't want to move there with me, because they'd have to leave their friends and other activities. I told the employer I needed to take care of my sons. He said my application would be kept on file and I should get back to him if my

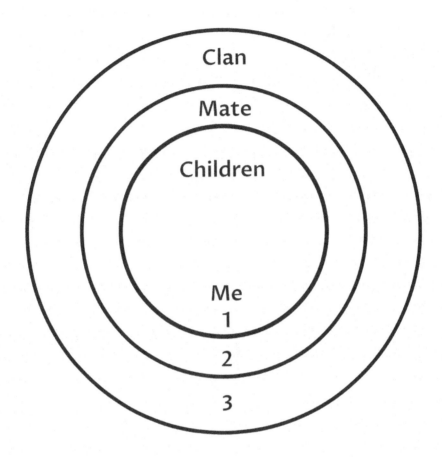

Chart 8: Distorted Hoop of Relations

situation changes. But I know the job won't stay open long. I could come back home every-other weekend, but I don't think that'll be enough. What should I do? This is tearing me up."

Me: "I feel for you and your predicament. At the same time, I'm concerned about how similar it sounds to past situations of yours. There are your kids to consider as well. Example can make an indelible impression on children, which means that there is a good chance that they'll carry on your legacy by patterning their lives after yours—and having to deal with issues like yours."

Rich: "I'm not sure I understand what you're getting at. I'm not worried about the example of my wife and me, because my sons know what is and isn't going on between us. I see my problem as not knowing how to do the best for my family. Do I do what benefits me over my sons, or do I sacrifice myself for them? Which example do I give them? I'm torn up inside over this."

Me: "Let me explain my perspective with some straight talk: In essence, your wife and you have decided to live unfulfilled lives and maintain the illusion of a relationship, ostensibly to benefit your sons. However, illusions cannot give them the example they need of parents in a caring relationship who are nurturing their children together. Instead, you and your wife have denied yourselves happiness for their sake, and they are learning to do the same. Just like you, they are going to think they are doing what's right for their children. You face that dilemma now: Do you go for a job that is soul-satisfying, or do you sacrifice yourself—again—for your children? *And* miss the opportunity to model for them the courage to follow one's heart?

"The bottom line: You can't give what you don't have. Unless you and your wife provide that example for them, they can't learn and grow from it, and they end up being emotionally crippled.

"I know this doesn't sound pretty, but it never does. I feel for you, because I know what it's like, for both you and your kids. My mom and dad put up with each other; she ended up chronically depressed, and he became an alcoholic. True to form, my two brothers and I struggled for decades in relationships, and we did all we could to become alcoholics.

The sad thing is that all we were doing was what we were genetically programmed to do—follow example. We were left to stumble
around and try to live life as best we could, and I hate to see other
kids having to grow up the same way and do the same thing."

Healing the Hoop

Once our dilemma is understood, we can take action to restore
Balance to our Hoop of Relations. I have found the following
four-point approach to be highly effective. It works because it is
not just a Band-Aid solution—it goes to the core of the imbalance
by rewiring our brains to restructure our lives.

A. **Change our living environment**. The simple and all-
powerful truth is that unless we remove ourselves from the
source of our sorrow, every effort we make to change ends up
being a continual struggle against our history. And history
usually wins.

B. **Make healthy friends**. Work and play, live and love, with
the people you emulate. There is no easier way to change, as
we become what we surround ourselves with. I call it *winning
by assimilation*.

C. **Discover ourselves**. When we know who we are, we know
our life direction. There are many ways to do this, and they
all involve Deep Listening. For a primer, you can reference
my book *Journey to the Ancestral Self: Remembering What It Is
to Be Human*.

D. **Live the Hoop of Relations**. Go back a few pages to *What
It Means*. Start the day by referring to it every day before you
share with someone, until you have the concept and process
memorized.

"Yeah, that sounds good for me; but what can I do for my kids?"
asked a parenting workshop participant after I presented this four-
step process.

I replied that when it comes to returning to the Original Instructions, there is no difference between parent and child—or more accurately, between your child-self and your biological child. "What you do," I continued, "is either directly or indirectly going to manifest in your children. Think of it as getting a two-for-one deal."

Chapter in a Page

We humans have an intrinsic way of relationship that naturally honors and supports the roles of parent and child. Imagine all the people we know surrounding us in circles, with our most intimate relationships in the circles closest to us, and our more distant relationships in the outer circles. These are what the Blackfoot elders described to me as the *Hoop of Relations*. Everyone we are in relationship with dwells within these hoops:

- **The Central Hoop** is home to our most intimate of relationships, which is with what is variously called our guardian angel, spirit guide, power animal, or dodem.

- **The Second Hoop** is for our most intimate relationship with another person. It could be our mate or an inseparable lifelong friend.

- **The Third Hoop** is the dwelling place of our children, and others with whom we have a deep and consistent connection, such as siblings, godchildren, nieces and nephews, aunts and uncles.

- **The Outer Hoop** encircles all the other relationships in our life, such as supportive communities of various kinds and extended family.

The Blackfoot elders explained that when we honor our innermost relationship (self/animal guide) first, our other relationships, in descending order of importance from self to clan, are naturally honored. Any switching around of the Hoops creates distortion, as we have to compress a large Hoop in order to fit it into a small-Hoop space, and we must somehow stretch a small Hoop in order to attempt to fill a large-Hoop space. Yet it is never too late to bring our Hoop of Relations back into Balance. Once our dilemma is understood, we can take action to restore Balance to our Hoop of Relations.

"This time his mother slapped him four times, rolling him over and over down the hill. When he stopped rolling, he sat up, with his little fat back toward his mother. She called him to come and get a root, but he didn't answer, did not even turn his head."

 **Chapter 38**

Let Them Go So They Can Grow

"I want the children raised as I was ... I don't want to settle. I love to roam over the prairies. There I feel free and happy, but when we settle down, we grow pale and die."[1] There could be no more fitting metaphor for how to parent the Blossoming Way than those words from Satanta, who grew up a free-ranging Kiowa on the Southern Plains. Yet in his adulthood, he was forced to drink the bitter tears of subjugation and crushed dreams—made all the more bitter because they were not only his but his peoples' children's as well.

Our own modern children, born wild as the wind and spontaneous as butterflies flitting from flower to flower, face the same internal fate as those Kiowa children when we parent them in the way of our directive and overly instructive culture. We protect and advise them, and we figure things out for them. As a result, they grow pale, and the adults they could have become die before they are born.

If we could only let them roam over the prairies of adventure and self-discovery, we could watch them Blossom instead!

It's Now or Never

As if modern parenting approaches aren't unnatural enough, we have to make a stressful chore of it. Being a housewife/husband is a full-time occupation, often in addition to full-time and inflexible careers outside the home. Add to that the cost and logistical issues that come with hired-out supplemental parenting, such as daycare, school, camp, and supervised recreational and sports activities.

We've grown so accustomed to this way of raising children that few of us question it. The upshot is that we tend to treat our children as empty shells, with us bearing the responsibility for filling them up. We saturate them with knowledge to inform them, values to guide them, and social etiquette to refine them. We perceive it, there's so much they need to absorb in so short a time.

In our efforts to raise our children according to those cultural expectations, we end up stunting—and sometimes destroying—them. That may sound harsh, and it ought to, because it is what happens. Certainly, the physical being is still there; however, she is no longer the free child originally born to you. Rest assured, she will struggle mightily to be herself; yet odds are she is going to succumb to the overwhelming onslaught and never become the person she could have been had she developed through her own unhindered experimentation and discovery of life.

Control-Style Parenting Victimizes Children

It may not be as obvious as with sexual exploitation or child labor, yet today's parenting practices victimize children. After going through the Control-Style Parenting wringer, most children are so defeated that they end up needing to be parented for the rest of their lives. Consciously or not, they rely on others to point out what's best for them.

We approach our children, of course, with the best of intentions, not realizing that our "best of intentions" is the problem. We would not do so if we trusted in the fact that our children were already complete beings unto themselves, born with memories, values, and preferences, and with a life direction unique to each of them. And if we knew that, those innate gifts and ways of being only need to be nourished.

Sadly, we have no Elders to tell us these things, we do not have the benefit of example, and we do not know from experience, as we did not grow up in a culture where children were allowed to Blossom. The three ways of learning—stories, example, and experience—have all been denied us.

But that is the past. We are on this healing journey to transform what was into what it is intended to be, as given to us in the Original Instructions. All through this book, we have been learning how to let our children go so they can grow. We have been reawakened to what our hearts already know: We are not here to teach and direct our children, but to honor them for the individuals they are by standing back and serving them in their growth.

In the next paragraph, we start putting what we now know into action with suggestions on how to honor our children's energy flow; and in the next chapter we learn how to do it supportively by talking *with*, rather than *to*, them. This work we are doing here and now is momentous, as I believe that every parent who contributes to the manifestation of one more Blossoming child contributes to the restoration of Balance to our world.

Honor Their Energy Flow

Everything that exists is energy in one form or another. Energy is constantly flowing and continually transforming. From the instant of conception, this energy form we call a child is on the move. She knows where she is going whether she can articulate it or not, and whether we understand it or not. It makes no difference to her— she is on a mission. A sunbeam has its own trajectory and reason for being, no matter what other sunbeams think or don't think about it. As with sunbeams, if we can relax and enjoy our children rather than trying to make something of them, we've taken a big step toward learning who they already are.

As our child grows, let us remember that it is energy, rather than an entity, that we are caretaking. Energy wants to flow, and a good energy caretaker helps keep the flow going, just as our child already does for herself.

322 Chapter 38 • Let Them Go So They Can Grow

This means helping her achieve what she is after without project-
ing our own preferences onto her. If she wants to touch a hot wood
stove (as in the Chapter 20 story), preventing her and telling her
she will hurt herself blocks her energy flow. One might say that she
learns little or nothing about *hot*; only about how to listen and obey.

There is one more thing she is likely to learn. If she honors
her energy flow—which here translates as curiosity and discovery through personal experience—she is going to be *compelled* to
explore that wood stove. Perhaps she'll touch it right after you leave
the room, or she may have to first work around her guilt for going
against an important person in her life.

The straight truth is that if we honor her flow, she learns hot;
and if we block her flow, she learns deceit. Blocking energy flow is
like damning up a river: The pressure is going to build and build,
until the dam bursts. Our child is compelled to experience the
wood stove for herself—it's her nature. However, she'll have to do
it when no one is looking, and she'll have to hide her actions (and
perhaps her burn).

The choice to aid her learning, rather than subvert the process
by injecting our own knowledge, is ours. On her own, she would
make a different choice, and we can empower that process by first
sensitizing to, then honoring, her energy flow. Through that simple step on our part, she gains tremendously in personal empowerment, relationship with her environment, and self-sufficiency.

How *No* Smothers

One additional harm of stymieing energy flow is the overuse of
the word *No*. It's not that *No* is a curse word; the problem lies in
its overuse, which makes it lose effectiveness. A child responds
naturally to *No* if he is not bombarded with it to the point where
he must ignore it in order to honor his flow. If *No* is used only when
necessary, he is likely to listen and respond appropriately. This
could be critically important in a situation of imminent danger.

As explored earlier in this book, a child normally learns experientially, which makes what he learns, his. When he comes head-on with a *No*, learning stops. No flow, no learning. This runs contrary to what many believe who use *No* as a teaching tool. He may appear to be learning, whereas in actuality he is being controlled.

The gaining of personal knowledge might stop, yet there is one thing he does learn: how to get entangled in codependent and exploitative relationships. When a parent uses *No* regularly, the child develops a pattern of dependence on the parent—and later other controllers—for direction and answers. This leaves him not only ripe for abuse, but sets him up for a lifetime of not hearing his own voice and knowing his own direction.

Here are three ways to get around saying *No*:

1. **Avoid giving advice.** The old proverb, *People give nothing so willingly as advice*,[2] shows how common the temptation is to step into the trap. Here is the antidote in an Italian proverb: "Give neither counsel nor salt until you are asked for it."[3] Instead of giving advice to children, let's give choices.

2. **Let them go so they can grow.** These seven words define Blossoming-supportive parenting. Instead of saying *No*, let your child carry on if the danger is slight. A bruise or a scare can be potent teachers, and the lessons are not easily forgotten. Overprotecting does no favors.

3. **Adjust a potentially dangerous situation,** when possible, so that you can safely let him go and grow, and still have the experience give a bit of a bite.

The Two Qualities of Growth

Parents and educators who are freewheeling with their *Noes* squelch two stellar character traits: *self-regulation* and *ambition*. It's disheartening for me to see these same people trying to instill the very traits that they have inadvertently deleted.

Ambition and self-regulation work as each others' counterpoints in guiding a child's flow. Fortunately, a child comes equipped with both, so we don't have to worry about one or the other taking off with our child. Ohiyesa referred to both of these traits in his childhood when he said, "I wished to be a brave man,"[4] and "Habits of perfect self-control were early established."[5]

Pretty-shield gives this example of how ambition and self-regulation, along with a little bite, work together when children are parented in the Blossoming Way:

> *A girl named Beaver-that-passes and I said we would be the hunters, that we would go out to a buffalo herd that was in sight and kill a calf. Knowing that we could not handle a bow, Beaver-that-passes borrowed her father's lance that was very sharp, and longer than both our bodies put together.*
>
> *We caught and saddled two gentle pack horses; and both the old fools went crazy before we managed to kill a calf. I helped all I could, but it was Beaver-that-passes who wounded a big calf that gave us both a lot of trouble before we finally got it down, and dead. I hurt my leg, and Beaver-that passes cut her hand with the lance. The calf itself looked pretty bad by the time we got it to our play-village. But we had a big feast, and forgot our hurts.*[6]

Bringing the Bite to the Child

Pretty-Shield tells another story of gaining self-regulation skills through experiential learning. It's about a Bear cub who had a vital lesson to learn but repeatedly refused to stay present for it. His mother decided she had to act. She "slapped him four times," said Pretty-Shield, "rolling him over and over down the hill. When he stopped rolling, he sat up, with his little fat back toward his mother. She called him to come and get a root, but he didn't answer, did not even turn his head."[7]

The mother Bear practiced what I call *Augmented Experiential Learning*. On rare occasions, it may become necessary for caregivers to enhance an experience in order to assure that it conveys a teaching essential to a child's well-being. If she has not grasped the importance of staying away from the neighbor's aggressive chained-up Dog, her caregiver could take her up close to the animal, so that she can experience the full force of his growling, lunging, and snapping jaws.

Augmented Experiential Learning is to be employed only when absolutely necessary, as there is grave risk of abuse. Physical punishment, the withholding of affection, and timeouts are common mistreatments, often justified by statements like, "I'm doing this for your own good."

Children are protected from being abused when they, rather than their caregivers, decide when experiential learning needs to be augmented. The young child made it clear to her caregiver that her draw to the neighbor's Dog could get her mauled to death if there was no enhancement of her learning experience.

Returning to Satanta's words, "I want the children raised as I was ... to roam over the prairies ... [to] feel free and happy," is not all that hard to provide for our children. The prairie of discovery lies ever before them, and they already know how to be free and happy. As we now know, all we have to do is get out of the way—and keep a discrete, watchful eye.

Chapter in a Page

We approach our children with the best of intentions, not realizing that our "best of intentions" are the problem. We would not do so if we trusted in the fact that our children were already complete beings unto themselves, born with memories, values, and preferences, and with a life direction unique to each of them. And those innate gifts and ways of being only need to be nourished. Sadly, we have no Elders to tell us these things, we do not have the benefit of example, and we do not know from experience, as we did not grow up in a culture where children were allowed to Blossom. The three ways of learning—stories, example, and experience—have all been denied us.

Everything that exists is energy of one form or another. Energy is constantly flowing and continually transforming. From the instant of conception, this energy form we call a child is on the move. She knows where she is going whether she can articulate it or not, and whether we understand it or not. It makes no difference to her—she is on a mission. A sunbeam has its own trajectory and reason for being, no matter what other sunbeams think or don't think about it. As with sunbeams, if we can relax and enjoy our children rather than trying to make something of them, we've taken a big step toward learning who they already are. As our child grows, let us remember that it is energy, rather than an entity, that we are caretaking. Energy wants to flow, and a good energy caretaker helps keep the flow going, just as our child already does for herself.

◇◇◇◇◇◇◇◇◇◇◇◇◇◇◇◇◇◇◇◇◇

Chapter 38 Endnotes

1 Kent Nerburn, *The Wisdom of the Native Americans*, 7.
2 Harold V. Cordry, *The Multicultural Dictionary of Proverbs* (McFarland, 2015), 8.

3   Alexander Margulis and Asya Kholodnaya1, *Russian-English Dictionary of Proverbs and Sayings* (McFarland, 2015), 39.

4   Kent Nerburn, *The Wisdom of the Native Americans*, 17.

5   Charles Alexander Eastman, *The Soul of the Indian*, 94.

6   Frank Bird Linderman, *Pretty-shield, Medicine Woman of the Crows*, 11.

7   Ibid, 59.

One does not bestow a gift by returning what was wrongfully taken. More than freeing our children, Blossoming-supportive parenting is about giving ourselves the opportunity to release control and recognize our children as fully actualized beings.

 *Chapter 39*

Talk *With* Rather Than *To*

Have you noticed that many people with expertise, or in positions of authority, talk as though they are delivering a monologue rather than engaging in a dialogue? Does listening to them ever get fatiguing to the point where you find it hard to stay focused on what they are saying? This could be because they are talking *to* you rather than engaging *with* you. When you are not being fully recognized, you are not being honored for who you are, so you naturally disengage.

It can be the same for our child when we give advice or explain something. Because we are bigger and have more experience than her, we tend to assume a position of authority over her; so she can feel talked down to, whether or not that was our intention.

The Patronizing Test

To determine whether you are coming across as authoritative or patronizing, imagine telling another adult what you are sharing with your child, using the same words and tone of voice. Now double the intensity of the reaction you think you'd get, and you have a sense of what it's like for your child.

Learning the Difference

When we talk *to* our child, she may learn more from *how* we say something than from *what* we are saying. I remember being talked down to as a child and turning around to do the same thing to my younger brothers; and I see the same thing being done by other children, even when talking to their dolls, toys, and pets. As with childhood patterns in the general, once *talking to* is established, it is likely to remain with our child for life.

How many adults do you know who would hardly notice if you substituted a cardboard cutout for yourself during a conversation? How many adults do you know who give the same spiel over and over, no matter who is "listening?" They are *talking to* rather than *talking with*.

Part of *talking to* can include *censorship,* which is the practice of choosing what is or is not appropriate to bring up with our child. We might think she is too innocent, it's none of her business, or it's over her head.

However, a child doesn't think the way we do. From a Child-Friendly Parenting perspective (covered in Part VII) our censoring is a form of judgment and control that disregards who our child is and marginalizes her from our life.

In response, our child is likely to piece together an answer for herself. Here is where major issues can arise—especially if she is trying to understand something that is troubling her. Without our empathetic presence and input, all she has to go on is her observations and prior experience.

As debasing as that could potentially be, there is still a more fateful outcome: our child being manipulated or exploited because she is desperate for answers to help her make sense of the situation.

An alternate approach is to consider how to explain things in an appropriate way. It is not *what* we say, but *how* we say it, that determines whether it is suitable or understandable. When my son Wabineshi was in his early teens, he asked what would happen to the school I worked for if it fell upon hard times financially. Instead of giving him a simplified answer based on the assumption that he could not grasp the complexities of the hypothetical situation, I chose to give him the same explanation I would give an adult, only in his vocabulary. He understood perfectly.

Had I avoided answering, or had he realized that I dumbed-down my answer to him, he could have interpreted that as there being a lurking fear in the future, which could have caused him undue anxiety.

Another more direct *talking to* practice is what I call *I want statements*. "I want you to do this," and "I don't want you to do that," are usually unconscious but blatant self-focused control efforts. They create a dilemma that forces our child to make a choice: Either honor her energy flow and go against what we want, or suppress her flow to please us. For her, it is a no-win situation, as even if her flow were in sync with our wishes, we have presented it in a way that she would be doing it for us.

The *I want* approach regularly degrades to a test of wills, which often results in a problem child. Over time, she becomes a rebel, then gets anointed as the black sheep of the family.

Or she may assume a placid outward appearance to mask a passive-aggressive personality: calm and easy-going on the outside, broiling and manipulative on the inside. She suppresses her own natural desires and inclinations and becomes a people-pleaser. Only she secretly resents those she is mollifying, which over time can sink her deeper and deeper into the depression that comes from not knowing and being oneself. A walking powder keg, she could blow up at any time, with those close to her at a loss to understand why.

Pitfalls to Recognize and Avoid

In stepping back, we may not be parenting in the classic sense, which is attempting to mold a whole person from a struggling little generic, imprintable form, yet we retain our caregiving role. If we are accustomed to Control-Style Parenting, we need to adjust to situations that hardly, if ever, came up for us. Here are the two most common, with suggestions for taking care of them.

1. **Caregiver burnout** occurs when one plays Surveillance Camera: keeping an ever-alert eye on children—especially very young ones—while they are simply doing their thing and there is no imminent danger. Such watching can be more fatiguing than joining— particularly when kids keep asking us to join in their play. The best solution I've found is to be involved in my own pursuit, at a respectful distance, while watching them out of the corner of my eye. It is best to be engaged with them only at special, designated times, to let them learn independently and allow for the evolution of the Children's Culture. This is as it would be in a Native camp. Children feel more themselves and function more autonomously when they are not overtly watched, and at the same time I am able to do something self-fulfilling.

2. **The "I thought *you* were watching them" panic** is easily avoidable. Whenever there are multiple adults present, there needs to be one designated caregiver, and the other adults need to know who it is. An easy and near-foolproof method is *pass the baton*, where a token such as a bandana or staff is held by the caregiver and passed on to the next person assuming the role. The person taking over notifies others he is doing so. If that is not possible, he posts his name at a predesignated central location, or something similar and reliable.

Stolen Goods

Some parents initially look upon Blossoming-supportive parenting as *allowing* children the freedom to be themselves. Is it ours to allow, or is it their birthright? One does not bestow a gift by returning what was wrongfully taken. More than freeing our children, Blossoming-supportive parenting is about giving ourselves the opportunity to release control and recognize our children as fully actualized beings.

Spoiling

"Wouldn't you spoil a child by raising him this way?" is a big fear I hear from mothers and fathers first exposed to parenting the Blossoming Way. I reply by telling them that the difference between creating the space for a child to be herself and spoiling her is hinged on two things: our consistency in providing that space, and her manipulative behavior if we are not consistent.

When we flip-flop between honoring and controlling our child's flow, she adapts by learning to manipulate our inconsistencies in order to create the opening she needs for her energy to flow. If she thinks we arbitrarily decide whether or not she can see her friends, we have unwittingly set her upon a quest to figure out how to arrange it so she can see them.

Consistency does not mean being unchanging. The sun's energy continually varies, and we continually adapt to it. The same is true of human energy. Consistency means honoring our child's present energy flow by adjusting to it. Rather than changing our mind, we are being mindful, and our child knows the difference—especially when we share our reasons and engage her in the process.

Fast Track to a Spoiled Child

1. **Enable** by overprotecting.
2. **Deny** learning experiences by spoon-feeding.
3. **Withhold** genuine affection by coddling.

When we get out of the child-controlling business and develop a flowing relationship with our child, she cannot be manipulative, because she doesn't have to try to get her way; she cannot become spoiled, because she is not being coddled or overprotected; and she cannot turn into a problem child, because she has nothing to rebel against. She can only be herself, and what more could a parent want?

Chapter in a Page

When we talk *to* our child, she may learn more from *how* we say something than from *what* we are saying. How many adults do you know who would hardly notice if you substituted a cardboard cutout for yourself during a conversation? How many adults do you know who give the same spiel over and over, no matter who is "listening?" They are *talking to* rather than *talking with*. Part of *talking to* can include *censorship,* which is the practice of choosing what is or is not appropriate to bring up with our child. Another more direct *talking to* practice is what I call *I want statements*. "I want you to do this," and "I don't want you to do that," are usually unconscious but blatant self-focused control efforts.

Some parents initially look upon Blossoming-supportive parenting as *allowing* children the freedom to be themselves. Is it ours to allow, or is it their birthright? More than freeing our children, Blossoming-supportive parenting is about giving ourselves the opportunity to release control and recognize our children as fully actualized beings. Some parents also see it as simply spoiling a child. I reply by telling them that the difference between creating the space for a child to be herself and spoiling her is hinged on two things: our consistency in providing that space, and her manipulative behavior if we are not consistent.

When we get out of the child-controlling business and develop a flowing relationship with our child, she cannot be manipulative, because she doesn't have to try to get her way; she cannot become spoiled, because she is not being coddled or overprotected; and she cannot turn into a problem child, because she has nothing to rebel against. She can only be herself, and what more could a parent want?

 *Epilogue*

Our Children, Our Future

From a greater perspective, our children don't need us as much as we need them. They are key not only to the continuation of our species, but to how—and if—we continue. And they are key to helping us adults become who we are intended to be. Without their example and guidance, we might just keep looking "out there" for ourselves, and keep finding only charades.

Regarding that second gift from our children, helping us with our own Blossoming, we have a lot of work to do. To grasp that, let's forget our children for a moment, and let's leave out the cultural context. Focusing on anything but ourselves right now is both an externalization and a disregarding of our children's gifts to us.

Besides, tending to the things around us fixes nothing ultimately. Sure, we might feel better for a while, as we've made some changes and we can see the results. But that's just slathering fresh frosting over a moldy cake. Rather than just trying to create change for our children and our institutions, you and I might do better looking our hypocrisy in the face and starting to practice what we preach.

To launch that process, I would like to suggest that you get together with your friends and start a Blossoming study group. You have this book as a guide, and you might like to incorporate the complementary works of other authors. To get you started, here are three classics I recommend:

- **For emotional healing:** *Running on Empty: Overcome Your Childhood Emotional Neglect,* by Jonice Webb

- **For Child-Friendly Parenting:** *Nisa: The Life and Words of a !Kung Woman,* by Marjorie Shostak
- **For trauma recovery:** *The Body Keeps the Score: Brain, Mind, and Body in the Healing of Trauma,* by Bessel van der Kolk

My dream is that through the shared experience of this book, we can all make a difference in how our children find joy, fulfillment, and healing. I wish you all the best in you and your children's Blossomings.

 *For Inspiration*

Proverbs and Sayings

Following is a collection of the pithy words of wisdom that can be found throughout this book. Some people like to adopt a new proverb each day as a topic for reflection. Others like to use them as themes for discussion with other parents. And some like to post a favorite in a conspicuous place, as a reminder. However you use them, they are sure to enrich your experience as a champion of our children's Blossoming.

A man [woman, or child] should not be struck
when he is down. *–Russian proverb*

All's well that ends well. *–William Shakespeare*

As the old cock crows, the young cock learns. *–Irish saying*

Become like a little child anew. *–Lao Tzu*

Be the change you wish to see in the world. *–Mahatma Gandhi*

Be ye as little children. *–Jesus*

Children have never been very good at listening to their elders, but they have never failed to imitate them. *–James Baldwin*

Do not offer salt or brains. *–English proverb*

Do not tickle the nose of a sleeping Bear. *–German saying*

Don't worry that [children] never listen to you; worry that they are always watching you. *–Robert Folghum*

Each child born has at birth a Bowl of perfect
Light. If he tends his Light, it will grow in strength
and he can do all things. *–Hawaiian Saying*

Every mother's child is handsome. *–American proverb*

Experience is the bitterest way to learn. *–Confucius*

Experience is the teacher of all things. *–Julius Caesar*

Faults of the source are left to the children.
(Hewa kumu waiho i keiki.) *–Hawaiian saying*

Give neither counsel nor salt until you
are asked for it. *–Italian proverb*

Give someone an inch and he'll take a mile. *–unknown*

Giving is receiving. *–Native saying*

He who has burnt his mouth always blows
on his soup. *–German proverb*

If you want to know a person, walk a mile
in his moccasins. *–Native saying*

It takes a village to raise a child. *–African proverb*

Lead with one hand, carry with one arm. (Ka'ika'i
i ka lima, hi'i i ke alo.) *–Hawaiian saying; refers to
a mother with children born too close together*

Like the one from whom he received what he learned.
(Ku i ka māna) *–Hawaiian saying; paid as a compliment to the
child who walks in the footsteps of the older children who reared him*

Man is most nearly himself when he achieves the
seriousness of a child at play. *–Heraclitus*

Many know how to flatter; few know
how to praise. *–Greek proverb*

Near is my shirt, but nearer is my skin. –*English proverb*

No man [woman, child] is an island. –*John Donne*

Now you will never become old … You will always remain fresh, young, a child, innocent. –*Osho*

Old habits die hard. –*unknown*

One can produce a child by sleeping with a mate, but he cannot produce a younger brother or sister. (Oke keiki he loa'a i ka moe, o ka pōki'i 'a'ole.) –*Hawaiian saying*

People give nothing so willingly as advice. –*French saying*

She lifted up the child (/koi !xo khāsi) –*!Korana saying; used to reflect the amount of care a child receives*

Show what youth can do. (Ho'olale i ka 'ai a ka u'i.) –*Hawaiian saying*

Small children give you a headache; big children give you a heartache. –*Russian proverb*

Strength comes from change. (Nutl el shihintsle angutle.) –*Mescalero Apache saying*

The fish whose mouth has been pierced by the hook will never again take another. (O ka huhū 'ino ka mea e ola 'ole ai.) –*Hawaiian saying*

The goodness of the taro root is judged by the young plant it produces. (I maika'i ke kalo i ka'ohā) –Hawaiian proverb

The memories of youth make for long, long thoughts. –*Saami saying*

The older one first cleared the path and then younger ones followed. (Nana i waele mua i ke ala, mahope aku mākou, na pōki'i.) –*Hawaiian saying*

The young ones chirped as the old ones sang. (Wie die Alten sungen, so zwitschern die Jungen) *–German saying*

There are no birds of this year in last year's nests. *–T. Fuller*

There are times when parenthood seems nothing but feeding the mouth that bites you. *–Peter De Vries*

These children are not your children, they are a gift to you to be cherished for only so long. *–Turtle Clan Mohawk Elder Sara Smith*

To teach is to learn twice over. *–Joseph Joubert*

We become what we surround ourselves with. *–Blackfoot Elder*

What parents do, children will do. (Ka hana a ka mākua, o ka hana no ia a keiki) *–Hawaiian saying*

What is learned in the cradle lasts till the grave. *–French Proverb*

What we first learn, we best know. *–Henry Scheib*

When an elephant is in trouble, even a frog will kick him. *–Hindu saying*

Who hears, forgets; who sees, remembers; and who does, learns. *–Xunzi*

You can do anything with children if only you play with them. *–German saying*

You carried a child who is running. (//o-i ʔie ta-sen-ts'i /ikaa.) *–Sandawe saying; suggests an avoidance of rescuing or enabling children*

You leave your child with the lions. (Sanā xamku-xa sana / ko-s xu.) *–!Korana saying; suggests learning through direct experience*

Youth doesn't mind where it sets its foot. *–Irish proverb*

Youth sheds many a skin. *–Irish proverb*

Glossary

acknowledgment: To recognize an accomplishment without rating it. Unlike complimenting, acknowledging a **child** reinforces his autonomy without manipulation.

All My Relations: The dwelling in kinship with all of life—the animals, plants, fire, air, water, earth, and unseen—that can be realized through **Becoming**.

Attachment Parenting (Attachment Mothering, Immersion Mothering, Babyreading, The Continuum Concept, Natural Childrearing): A childrearing philosophy that offers methods to encourage a close relational connection between mother and child, based on the emotional attunement of one to the other. The connection is based on the mother's sensitivity, empathy, and immediate responsiveness, and on continuous bodily closeness and touch.

Augmented Experiential Learning: When a caregiver enhances an experience to assure that it conveys a teaching essential for a **child**'s well-being. Should be employed only when absolutely necessary, as there is grave risk of abuse.

babywearing: The practice in which a mother holds her baby or toddler close to the body using a baby carrier. A common practice used by traditional cultures and progressive Westerners.

Balance: The state of personal centeredness that results from following inner guidance and living in harmony with life.

Becoming: The ability to assume another identity for the purpose of gaining firsthand, intimate knowledge of the feelings, thoughts, motivations, and circumstance of the entity.

Behaviorist Parenting: A parenting method based on the **Behaviorist Theory of Reinforcement** that emerged after the advent of the Industrial Revolution. Its signature practices are bottlefeeding, the use of cribs, playpens, and strollers, and **positive-negative reinforcement**.

Behaviorist Theory of Reinforcement: A theory developed alongside Newtonian physics based on the idea that animals can be conditioned to act in certain ways in response to the use of **reward-punishment**; and since we humans are animals, the same must be true of us.

Blossoming: A continually unfolding process of movement, growth, and change.

child: A young, semi-autonomous human with a unique **Life Journey**.

Child-Friendly Parenting: A style of parenting focused on seeing the **child** as an autonomous being with a unique **Life Journey**. Involves teaching children to live as verbs rather than nouns; giving experiences rather than things; minimizing personal possessions; encouraging inquisitiveness; and sharing ancestral stories.

child-self (inner child): The aspect of psyche that holds our child-like innocence, playfulness, and passion. Can be obfuscated, wounded, and/or disregarded by **Civilized** existence and **Behaviorist Parenting** practices.

Children's Culture: A semi-autonomous group of at least four **children**, typically of varying ages, that facilitates maturation and social consciousness. It is perpetuated through games, riddles, jump rope rhymes, stories, and other forms of play.

chronic clinginess: A repeated behavior characterized by the **child** insisting or manipulating to be continually held, and/or to keep the caretaker continually engaged with him.

Circle of Life (Hoop of Life, Web of Life): The community of Plant, Animal, Mineral and Sky beings who live together in **Balance**.

Circle Way (Old Way, Ancestral Way, the Original Instructions, the Beauty Way): The manner in which all things are related to, and affect, each other; a way of life that allows one to remain centered and not only see, but also benefit from all in life that appears beyond control.

Civilized: The lifestyle that results from living out of **Balance** with the **Circle of Life**; characterized by isolation from Nature, environmental degradation, regimentation, hierarchical structures, materialism, and loss of individuality.

clan: The common formation of living for **Native** hunter-gatherers and the environment conducive to **Collective Parenting**. Includes **extended family** and non-blood relatives.

clan memory: The **clan**'s cumulative knowledge that is passed down from one generation to the next.

codependency: A state of relating in which one person relies excessively on another for approval and a sense of identity. Can manifest as people-pleasing, **chronic clinginess**, or grandiosity.

Control-Style Parenting: A style of parenting in which the parents use the **child** to meet their needs. Involves power struggles and **reward-punishment** tactics.

cradleboard: A rigid-backed baby carrier used by many temperate and far-northern climate Native peoples, particularly when their babies are between the infant and walking stages.

Cute Doll Syndrome: A **Control-Style Parenting** tactic in which the parents manipulate the **child** to do and be what they prefer.

Deep Listening: Holding calm, receptive, nonjudgmental space for a speaker, to encourage and support the expression of her truth.

ego: The aspect of personality that creates self-consciousness and individual identity; our fear-based identity.

extended family: A multigenerational environment that often includes the biological parents, grandparents, aunts, uncles, and other close relatives.

empathy: The awareness that others feel hurt in the same way we do, and that others tend to return favors or pleasure received.

Gifting Way: An approach to life that involves a healthy relationship with one's **child-self**; an open and sharing attitude; and following the natural law that giving is receiving.

Heartvoice: The expression of the **Heart-of-Hearts**, which is spoken and heard by the entire physical-mental-emotional being.

Heart-of-Hearts: The center of one's being and seat of personal **Balance** where feelings, intuition, **ancestral wisdom**, the senses, and mental input come together to give perspective and guidance.

Indian: A member of any of the various groups of America's indigenous inhabitants. The term is used in this text rather than the more commonly accepted Native American because most of the author's **Native** friends and associates prefer it, so he uses it out of respect for them. They state that they identify first with their respective nations, rather than with America, and they dwell on Turtle Island rather than America.

(isolated) nuclear family: A stripped-down version of the **extended family** that includes only the biological parents and their offspring.

Life Journey (Life Path): The unique direction of one's life.

Native: A plant or animal living a **natural** life in their **natural** habitat; a person living a hunter-gatherer lifestyle.

natural: Intrinsic to a species or system.

peer group: A group of **children** of the same age.

praise-isolation: A **reward-punishment** model that involves accolades when the **child** behaves in desirable ways to the parents, and timeouts when the child behaves in undesirable ways.

primal memories (ancestral wisdom, the genetic library, intuition, superconsciousness, Dreamtime, or the Voice of Spirit): The seat of long-term memory, emotions, sensory processing, and deep guidance from our forebears that we have accrued along our evolutionary path. May be genetically imprinted. Often appears in the guises of metaphor and story.

real love: An intrinsic longing to manifest what it is to be human.

reward-punishment (positive-negative reinforcement): A commonly employed tactic for getting children to do what adults want them to do. Involves rewarding children for desirable behaviors and punishing them for undesirable behaviors. Based on the **Behaviorist Theory of Reinforcement.**

rite of passage: An initiation ritual that signifies a completion of a milestone and a rebirth in itself. One can have several rites of passage throughout their lifetime.

Shared Parenting (Collective Parenting, Communal Parenting, Non-Nuclear Parenting, Non-Immediate Attachment Parenting): Our biologically programmed method of parenting in which every adult cares for all of the **children** in the **clan**, and every child relates to all clan adults as parents.

Teaching Trail: A way of living that entails engaging in our life process, becoming sensitized to our feelings and needs, exploring possibilities, gaining knowledge, learning skills, and growing in relationship.

Truthspeaking: Concise, straight-from-the-heart expression of personal reality; engenders trust and strengthens relationship. (For more information, see *Truthspeaking: Ancestral Ways to Hear and Speak the Voice of the Heart* by Tamarack Song.)

Vision Quest: One of many types of **rites of passage** in which the person fasts in the wilderness until they have visions.

Native Terms

'aha (Hawaiian): Extended family.

aina uudelleen (Saami): Learning through direct experience.

Bimadisiwin (Ojibwe): **Circle of Life**.

Cante wasteya nape ciyuzapelo (Lakota): A greeting that translates to *With good heart I take your hand.*

dikinaagan (Ojibwe): Literally translated to *Made by the hand of a person from the body of a tree.* A tumpline-carried **cradleboard** indigenous to the upper Great Lakes area.

ena (Yupik): Female subterranean communal lodge.

gaay (Gamilaraay Aborigine): **child**.

ha'ole (Hawaiian): foreigner.

hiapo (Hawaiian): oldest sibling.

Keiki (Hawaiian): **child**.

kokea (Saami): Earned knowledge through direct experience.

Ku i ka welo (Hawaiian): Literally translates to *children and adults fitting into the clan ways.* A phrase used to describe the Hawaiian style of **Shared Parenting**.

kupuna (Hawaiian): grandparents.

makua (Hawaiian): parents.

māna (Hawaiian): Food masticated by an older person and conveyed to the mouth of a small child.

Nakanagana (Ojibwe): **All My Relations**.

Nokomis (Ojibwe): Grandmother.

'ohana (Hawaiian): **clan**.

poho (Ainu): **child**.

qasgiq (Yupik): Male subterranean communal lodge.

rebozo (Spanish): A baby carrier typically used by Latin American women.

ti ! kã-p =xam-p (!Korana): my younger brother.

Wabineshi (Ojibwe): Little Morning Bird; the name of the author's son.

wi-ye-a (Awabakal Aborigine): Learning through direct experience.

won-nai-ki-lo-a (Awabakal Aborigine): child-like.

Index

Acknowledgments

What you hold in your hands is more of a journal than a book. It evolved out of the need for Circle Way-based guidance in real-life situations with traditional families, single parents, Shared Parenting, and intentional communities. As a result, hundreds of people have contributed their tears, talents and aspirations during the forty-plus years this book has been in gestation. Please know that the omission here of any individual whose spirit graces these pages is due only to the limitations of my long-term memory.

I would first like to recognize my Elders, beginning with my grandparents Lena, Nicola, Leonora, and Julius, who gifted me with their Old Country childrearing traditions. Guidance in Native practices came from my American Indian Elders, most notably Bawdwaywidun, Kamgabwikwe, Keewaydinoquay, and Makwa Geesis.

Oftentimes when I had questions about the Original Instructions on how to raise children, my Indian Elders would send me to the people they consulted for answers: the wingeds and four-leggeds. In particular, I would like to acknowledge Dove and Wolf for welcoming me into their families and treating me as one of their own.

A good share of the credit for this book goes to the hundreds of children and parents who contributed their stories and teachings. Of particular note is what I learned from living in intentional communities, where children and childrearing practices are typically top priorities. First came northern Wisconsin's Coldfoot Creek

Community, with its twenty-two members. Next was the Family House at the Teaching Drum Outdoor School, which averaged ten adults and three-to-four children. Of special note is the unique community experience that occurred in 2012-2013, with the Teaching Drum's Family Wilderness Guide Program. Seventeen children and twenty-five adults, ranging in ages from two to seventy-five and spanning three generations, came together to live for a year in a primitive camp deep in a national forest.

Each and every person from this great extended family of mine lives in the pages of *Blossoming the Child*. I wish to recognize as many of them here as is practical, by their everyday names, as I know them. For those who do not appear here, it is due to my memory lapse rather than being a statement of lesser regard:

Children: Hope, Charra, Jesse, Jami, Kai, Stella, Sam, Lily, Bryn, Amos, Susan, René, Sage, Takeshi, Cedar, Zinnia, Rabin, Katrina, Ian, Genevieve, Kyle, Jason, Logan, Zena, Julia, Moritz, Rasmus, Jokim, Zehpyr, Gio, Zander, Baldur, Cicada, Diindiis, Talika, Janika, Canto, Izaiah, Andre, Kiara, Lena, and Silas.

Parents: Jennine, Ron, Eagle, Victoria, Ahwe, Wohabe, Ray, Scott, Elsa, Angela, Joe, Orca, Mountain, Stephanie, Justin, Jim, Lia, Sabrina, Alex, Ma'iingan, Brum, Kerstin, Ernst, Katya, Caroline, Susan, Elke, Sarah, Abel, Coyotequai, and Margaret.

Next, I wish to acknowledge the researchers, therapists, and writers, too numerous to list here, who have either directly or indirectly contributed.

The form and substance of what you hold is courtesy of the book production team: managing editor Alex Steussy-Williams, text editors Andrew Huff, Leah Moss, Samantha Sprole, and Brett Winters, and indexers Brett Schwartz, Alegre Hall-Moon, and Linda Lee — with Alegre and Linda giving a supreme effort to complete the project by deadline. Nan Casper transcribed, Kati Green and Christine Metropulos-Friedrich rendered the chapter illustrations, and the cover was created by Amber Braun and a person who wishes to remain anonymous. That person also took on the monumental task of synthesizing reader input. Michael Patterson provided me with an extensive library of parenting books. Jim Arneson of JamesBookDesigns.Weebly.com executed the design and layout, and Tony Roberts of The Roberts Group Editorial and Design crafted the e-book version.

I needed a quiet nook for the final rewrite, which friend and neighbor Catherine Marshall provided with her little dacha (Russian for *summer cottage*) on a beautiful woodland rise overlooking the lily-dappled waters where my family harvests wild rice every autumn.

To everyone involved in this grand labor of love for our children—and ourselves—I extend my deepest gratitude, along with my fondest wishes for your continued personal Blossoming.

One person has been with me through the entire creative process. We've had the pleasure of nurturing our children and grandchildren together, and we've been privileged to guide many others in the fledging of theirs. I trust that my dear mate and soul companion, Lety Seibel, has a sense of the depth of gratefulness for her presence in my life that mere words could hardly begin to convey.

To learn more about Tamarack Song's work, please visit these sites.

BROTHER WOLF FOUNDATION

Since 1972, a voice for:
Renewing *the age-old human-Wolf relationship, and*
Creating *safe space for Wolves to run free.*
www.brotherwolffoundation.org

HEALING NATURE TRAIL & CENTER

Where Towering Pine and Whispering Breeze
Revitalize *body, mind, and spirit*
Release *pain, stress, and sorrow*
Renew *relationship with all of life.*
www.healingnaturecenter.org

TEACHING DRUM OUTDOOR SCHOOL

Where wilderness is the classroom,
Ancient Voices are the teachers,
knowing self and balance are the quest.
www.teachingdrum.org

SNOW WOLF PUBLISHING

Crafter of quality books for
Remembering *what it is to be human,*
Restoring *our primal health, and*
Rediscovering *the world of Nature.*
www.snowwolfpublishing.org

About the Author

Tamarack Song is a cofounder of the Healing Nature Center, and he is the founder of the Brother Wolf Foundation, Teaching Drum Outdoor School, and Snow Wolf Publishing, where he is a writer-in-residence. He has served as a Childcare Trainee Supervisor for the University of Victoria, British Columbia, and his doctorate work is in recovery from childhood trauma and Nature-based healing. Yet he gives the  most credit for his parenting insight to the indigenous approach he learned from Native Elders, and to what he experienced directly by living with a flock of Doves and a pack of Wolves.